Careers in Hospitality & Tourism

Careers in Hospitality & Tourism

Editor

Michael Shally-Jensen, Ph.D.

SALEM PRESS

A Division of EBSCO Information Services, Inc.

Ipswich, Massachusetts

GREY HOUSE PUBLISHING

Library of Congress Cataloging-in-Publication Data

Careers in hospitality & tourism / editor, Michael Shally-Jensen, Ph.D.

   pages : illustrations ; cm. -- (Careers in--)

   Includes bibliographical references and index.
   ISBN: 978-1-61925-477-0

   1. Hospitality industry--Vocational guidance. 2. Tourism--Vocational guidance. I. Shally-Jensen, Michael. II. Title: Careers in hospitality and tourism

TX911.3.V62 C375 2014
647.94/023

First Printing

PRINTED IN THE UNITED STATES OF AMERICA

CONTENTS

PUBLISHER'S NOTE

Careers in Hospitality & Tourism contains twenty-five alphabetically arranged chapters describing specific fields of interest in hospitality and tourism. These chapters provide a current overview and a future outlook of specific occupations in these industries. Merging scholarship with occupational development, this single comprehensive guidebook provides hospitality and tourism students and readers alike with the necessary insight into potential careers, and provides instruction on what job seekers can expect in terms of training, advancement, earnings, job prospects, working conditions, relevant associations, and more. *Careers in Hospitality & Tourism* is specifically designed for a high school and undergraduate audience and is edited to align with secondary or high school curriculum standards.

Scope of Coverage

Understanding the interconnected nature of the different and varied branches of hospitality and tourism is important for anyone preparing for a career in these fields. *Careers in Hospitality & Tourism* comprises twenty-five lengthy chapters on a broad range of branches and divisions within these industry segments, including traditional and long-established fields such as Bartender, Hotel Manager, and Travel Agent, as well as in-demand and cutting-edge fields such as Fitness Trainer and Event Coordinator. This excellent reference also presents possible career paths and occupations within high-growth and emerging fields in these industries.

Careers in Hospitality & Tourism is enhanced with numerous charts and tables, including projections from the US Bureau of Labor Statistics, and median annual salaries or wages for those occupations profiled. Each chapter also notes those skills that can be applied across broad occupation categories. Interesting enhancements, like **Fun Facts**, **Famous Firsts**, and dozens of photos, add depth to the discussion. A highlight of each chapter is **Conversation With** – a two-page interview with a professional working in a related job. The respondents share their personal career paths, detail potential for career advancement, offer advice for students, and include a "try this" for those interested in embarking on a career in their profession.

Essay Length and Format

Each chapter ranges in length from 3,500 to 4,500 words and begins with a Snapshot of the occupation that includes career clusters, interests, earnings and employment outlook. This is followed by these major categories:

- **Overview** includes detailed discussions on: Sphere of Work; Work Environment; Occupation Interest; A Day in the Life. Also included here is a Profile that outlines working conditions, educational needs, and physical abilities. You will also find the occupation's Holland Interest Score, which matches up character and personality traits with specific jobs.

- **Occupational Specialties** lists specific jobs that are related in some way, like Chef, Sous Chef, Restaurant Cook, Fast-Food Cook and Pastry Chef. This section also includes a list of Duties and Responsibilities.
- **Work Environment** details the physical, human, and technological environment of the occupation profiled.
- **Education, Training, and Advancement** outlines how to prepare for this occupation while in high school, and what college courses to take, including licenses and certifications needed. A section is devoted to the Adult Job Seeker, and there is a list of skills and abilities needed to succeed in the job profiled.
- **Earnings and Advancements** offers specific salary ranges, and includes a chart of metropolitan areas that have the highest concentration of the profession.
- **Employment and Outlook** discusses employment trends, and projects growth to 2020. This section also lists related occupations.
- **Selected Schools** list those prominent learning institutions that offer specific courses in the profiles occupations.
- **More Information** includes associations that the reader can contact for more information.

Special Features

Several features continue to distinguish this reference series from other career-oriented reference works. The back matter includes:
- Appendix A: Guide to Holland Code. This discusses John Holland's theory that people and work environments can be classified into six different groups: Realistic; Investigative; Artistic; Social; Enterprising; and Conventional. See if the job you want is right for you!
- Appendix B: General Bibliography. This is a collated collection of annotated suggested readings.
- Subject Index: Includes people, concepts, technologies, terms, principles, and all specific occupations discussed in the occupational profile chapters.

Acknowledgments

Special mention is made of editor Michael Shally-Jensen, who played a principal role in shaping this work with current, comprehensive, and valuable material. Thanks are due to the many academicians and professionals who worked to communicate their expert understanding of hospitality & tourism to the general reader. Finally, thanks are also due to the professionals who communicated their work experience through our interview questionnaires. Their frank and honest responses provide immeasurable value to *Careers in Hospitality & Tourism*. The contributions of all are gratefully acknowledged.

EDITOR'S INTRODUCTION

An Overview

At the core of the hospitality and tourism industry today are two mainstays of American business: hotels (and similar forms of lodging) and restaurants (and related food service operations). Both of these are highly developed, or "mature," industry sectors marked by ongoing growth and competition. Closely allied with them are two other industry sectors, namely, leisure services and transportation. These too are well-developed industry fields with changing dynamics of their own. The hospitality and tourism industry as a whole is a multibillion-dollar one that depends on business travelers and private vacationers for its revenues, as well as the many millions of local users of leisure and entertainment services. The businesses involved in this industry—ranging from airlines to restaurants to resort facilities—tend to be large and to employ many individuals working in a variety of specialized occupations.

Elements of the Industry

On the hotel, or lodging, side are a number of established institutional types. These include:

- commercial hotels, which typically have room service, a coffee-shop, dining room, cocktail lounge, laundry and valet service as well as access to computers and Wi-Fi;
- airport hotels, which are conveniently located for travelers and typically provide regular bus or limousine service to the airlines;
- motels and economy hotels, which provide limited services and are known for their low prices and basic accommodations;
- suite hotels, which offer attractive, often spacious layouts and designs; and
- casino and resort hotels, which typically are quite luxurious and can be destinations in their own right in that they provide entertainment and leisure activities for guests.

In addition to these there are conference centers, designed to provide meeting space and accommodations for groups; and bed & breakfast inns, which typically are converted homes.

Restaurants are even more varied. They may be classified by cuisine (e.g., Italian, Chinese, Mexican), by the kind of food offered (e.g., seafood, steak, vegetarian), by style (formal or informal), by meal type (breakfast, lunch, dinner), by method of preparation and delivery (fast food, short order, buffet style), and by other factors such as cost, location, service, and whether the restaurant is part of a chain or is independent. Restaurants are closely allied with another part of the food service sector: drinking establishments. The latter, too, come in a variety of forms (bars, pubs, taverns, brewpubs, restaurant bars, etc.), all of which share the common purpose of serving alcoholic beverages to patrons.

In the leisure services area is an array of specialized personal and group services ranging from trip planning, event planning, and recreational activities to gambling/gaming operations, rental services, health and beauty services, and more. Like the other areas of the hospitality and tourism industry, this sector too draws its life from the expenditures of visiting travelers and local users of leisure goods and services.

Forms of transportation are likewise varied and extend well beyond the hospitality and tourism industry to other areas of commerce. Within the hospitality and tourism industry, the main forms of transportation are: airlines, which connect travelers to all major cities and many smaller ones; cruise ships or steamship lines, which carry travelers to ports across the seas and oceans; rail lines and bus lines, which transport travelers across continents and inside cities; and taxicabs and limousines, which offer localized—even door-to-door—transportation.

Hotel and Restaurant History

The practice of feeding guests and renting overnight space to travelers is ancient. Only in more recent times did the modern concepts of the hotel and restaurant emerge. City Hotel opened in New York City in 1794. Similar operations soon appeared in Baltimore, Boston, and Philadelphia. Boston's Tremont House, opened in 1829, was the first hotel to offer first-class service—including indoor toilets and baths. The Tremont's restaurant featured fine French cuisine.

American food service is linked to use of the ice-box (1803), the gas stove (1825), and the dishwashing machine (1860), among other appliances. In 1827 Delmonico's Restaurant in New York City was opened. Becoming one of the best known restaurants of the nineteenth century, it drew its clientele from the city's elite. In San Francisco, in contrast, the Gold Rush gave rise (in 1849) to the first self-service restaurant.

In 1908, the Statler Hotel opened in Buffalo, NY, marking the beginning of the modern commercial hotel era. Many services now considered standard were introduced by the Statler, including such amenities as a light switch next to the door, private bath, ice water, and a morning newspaper. The Statler set the standard of the day by being clean, comfortable, and affordable.

In the 1920s, hotel building entered a boom phase and many famous hotels were opened, including the Waldorf Astoria, New York's Hotel Pennsylvania, and the Chicago Hilton and Towers (originally named the Stevens). Motels began to replace roadside cabins as use of the automobile spread. Offering clean rooms with adjacent parking, motels enjoyed great popularity with the traveling public. By the 1950s and 1960s, the practice of franchising had appeared. Franchising enabled entrepreneurs to expand their operations without the use of substantial capital.

Also in the 1950s and 1960s frozen food began to change the restaurant business, led by fast food restaurants and large institutions (airlines, hospitals). The ease of transporting and using frozen foods allowed kitchens everywhere to reduce the size of their food-prep areas and the time it took to organize and prepare foods.

For much of their history, hotels and restaurants were owned and operated by individuals. However, as franchises and chains began to appear, individually owned operations found themselves increasingly at a competitive disadvantage. From the 1980s onward, mergers and acquisitions became common within the industry, and hotel and restaurant brands became hotly traded commodities. These chain brands tend to yield a more predictable and steady income stream as compared to individually owned properties.

For decades one of the main sources of income for restaurants, particularly upscale restaurants, was their bar business. High bar income resulted from steady alcohol consumption by guests, relatively low unit (per-drink) costs, and relatively high unit price tags. However, by the end of the 1980s, public awareness about the dangers of drinking and driving, together with stiffer drunk-driving laws, greatly impacted bar profits. In addition, in the 1990s smoking became outlawed in restaurants and bars in many American cities, leading to a further decline in bar patrons and, therefore, alcoholic beverage sales.

Today, specialty restaurants and coffee houses are two of the main drivers of the restaurant industry. These allow for unique meals—ethnic specialties, regional favorites, fresh combinations of ingredients—at a low price in a casual atmosphere. These places draw customers by offering a new, different dining experience in a friendly, social environment.

Employment Trends

Although employment in the leisure and hospitality industry fell by nearly a half-million jobs during the 2007-2009 recession, there are signs that it is experiencing an uptick. Initially, the industry did not feel the full impact of the recession. Employment peaked, in fact, in January 2008, one month after the start of the recession. Two years later, in January 2010, it hit a low point, which is notable in that it came a full seven months after the end of the recession. In all, during the recession about half of the employment decline in the industry was in the food services (and drinking establishments) subsector, where 230,000 jobs were lost. Hotel and accommodations employment lost about 28 percent of the industry total, or 129,000 jobs. Recreation and entertainment shed 21 percent of the total, or 95,000 jobs; particularly hard hit were the areas of gambling and amusements. Similarly, all fields of transportation, but particularly the leisure sector, slowed and experienced employment shrinkage.

In the early months of 2014, however, employment in these industries returned to pre-recession levels—or even slightly better than pre-recession levels. Some 14 million people are currently employed in the industry. Although hiring continues apace, with over one million hires occurring each quarter, job losses occur at about the same rate. This means that there is substantial turnover, yet opportunities exist for motivated individuals. The number of newly created positions remains quite low and competition remains strong. The unemployment rate (i.e., the percentage of those looking for work) in the hospitality industry has in recent months failed to climb above the unemployment rate for all industries taken together. It hovers between 8 percent and 10 percent, as compared to the 7 percent to 8 percent rate for the rest of the economy.

Still, many individual occupations in the industry match or nearly match the 11 percent growth rate projected for all industries over the next decade by the Bureau of Labor Statistics—and a number of such occupations (e.g., fitness trainer, interior designer, cosmetologist) exceed that projected growth mark. Overall, the outlook is reasonably good.

Business Trends

In the wake of previous mergers and acquisitions, which often brought hotel/restaurant and non-hotel/restaurant companies together under one corporate umbrella, there is now a trend among companies toward selling off unrelated brands in an effort to get back to their core business. One of the key measures in the hospitality industry is "usage rate," or, its opposite, "vacancy rate." Restaurants, hotels, and airlines seek to maximize the number of customers they serve on a given day, or given flight, similar to the way a factory owner seeks to make optimal use of his or her factory rather than pay fixed costs while the factory sits idle. Thus, a development in recent years has been the emergence of so-called hospitality consolidators, services that provide travelers with comparative information regarding room rates, airline ticket rates, space availability, times, restaurant/meal information, and so on. These services, which customers access for free (usually) online, have led to increased usage rates and, on the whole, heightened customer satisfaction regarding value in the utilization of hospitality offerings. Several years ago, customers would call a toll-free number to make room or flight reservations. Today, about two-thirds of all reservations are made via the internet.

At the same time, a form of product segmentation has occurred. Luxury and first-class hotels have created more amenities and products for their customers while economy and budget motels have cut back services in order to maintain their lower prices. Also, specialized extended-stay and suite hotels have become more popular. Hotels with indoor water parks and similar themed entertainment are one of the latest trends. Another segment that many hotel companies are involved in recently is timeshares; the development, sale, and management of timeshares have become particularly popular with the large chains. Franchising continues to flourish in the hotel and, to a lesser extent, the restaurant industry.

Other recent trends in the hotel industry include luxury mattresses, complimentary breakfast, high definition TV, high-speed Internet access, Wi-Fi, and room suites. Another recent trend for hotels is to set up their lobbies as flexible spaces. For example, part of the lobby may be used for a breakfast area in the morning and a bar at night. This may include sliding walls, decorative lighting, and music. One reason for this is to generate more income per square foot.

Hospitality businesses continue to find competitive advantage in some of the classic principles of the trade (location, reputation) as well as in investing in upkeep and, where appropriate, expansion of facilities (particularly in the luxury sector). Although hospitality consolidators play a large role in driving customers toward businesses, marketing operations continue to be very important as well. Marketing campaigns are often helped by having a themed component to the business or facility. Extremely important too is the quality of the personnel working in direct contact with customers. In the hospitality trade, a staff's ability to communicate authenticity, professionalism, and sincere concern for the happiness and well-being of customers is something that all successful organizations expect and, in fact, rely on to give them a competitive advantage.

—Michael Shally-Jensen

References

Bureau of Labor Statistics. "Employment Increases in Leisure and Hospitality, Professional and Business Services in June." July 8, 2013. www.bls.gov/opub/ted/2013/ted_20130708.htm

Davila, Eliot. "Employment in Leisure and Hospitality Departs from Historical Trends during 2007-09 Recession," Monthly Labor Review, April 2011, pp. 49-52.

Internal Revenue Service. "Hotel Industry Overview." May 14, 2013. www.irs.gov/Businesses/Hotel-Industry-Overview---Complete-Version

Schonwalder, Helmut. "Food Service History" and "Hotel History." 2011. schonwalder.org/a_businesscard_b.htm

Shaffie, Anam. "A Look at the Hospitality Industry." August 23, 2012. examiner.com

Administrative Support Manager

Snapshot

Career Cluster(s): Business Administration, Hospitality & Tourism, Distribution & Logistics

Interests: Working with people, office management, administrative best practices

Earnings (Yearly Average): $88,660

Employment & Outlook: Average Growth Expected

OVERVIEW

Sphere of Work

Administrative support managers oversee the efficient and effective delivery of front-line business services and/or back-office administrative operations within their organizations. This includes hiring and training support staff, temporary workers, administrative and clerical workers, shift workers, and other staff. It also includes ensuring that scheduled work shifts are covered, setting administrative priorities and goals for short- and long-term projects, and developing best practices (i.e., business efficiencies) and workflow procedures for their employees.

Administrative support managers may be found in all industries, wherever administrative and clerical tasks are performed. In many cases their work extends beyond office functions to customer service and related functions.

Work Environment

Administrative support managers usually work in office environments or similar venues in close proximity to the staff whose work they oversee. The manager's support staff may perform such duties as receptionist duties, customer assistance, data entry, clerical tasks, bookkeeping, and secretarial work as well as other office and support functions as needed. In addition to supervising staff, administrative support managers can usually expect to perform some administrative duties themselves. Administrative support managers usually work approximately forty hours per week during normal office hours but are sometimes required to work longer hours as needed.

Profile

Physical Strength: Light Work
Education Needs: High School Diploma (minimum), Technical/Community College, Bachelor's Degree (often) Apprenticeship
Licensure/Certification: Usually Not Required
Physical Abilities Not Required: No Heavy Labor
Opportunities For Experience: Apprenticeship, Military Service, Volunteer Work, Part-Time Work
Holland Interest Score*: CES

* See Appendix A

Occupation Interest

This occupation suits people who combine advanced administrative and organizational capabilities with the ability to lead, supervise, and motivate others. Administrative support managers have generally proven their administrative capabilities by first excelling in an entry-level administrative position. Successful administrative support managers enjoy working with people and have strong oral and written communication skills, allowing them to delegate, set high expectations, and provide constructive feedback with tact and confidence. Although they work independently in a supervisory role, administrative support managers must also be comfortable collaborating with members of their team at certain times.

A Day in the Life—Duties and Responsibilities

An administrative support manager's day is likely to involve a combination of administrative and supervisory duties. This is a job in which success usually requires a blend of advanced skills in several areas, including management, technology, administrative duties, the ability to coordinate with other departments, and communication skills.

During a typical day, managers may organize and lead meetings with their staff to discuss assigning and scheduling the day's or week's work priorities. They may meet with staff individually to receive verbal updates on work progress, provide one-on-one feedback, and to check the accuracy and overall quality of work. Managers may spend a considerable amount of time helping staff to resolve problems that arise. In this regard, they are expected to be able to interpret and apply company policy to a wide range of different scenarios. Sometimes they may also be expected to develop or adapt policies or protocols in response to new or special circumstances. Administrative support managers may also be required to prepare and administer budgets, contribute to strategic planning processes, and develop new workflows and procedures. They may sometimes be expected to perform some basic administrative duties themselves or to cover others' duties.

To ensure that the employer's administrative and support needs are adequately and appropriately met, administrative support managers also coordinate often with members of other departments within the organization, as well as with customers and corporate management. Some workdays may include hiring and training new staff and conducting staff performance reviews. The administrative support manager may be required to maintain a weekly or monthly log of his or her employees' hours and submit timesheets to the human resources or payroll departments.

Duties and Responsibilities

- Determining work procedures and administrative and support staff schedules
- Assigning duties to staff workers
- Examining work for quality and timeliness
- Maintaining harmony among workers
- Performing administrative tasks of one's own
- Overseeing budget and time reports as necessary
- Hiring, training, evaluating, and disciplining clerical and other employees

OCCUPATION SPECIALTIES

General Services Managers

General services managers plan, coordinate, and direct a broad range of services that allow organizations to operate efficiently. An organization may have several managers who oversee activities that meet the needs of multiple departments, such as customer service, recordkeeping, security, building maintenance, and recycling.

Contract Administrators

Contract Administrators handle the purchasing of services or equipment and supplies from outside contractors. They review bids and decide which contractors to use to meet their company's needs.

Facilities Managers

Facilities Managers oversee buildings, grounds, equipment, and supplies. Their duties fall into several categories, including overseeing operations and maintenance, planning and managing projects, and dealing with environmental factors. Facility managers also are responsible for directing staff, including maintenance, grounds, and custodial workers.

WORK ENVIRONMENT

Physical Environment

Administrative support managers usually work in comfortable indoor settings such as offices or similar facilities. The specific physical environment will be influenced by the size and type of the employer and the industry in which they operate. There is a wide range of settings, from small organizations to large and busy operations.

Relevant Skills and Abilities

Communication Skills
- Expressing thoughts and ideas clearly
- Speaking and writing effectively

Interpersonal/Social Skills
- Cooperating with others
- Motivating others
- Working as a member of a team

Organization & Management Skills
- Managing time
- Meeting goals and deadlines
- Paying attention to and handling details

Technical Skills
- Working with office machines/ technologies

Human Environment

Administrative support supervisors interact on a daily basis with a wide range of people within and outside of the workplace. These professionals spend a significant amount of time leading, managing, and motivating employees. They frequently interact with colleagues and report to upper-level managers or executives.

Technological Environment

Daily administrative operations require the use of standard office technologies, including computers, telephones, e-mail, photocopiers, and the Internet. Administrative support managers must be proficient in the use of basic office software such as word processing programs, contact management software, spreadsheets, and presentation programs. They may also need to use specialized systems, including tracking databases and enterprise-wide resource platforms.

EDUCATION, TRAINING, AND ADVANCEMENT

High School/Secondary

High school students can best prepare for a career as an administrative support manager by taking courses in English, composition, and business writing. Courses that develop general business skills may include accounting, entrepreneurship, bookkeeping, business management, and applied mathematics. Administrative and clerical skills may be developed by taking subjects such as business computing, typing, and shorthand. Subjects such as history and social studies help the student to develop his or her general research and analytical skills. Studies in psychology may be beneficial for developing understanding about human behavior and motivation.

Becoming involved in part-time administrative or clerical work while still in high school is an excellent way to gain entry-level experience in the administrative profession. High school students may also gain volunteer administrative experience with local community and sporting organizations as well as with scholastic clubs and societies. A wide variety of extracurricular activities provide leadership opportunities.

Suggested High School Subjects
- Applied Communication
- Bookkeeping
- Business
- Business & Computer Technology
- Business Data Processing
- Business English
- Business Math
- Keyboarding
- Psychology

Famous First

The first staffing agency, which provided office personnel on a temporary basis to employers, was Manpower Inc. founded in Milwaukee, Wisc., in 1948. The firm later opened offices in Chicago, Montreal, and elsewhere. Almost all of the initial "temps" Manpower placed were women, but eventually that changed. In 1976 Manpower was bought by the Parker Pen Company. It became independent again in 1986, and the next year was bought by a U.K. corporation. It again became independent in 1991, and today boasts annual revenues of about $22 billion.

College/Postsecondary

Administrative support managers are not generally required to possess formal postsecondary educational qualifications; however, an associate's or bachelor's degree in business, administration, or another relevant field may lead to improved career opportunities. In addition to universities and technical or community colleges, the International Association of Administrative Professionals (IAAP) and Association of Executive and Administrative Professionals (AEAP) offer accredited and non-accredited training options for administrative professionals. Some employers in this profession value on-the-job experience or professional development courses more than postsecondary degrees.

Related College Majors
- Business Administration & Management
- Office Supervision & Management

Adult Job Seekers

Adults seeking a career transition or returning to an administrative support manager role are advised to refresh their skills and update their resume. Advanced administrative skills, leadership, and supervisory experience should be highlighted in the candidate's resume and application letter. Networking, job searching, and interviewing are critical, and those without prior experience may find it helpful to obtain specialized training. Aspiring administrative support managers may also find it beneficial to consider related roles, such as office manager, administrative assistant, and any staff supervisor positions. Advancement opportunities in this field generally depend on the size and type of employer and an individual's breadth of experience. Larger organizations are likely to provide more scope for career and salary development.

Professional Certification and Licensure

There are no formal professional certifications or licensing requirements for administrative support managers; however, gaining recognition as a Certified Administrative Professional may improve one's job prospects. This certification is awarded by the International Association of Administrative Professionals. To become certified, candidates must demonstrate work experience, have employer sponsorship, and complete a written exam. Continuing education is required for certification renewal. It is beneficial to consult credible professional associations and current or prospective employers regarding the value of pursuing any voluntary certification.

Additional Requirements

Administrative teams are often under pressure to become more efficient and effective. Office should stay knowledgeable about relevant technology and computer software that offer improved cost effectiveness and improved quality control or efficiency. Honesty, integrity, and professional ethics are also important in this field, as administrative support managers may have access to sensitive company documents or financial information.

EARNINGS AND ADVANCEMENT

Earnings of administrative support managers depend on the type, size and location of the employer, and the level of responsibility and level of specialized knowledge needed by the employee. Employers in major metropolitan areas tend to pay higher salaries than those in rural areas.

Administrative support managers earned mean annual salaries of $88,660 in 2012. The salary range was rather broad, however, extending from $44,330 at the low end to $143,070 at the high end. Administrative support managers may receive paid vacations, holidays, and sick days; life and health insurance; and retirement benefits. These are usually paid by the employer.

Metropolitan Areas with the Highest Employment Level in this Occupation

Metropolitan area	Employment	Employment per thousand jobs	Hourly mean wage
New York-White Plains-Wayne, NY-NJ	12,980	2.52	$58.01
Chicago-Joliet-Naperville, IL	10,130	2.78	$39.12
Los Angeles-Long Beach-Glendale, CA	8,770	2.26	$47.87
Atlanta-Sandy Springs-Marietta, GA	8,250	3.65	$44.51
Boston-Cambridge-Quincy, MA	7,260	4.24	$50.53
Houston-Sugar Land-Baytown, TX	6,620	2.51	$47.11
Minneapolis-St. Paul-Bloomington, MN-WI	5,900	3.37	$40.32
Washington-Arlington-Alexandria, DC-VA-MD-WV	5,590	2.39	$47.61

Source: Bureau of Labor Statistics

EMPLOYMENT AND OUTLOOK

There were approximately 264,000 administrative support managers employed nationally in 2012. Employment is expected to grow about as fast as the average for all occupations through the year 2022, which means employment is projected to increase 9 percent to 15 percent. Most job openings will result from the need to replace workers who transfer to other occupations or leave the work force.

Employment Trend, Projected 2012–22

Administrative Support Managers: 12%

Total, All Occupations: 11%

Management Occupations: 7%

Note: "All Occupations" includes all occupations in the U.S. Economy. Source: U.S. Bureau of Labor Statistics, Employment Projections Program

Related Occupations
- Food Services Manager
- Health & Fitness Center Manager
- Hotel /Motel Manager

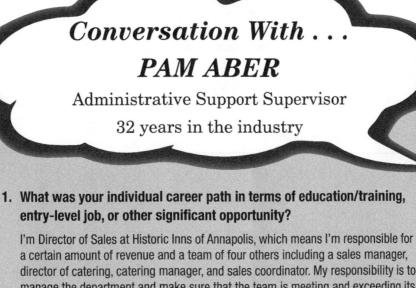

Conversation With . . .
PAM ABER
Administrative Support Supervisor
32 years in the industry

1. What was your individual career path in terms of education/training, entry-level job, or other significant opportunity?

I'm Director of Sales at Historic Inns of Annapolis, which means I'm responsible for a certain amount of revenue and a team of four others including a sales manager, director of catering, catering manager, and sales coordinator. My responsibility is to manage the department and make sure that the team is meeting and exceeding its revenue goals. I do payroll, and I hire and fire.

I received a BA in recreation with a minor in PR from Ohio State University. During that time I worked part-time for a travel agency and for Marriott as a concierge. So that gave me experience before I even graduated. Hospitality is all about getting promoted and getting the experience.

When I graduated from college, I went to Disney and was a group coordinator; from there I just kept growing into different categories as far as catering and sales. I finally found my true skill is selling, so I stayed on a career path as a sales manager with various hotels, including Kimpton Hotels. I was finally given an opportunity as associate director of sales and really liked it. At that point, I was 20 years out of college and had moved a lot for my husband's job.

I've had a well-rounded hotel career with all sorts of sales markets, catering jobs including weddings...I've done it all.

2. What are the most important skills and/or qualities for someone in your profession?

In the hospitality industry, you're basically selling yourself to these clients. When you're working the front desk, you're probably the first person a guest is going to come in touch with. If that person meets you and you don't have a smile, they may think, "I'm not sure I want to stay at this hotel."

A college degree is very important and if girls and guys can get a college degree that's great. But I see so many of these kids who are struggling and feel they have to have a degree. That's not the case in our industry. In our industry, with the right person, we can train them. I pulled in a sales manager, now a catering manager, who didn't have a college degree. She had worked as a restaurant manager and had the right personality and the right drive: she's friendly, bubbly, enthusiastic, a driver, polite, and knows what the client wants. She's going to night school now and she's 38 years old.

You need to think about what you want to do, then you can reach out to your supervisors and let them know where you want to go. My sales manager here, who is new to the industry, would like to become a director of sales. So, my ultimate responsibility is to help her get there.

3. What do you wish you had known going into this profession?

I wish, when I was in high school, that I had known a profession like this existed. I didn't know somebody in hotels actually coordinated weddings, or that there was a sales person talking to clients and booking meetings.

4. Are there many job opportunities in your profession? In what specific areas?

A hotel is a 24-hour business. There are hotels everywhere, and there are job opportunities everywhere. Sometimes you have to be willing to re-locate.

5. How do you see your profession changing in the next five years? What role will technology play in those changes, and what skills will be required?

The economy is changing for the better and I think there are growth opportunities in the branded hotels and hotel management companies that are constantly buying hotels.

With technology, the pace is a lot faster. You become more productive. Our company keeps looking at different reservation systems that are all based on productivity to really focus on the guest services end.

6. What do you enjoy most about your job? What do you enjoy least?

I love the interaction I have with my team. I love the interaction with my clients; they become my best friends almost. It's hard to deal with a dissatisfied guest. In the hospitality industry, you want a happy guest. They're paying good money to have a good experience.

7. Can you suggest a valuable "try this" for students considering a career in your profession?

Hotels are always looking for interns. Some hotels will pay interns, some will not. If you can get an internship for two or three months and learn all the facets, that's great. Some are just sales and catering, where you get into the day-to-day routine. It will give you a really good look: am I cut out for this? We also work really well with our local community college's hospitality department. It's so important, while in school, to really engage yourself in work.

SELECTED SCHOOLS

Most colleges and universities offer bachelor's degrees in business administration and management; some have programs in administrative services management and/or hospitality and tourism. The student may also gain initial training at a technical or community college. Below are listed some of the more prominent four-year institutions in this field.

California State University, Fullerton
Mihaylo College of Business and Economics
800 N. State College Boulevard
Fullerton, CA 92834
657.278.4652
business.fullerton.edu

Colorado State University
College of Business
1201Campus Delivery
Fort Collins, CO 80523
970.491.6471
biz.colostate.edu

Drexel University
LeBow College of Business
3141 Chestnut Street
Philadelphia, PA 19104
215.895.2111
www.lebow.drexel.edu

Florida International University
Landon Undergraduate School of Business
11200 S.W. 8th Street – CBC 301
Miami, FL 33199
305.348.2751
business.fiu.edu

Penn State University
Smeal College of Business
202 Business Building
State College, PA 16802
814.865.1947
www.smeal.psu.edu

University of Illinois, Springfield
1 William Maxwell Lane
Springfield, IL 62703
217.206.6600
www.uis.edu

University of Iowa
Henry B. Tippie College of Business
21 E. Market Street
Iowa City, IA 52242
319.335.0860
tippie.uiowa.edu

University of Maryland
Robert H. Smith School of Business
Mowatt Lane
College Park, MD 20742
301.405.2189
www.rhsmith.umd.edu

University of Massachusetts, Amherst
Isenberg School of Management
121 Presidents Drive
Amherst, MA 01003
413.545.5610
www.isenberg.umass.edu

University of Wyoming
College of Business
1000 E. University Avenue
Laramie, WY 82071
307.766.1121
www.uwyo.edu/business

MORE INFORMATION

American Society of Administrative Professionals
121 Free Street
Portland, ME 04101
888.960.2727
www.asaporg.com

American Staffing Association
277 S. Washington Street, Suite 200
Alexandria, VA 22314
703.253.2020
www.americanstaffing.net

Association of Executive and Administrative Professionals
900 South Washington Street
Suite G-13
Falls Church, VA 22046
703.237.8616
www.theaeap.com

International Association of Administrative Professionals
10502 NW Ambassador Drive
Kansas City, MO 64153
816.891.6600
www.iaap-hq.org

International Facility Management Association
800 Gessner Road, Suite 900
Houston, TX 77024
713.623.4362
www.ifma.org

National Contract Management Association
P.O. Box 758747
Baltimore, MD 21275
571.382.1127
www.ncmahq.org

Kylie Hughes/Editor

Bartender

Snapshot

Career Cluster: Hospitality & Tourism

Interests: Beverages, customer service, bar & restaurant environments

Earnings (Yearly Average): $21,630

Employment & Outlook: Average Growth Expected

OVERVIEW

Sphere of Work

A bartender is a worker in the service industry who serves alcoholic and nonalcoholic beverages to patrons in a bar, restaurant, pub, hotel, or other private function setting. Bartenders usually work behind the main bar of an establishment, where they mix and serve drinks and collect payment from customers. They are often responsible for taking and serving food orders and for maintaining the establishment's bar inventory, including liquor, beer, and wine, cocktail garnishes, and glassware. Bartenders are usually responsible for the cleanliness of their area and for other managerial duties behind the bar.

Work Environment

Bartenders typically work in the indoor bar or lounge area of a restaurant, club, hotel, or other establishment. If working at a private event or large catering function, a bartender may work outside. Bartenders usually report to a restaurant or club owner, or applicable supervisor or manager, and interact with waitstaff and barbacks (bar assistants), bar patrons, and other customers. Bartenders may work forty hours per week or less, most often at night and on weekends. Some bartenders may be required to work split shifts. Part-time bartending and waitstaff positions are generally far more prevalent than full-time positions, so bartenders must be flexible with their schedules.

Profile

Working Conditions: Work Indoors
Physical Strength: Medium Work
Education Needs: On-The-Job Training, High School Diploma Or GED
Licensure/Certification: Usually Not Required
Physical Abilities Not Required: No Strenuous Labor
Opportunities For Experience: Internship, Apprenticeship, Volunteer Work, Part-Time Work
Holland Interest Score*: SEC

* See Appendix A

Occupation Interest

Individuals interested in pursuing a career in bartending should enjoy interacting with others for long periods. They should also be in good physical shape, as the job may require standing up for the majority of the shift. They should also demonstrate an interest in basic calculations, as bartenders constantly deal with the exchange of money (albeit aided by electronic cash registers) and the measuring out of drink ingredients. An interest in the culinary arts, particularly preparing food and drink and recommending beverage pairings with food, is helpful for anyone considering bartending.

A Day in the Life—Duties and Responsibilities

Most bartenders report to work in the afternoon to prepare for an evening shift. Bartenders typically arrive at a restaurant, club, hotel, or other establishment and immediately begin working behind the bar. Before customers arrive, a bartender might clean the bar area, organize the beverages and glassware, and prepare the bar for customers; this might include cutting fruit for garnishing, restocking inventory, and preparing any drink specials.

During a shift, bartenders usually receive drink and food orders from patrons and service staff. They are responsible for mixing and preparing drinks accurately and in a timely fashion, and according to a set recipe or customer request. Bartenders also handle all monetary transactions, including making change and operating a credit card machine or point-of-sale terminal, and enforce the legal drinking age. Bartenders often use restaurant equipment like dishwashers, refrigerators, blenders, drink machines, shakers, and automatic measuring devices. They carry heavy loads of glassware, trays of food and drinks, and other supplies. At the end of each shift, bartenders take inventory of the bar supplies and place orders with suppliers accordingly.

In addition to their typical service duties, bartenders may take on managerial responsibilities as needed. These may include greeting and conversing with customers, dealing with outside vendors, opening and closing the bar or restaurant, refusing service to overly intoxicated customers, and managing the waitstaff.

Duties and Responsibilities

- Mixing ingredients such as liquor, soda, water, sugar, bitters, or fruit juice
- Serving cocktails, wine, and draught or bottled beer
- Ordering liquor and supplies
- Checking customer IDs for proof of age
- Collecting money (and tips) for drinks served
- Cleaning glasses and other utensils and equipment

Fun Facts

Before Prohibition, Shlitz Brewery owned more property in Chicago than anyone else except the Catholic Church.

To 'mind your P's and Q's' refers to English drinks being served in pints and quarts. Back in the day, bartenders advised customers to mind their own pints and quarts when they were becoming unmanageable.

Source: *Bartender Magazine*/Bartender.com

OCCUPATION SPECIALTIES

Bar Attendants

Bar Attendants sell and serve alcoholic beverages to patrons in neighborhood taverns or combination bar and package-goods stores. Attendants usually do not serve mixed drinks.

Barbacks

Barbacks, or runners, are bar assistants who stock the bar with liquor, glassware, and other supplies, bus tables, and wash glasses.

WORK ENVIRONMENT

Relevant Skills and Abilities

Interpersonal/Social Skills
- Being able to work independently
- Cooperating with others

Interpersonal/Social Skills
- Working as a member of a team

Organization & Management Skills
- Following instructions
- Making decisions
- Paying attention to and handling details
- Performing routine work

Technical Skills
- Working with your hands
- Working with data or numbers

Physical Environment

Most bartending is performed at restaurants, hotels, clubs, bars, pubs, and other service establishments. Bartenders usually work behind the bar in these settings. Most bar environments are noisy, bustling, and dimly lit. For some, exposure to second-hand smoke is a daily occurrence (though less common now than in the past owing to no-smoking ordinances). Standing for the duration of one's shift is common.

Human Environment

Bartenders usually work under the direction of the general manager or owner of an establishment. They must also work and interact with waitstaff, bus people, barbacks, hosts and hostesses, and customers. Being able to speak clearly and loudly is important. A bartender must also learn to deal with unruly customers and be comfortable refusing service to overly inebriated or underage customers.

Technological Environment

Bartenders use a variety of kitchen equipment to aid them in the preparation of food and beverages. They use large appliances like dishwashers, refrigerators, and freezers as well as drink machines, blenders, and automatic measuring tools. They also operate a cash register or restaurant computer to record and calculate customer transactions.

EDUCATION, TRAINING, AND ADVANCEMENT

High School/Secondary

High school students interested in becoming bartenders should prepare themselves by taking courses in communications, foods and nutrition, basic mathematics, home economics, and computer technology. Prospective bartenders might involve themselves in extracurricular social groups or clubs at the high school level. They can supplement their education by taking courses in the culinary arts.

Suggested High School Subjects
- Business
- Business Math
- English
- Food Service & Management

Famous First

The first singles bar designed specifically for that purpose was T.G.I. Friday's, opened in New York City by Alan Stillman in 1965. A salesman, Stillman lived in a neighborhood inhabited by other salesmen, airline flight attendants, secretaries, fashion industry people, and other single professionals. He decided he would create a restaurant featuring a prominent bar and a cocktail-party atmosphere where singles could meet. The original restaurant proved so successful that by 1971 T.G.I. Friday's had become a franchise restaurant chain.

Postsecondary

After high school, students interested in becoming a bartender often attend vocational institutions that offer advanced classes and courses in the culinary arts. Many culinary programs provide instruction in food management, food purchasing, food service sanitation, beverage management, mixology and liquor laws, introduction to nutrition, and related subjects. Some programs may also offer work-study or work-exchange initiatives in order for students to gain experience in a restaurant or bar. Work-study opportunities may include apprenticeships, job shadowing, internships, or volunteer work.

Alternatively, bartenders can enroll in short bartender-training courses, often called mixology courses, that teach prospective bartenders how to serve alcoholic and nonalcoholic drinks, create and mix specialty beverages, follow standard recipes, and manage a bar.

Related College Majors
- Business Administration & Management
- Office Supervision & Management

Adult Job Seekers

People looking to become bartenders are usually required to be of legal drinking age. Aspiring bartenders should have some experience working in the service industry as a bartender assistant (such as a barback), waitress or waiter, dining room attendant, or other related position. Bartenders seeking employment can start by looking in the classified listings of local news outlets, performing searches on jobs websites, or inquiring in person at local establishments. Adult job seekers may also benefit from the networking opportunities, seminars and workshops, and job placement services offered by professional bartender associations such as the National Bartenders Association.

Advancement is limited in many establishments. Some experienced bartenders become supervisors in their establishments or start their own businesses.

Professional Certification and Licensure

In some cases, it is necessary for bartenders to obtain a bartending license or health certificate before becoming employed at a restaurant or other establishment. Bartenders usually receive their license after participating in and completing a short bartender training course. Licensure requirements for serving alcohol vary by state. Interested individuals should check the requirements of their home state and of the establishments where they wish to work.

Additional Requirements

Bartending is an extremely social occupation. Prospective bartenders must truly enjoy interacting with and listening to customers and other staff.

They must be prepared to thrive in a busy, loud, and sometimes frenetic environment. Bartenders must also be detail-oriented, organized individuals who are driven to run a successful bar and to take responsibility for any errors in management. Bartenders must also be able to think on their feet; they may receive requests for rare or specialty drinks and must be able to improvise if needed. Physical stamina and speed are also required, depending on the establishment.

EARNINGS AND ADVANCEMENT

Earnings depend on the employer, business location, union affiliation and employee's experience. Bartenders receive their earnings from a combination of hourly wages and tips. Bartenders had mean annual earnings, including tips, of $21,630 in 2012. The lowest ten percent earned less than $16,756, and the highest ten percent earned more than $33,381.

Bartenders may receive paid vacations, holidays, and sick days; life and health insurance; and retirement benefits. These are usually paid by the employer. Bartenders may also receive free or reduced meals at work and may be furnished bar jackets or complete uniforms.

Metropolitan Areas with the Highest Employment Level in this Occupation

Metropolitan area	Employment	Employment per thousand jobs	Hourly mean wage
New York-White Plains-Wayne, NY-NJ	18,950	3.67	$11.76
Chicago-Joliet-Naperville, IL	17,990	4.94	$10.59
Los Angeles-Long Beach-Glendale, CA	12,230	3.16	$11.04
Las Vegas-Paradise, NV	10,310	12.60	$13.40
Minneapolis-St. Paul-Bloomington, MN-WI	8,790	5.02	$9.73
Boston-Cambridge-Quincy, MA	8,230	4.81	$14.11
Houston-Sugar Land-Baytown, TX	7,970	3.02	$10.07
Philadelphia, PA	7,810	4.28	$11.75

Source: Bureau of Labor Statistics

EMPLOYMENT AND OUTLOOK

There were approximately 538,220 bartenders employed nationally in 2012. Employment is expected to grow on par with the average for all occupations through the year 2022, which means employment is projected to increase about 12 percent. Faster growth has slowed somewhat due to the fact that diners increasingly are eating at more casual dining spots, such as coffee bars and sandwich shops, rather than at the full-service restaurants and drinking places that employ more of these workers.

Job openings will arise from the need to replace bartenders who transfer to other occupations or stop working for a variety of reasons. There is substantial turnover in this occupation, and the limited formal education and training requirements allow easy entry. The fact that bartending is most often a part-time job is attractive to persons seeking a supplemental income or a short-term job rather than a career. However, bartenders must be 21 years of age, and some employers prefer to hire people 25 years of age or older.

Employment Trend, Projected 2012–22

Bartenders: 12%

Total, All Occupations: 11%

Food and Beverage Serving Workers: 10%

Note: "All Occupations" includes all occupations in the U.S. Economy. Source: U.S. Bureau of Labor Statistics, Employment Projections Program

Related Occupations
- Cook/Chef
- Food & Beverage Service Worker
- Waiter/Waitress

Conversation With . . .
MacGuyver
Bartender, 30 years

1. What was your individual career path in terms of education/training, entry-level job, or other significant opportunity?

As I have moved through life, I have found myself doing many things ranging from baking bread to tree-trimming and even law enforcement. The one thing that has remained a constant is bartending. As I got older, I began to realize my lifelong dream of flying. Bartending has given me both the flexibility with my schedule, as well as the money, to become a certified flight instructor with a wide variety of flight certifications.

I started as a bartender in 1985 right after high school when I moved to Florida and have been at Pusser's for 20 years. I also hold an associate's degree in criminal justice with a law enforcement minor, and a law enforcement certification from the state of Maryland.

2. What are the most important skills and/or qualities for someone in your profession?

Organization, drink knowledge, team skills, patience and understanding are key.

I train a lot of bartenders, and I tell them that organization is their first priority. Knowing how to make drinks is secondary. Working seamlessly with your partner is next on the important list. The skills to do the job should be automatic. I teach bartenders to set up their work area in an efficient manner and do things the same way each time so they don't have to think about each step. You just achieve them automatically.

It is important to be patient with customers when you're busy. They are often difficult to deal with because of the effect of alcohol but remember, they pay your bills.

Also, as a bartender you're the face of the business because you're often the first impression of a bar or restaurant. This is one of the most important things to teach a new bartender from the beginning.

Those who find the most success in this industry start as a server in a restaurant, or as a bar-back (bartender's assistant).

3. **What do you wish you had known going into this profession?**

I wish I had been told how easy it is to lose sight of your goals, how hard this job is on your body, and how unlikely it is to find a bartending job with retirement benefits.

Most people who get into bartending do it with the intention of moving into a career job outside the bar industry. Given the bartender's hours, it is easy to do that and to keep your bar job as a second income. However, this is a fairly lucrative position and, with cash in your pocket, it is easy to lose sight of goals that would otherwise be important to you.

This is also a physical job with a lot of standing and a lot of walking at high speed in a confined space. If you do this job, go to the gym. This does not mean to get pumped like a power lifter, but good joint strength is important for longevity.

Finally, save your money. Organize your retirement planning and savings because Uncle Sam won't. If you start saving early, even a bartender can retire on a golf course or Florida beach.

4. **Are there many job opportunities in your profession? In what specific areas?**

Job opportunities are limited but that's not to say they don't exist. There are bars everywhere: on cruise ships, ski resorts, theaters, golf courses, you name it. Movie stars start out as bartenders. I work for a company that has properties in the British Virgin Islands and offers seasonal exchange positions.

5. **How do you see your profession changing in the next five years? What role will technology play in those changes, and what skills will be required?**

Other than the occasional new liquor trend, this is a fairly constant business. I'm sure someday we will be replaced by robots or vending machines but that's not gonna happen in this century.

6. **What do you enjoy most about your job? What do you enjoy least?**

The best part of this job by far is the social aspect. I am an outgoing type A guy. I like people. I work with great people from the management to the bottom of the totem pole. Everyone brings something, but the customers and sharing stories with new people every day is a unique experience. I have seen movie stars, sports personalities and government officials in my bartending time. Once the great Chuck Yeager even talked to me about flying.

The worst part of the job is watching coworkers who become dependent on alcohol. This is an unfortunate side effect of this industry and most people don't see it coming until it's too late.

7. Can you suggest a valuable "try this" for students considering a career in your profession?

Most people who want to bartend have probably made a drink or two in their day, but those who are serious may try sitting in a busy bar and, rather than being social with their buddies, spend some time watching the bartender. A lot can be learned from actually seeing the process.

SELECTED SCHOOLS

Many large urban centers have culinary/food service training schools that cover bartending skills. The student may also explore online courses in mixology. Another tried-and-true method is that of apprenticeship, whereby a person starts out as a dishwasher or a bar assistant and learns the trade from an experienced bartender.

MORE INFORMATION

Culinary Institute of America
1946 Campus Drive
Hyde Park, NY 12538
845.452.9600
www.ciachef.edu

National Bartenders Association
Atlanta, GA
770.864.7811
www.bartender.org

National Restaurant Association Educational Foundation
175 West Jackson Boulevard
Suite 1500
Chicago, IL 60604-2814
800.765.2122
www.nraef.org

UNITE HERE! Headquarters
275 7th Avenue
New York, NY 10001-6709
212.265.7000
www.unitehere.org

Briana Nadeau/Editor

Bellhop/Bell Captain

Snapshot

Career Cluster: Hospitality & Tourism

Interests: Customer service, assisting others, working on your feet

Earnings (Yearly Average): $23,090

Employment & Outlook: Average Growth Expected

OVERVIEW

Sphere of Work

Bellhops and bell captains are part of the front-desk teams at large (and often luxury) hotels. A bell service team member greets guests as they arrive, directs them toward the front desk for check-in, carries luggage into and out of the hotel, arranges taxis and other transportation for the guests, and guides guests to their rooms. Bell captains manage the hotel's bellhop teams in addition to their bell service duties. Essentially, as is the case with many members of the hotel staff, the bellhop and bell captain's responsibility is to ensure that guests feel welcome and comfortable during their stay.

Work Environment

A bellhop's or bell captain's work primarily revolves around the hotel's main lobby area, where they greet guests as they arrive and depart. As part of their duties, they may carry luggage to and from guest vehicles, answer questions, and call for transportation. They may also be stationed in the hotel's lobby, storing luggage and coats for guests and directing them to conference rooms, the front desk or concierge, or other areas of the hotel. Additionally, bellhops and bell captains often accompany guests to their rooms, carrying luggage, opening doors, and providing guests with a tour of the room's amenities.

Profile

Working Conditions: Work Both Indoors And Outdoors
Physical Strength: Medium To Heavy Work
Education Needs: On-The-Job Training, High School Diploma Or GED
Licensure/Certification: Usually Not Required
Physical Abilities Not Required: No Strenuous Labor
Opportunities For Experience: Part-Time Work
Holland Interest Score*: ERS, ESR

* See Appendix A

Occupation Interest

Individuals interested in becoming bellhops and bell captains must be very personable and outgoing. They must be organized and able to handle multiple tasks at once. In addition, bellhops and bell captains must be able to stay on their feet for most of the day and carry heavy loads. Furthermore, bellhops and bell captains must be friendly, courteous, and diplomatic. Both positions require good communication and problem-solving skills, while bell captains must have managerial skills as well.

A Day in the Life—Duties and Responsibilities

A bell service team member spends the majority of the workday in a hotel lobby and in front of the hotel. They are present from the moment a guest arrives at the hotel until the guest is settled in his or her room. In this role, they greet a guest as he or she pulls up to the hotel, carry the guest's luggage into the lobby, and guide him or her to the front desk for check-in. The bellhop or bell captain then carries the guest's luggage to his or her room and, once inside, shows the room's amenities, such as the television, phone, bathroom, and other features. In some cases, bellhops and bell captains may move and park guest vehicles as well. When a guest departs, the bell service team may transport a guest's luggage or baggage from the hotel room to the guest's vehicle.

In addition to providing services to incoming and outgoing guests, a bellhop may serve as a hotel lobby's "jack of all trades." He or she may deliver messages to guests, provide directions to points of interest, run errands, arrange for mail and package delivery, and inspect rooms to make sure they are satisfactory. A bell captain performs most of these tasks and directs the rest of the bell service team. Like any traditional manager, bell captains coordinate schedules and shifts and address any team concerns that may arise.

Duties and Responsibilities

- **Transferring trunks, packages, and other luggage to rooms**
- **Escorting incoming guests to their rooms**
- **Informing patrons of available services of the hotel**
- **Paging guests, delivering messages, and running errands**
- **Setting up conference rooms and display tables for sales agents**
- **Arranging for outgoing mail shipments for guests**

OCCUPATION SPECIALTIES

Baggage Porters

Baggage Porters deliver luggage to and from guests' rooms, and set up rooms for sales personnel.

Room-Service Clerks

Room-Service Clerks deliver and remove packages, laundry, groceries and other articles to and from guests' rooms and record all information pertaining to services rendered to guests.

Doorkeepers

Doorkeepers serve residents and guests by opening doors, hailing taxicabs, answering inquiries and assisting guests into automobiles.

WORK ENVIRONMENT

Physical Environment

Bellhops and bell captains work mostly in the hotel lobby and at the entrance of the hotel itself. They may work outside the hotel entrance in any weather condition. A hotel lobby is often very crowded with guests and visitors, and bellhops and bell captains must work together to ensure that each guest receives the service he or she requires.

Relevant Skills and Abilities

Communication Skills
- Speaking effectively

Interpersonal/Social Skills
- Being able to remain calm
- Being sensitive to others
- Cooperating with others
- Respecting others' opinions
- Working as a member of a team

Organization & Management Skills
- Performing duties that change frequently
- Performing routine work

Other Skills
- Keeping a neat appearance
- Having a willingness to please

Human Environment

Bellhops and bell captains must work together in a team environment. They also need to work with other important hotel staff members, including sales managers, front-desk managers, concierges, maintenance personnel, parking valets, and general managers. Above all, they must work well with customers (including the occasional "touchy" customer who gets upset easily).

Technological Environment

Bellhops and bell captains must be well versed in the amenities available in guest rooms, such as telecommunication services, television functionality, and bathroom fixtures such as a whirlpool or hot tub. Bell captains must also have familiarity with computer

EDUCATION, TRAINING, AND ADVANCEMENT

software such as email, word processing, and spreadsheet applications to perform their managerial duties.

High School/Secondary

High school students who are interested in becoming a bellhop or bell captain should complete their state-required high school coursework. Foreign language courses are also recommended for interested students, as working in the hospitality industry often requires interaction with guests from all over the world.

Suggested High School Subjects
- English

Famous First

The first use of the familiar red cap worn by bellhops was by an African American train porter, John Williams, in New York's Grand Central Station in 1890. Williams employed a red cap during a busy Labor Day weekend to distinguish his outfit from the blue outfits and hats worn by other train personnel and to make himself stand out in the crowd. The tactic proved successful and red caps (and uniforms) were eventually adopted by hotel porters, or "bellboys" as they were originally called. They long remained part of the standard uniform, but today are seen far less frequently than before.

Postsecondary

A college degree for bellhops and bell captains is typically not required. However, continued training in foreign languages and hospitality management can help a bellhop advance within the hotel and the industry. For those students studying toward a degree in hospitality management or a related field, many trade or technical schools have partnered with hotels to provide students with opportunities to work in a hotel setting, giving them the ability to understand the business.

Adult Job Seekers

Adults seeking to become members of the bell service team are encouraged to apply directly for positions at hotel human resource departments or online. Candidates should emphasize their interpersonal skills, willingness to help others, and organizational abilities. Some hotel associations and hospitality-oriented websites post openings and hold job fairs at which these positions are often available.

Professional Certification and Licensure

Bellhops and bell captains are typically not required to obtain any professional certification. However, they are usually required to hold a valid driver's license and maintain a clean driving record, especially for positions in which they will be asked to park and move guest vehicles.

Additional Requirements

Most luxury hotels expect their bellhops to have experience in the hotel industry prior to joining their bell service team. Bell captains in particular should have experience working with and leading bell service teams as well as performing the duties of a bellhop. Therefore, aspiring bell service team members should be willing to learn this craft early in their careers, possibly through job shadow programs.

EARNINGS AND ADVANCEMENT

Earnings depend on the type, size, geographic location, and union affiliation of the employer. Nationally, bellhops and baggage porters earned an average annual salary of $23,090 in 2012. The lowest ten percent earned $16,580 and the highest ten percent earned $32,220. Tips for bellhops generally depend on the size and location of the hotel. Baggage porters working in airports usually receive larger tips than those employed by other transportation facilities. If average tips bring them above the minimum wage level, they may receive less than the minimum hourly wage.

Bellhops and baggage porters may receive paid vacations, holidays, and sick days; life and health insurance; and retirement benefits. These are usually paid by the employer. They may also receive reduced rates on meals during working hours and free room and board in resort hotels.

Metropolitan Areas with the Highest Employment Level in this Occupation

Metropolitan area	Employment[1]	Employment per thousand jobs	Hourly mean wage
New York-White Plains-Wayne, NY-NJ	3,810	0.74	$14.34
Miami-Miami Beach-Kendall, FL	2,780	2.78	$11.82
Las Vegas-Paradise, NV	2,580	3.15	$12.50
Washington-Arlington-Alexandria, DC-VA-MD-WV	2,280	0.97	$11.15
Orlando-Kissimmee-Sanford, FL	1,680	1.66	$9.66
Los Angeles-Long Beach-Glendale, CA	1,460	0.38	$11.37
Chicago-Joliet-Naperville, IL	1,200	0.33	$11.24
Seattle-Bellevue-Everett, WA	1,070	0.76	$10.50

Source: Bureau of Labor Statistics

EMPLOYMENT AND OUTLOOK

There were approximately 40,500 bellhops and baggage porters employed nationally in 2012. Employment is expected to grow about as fast as the average for all occupations through the year 2022, which means employment is projected to increase about 11 percent.

Employment Trend, Projected 2012–22

Bellhops and Bell Captains: 11%

Total, All Occupations: 11%

Unskilled Occupations: 7%

Note: "All Occupations" includes all occupations in the U.S. Economy. Source: U.S. Bureau of Labor Statistics, Employment Projections Program

Related Occupations
- Counter & Rental Clerk
- Flight Attendant
- Waiter/Waitress

Conversation With . . .
SID BELAOUN
Bellman, 8 years

1. **What was your individual career path in terms of education/training, entry-level job, or other significant opportunity?**

   I had been working as a lifeguard and wanted a change. I took a job as bellhop at the Park Plaza Hotel, where I worked for four years. I moved to The Lenox because it was a step up. I did a week of training upon being hired.

2. **What are the most important skills and/or qualities for someone in your profession?**

   To be a bellman, you have to be happy to do the job, because it will show in your interactions with people. You must be open to meeting different people from different parts of the world. You have to be interested in making guests feel comfortable. You must be organized and efficient. You need to be knowledgeable about the city. Also, you need to be physically fit because of the amount of luggage you will be lifting.

3. **What do you wish you had known going into this profession?**

   When I started, I wish I had known more about the city of Boston. I wish I had known more about the city's history, as well as directions, attractions, restaurants—all of that, anything that a guest of the hotel or tourist might ask you about.

4. **Are there many job opportunities in your profession? In what specific areas?**

   There are opportunities if you want them. A bellman can move up to bell captain. But I have been happy doing what I have been doing. I love the guests, and every day I am still learning something new.

5. How do you see your profession changing in the next five years? What role will technology play in those changes, and what skills will be required?

I don't see the profession changing much in the next five years. It may be one of the few areas where technology will not affect the job. The core of being a bellman is human interaction with other people, and I believe that will always be the case.

6. What do you enjoy most about your job? What do you enjoy least?

I enjoy the friendship and what is around you. I love it when I get a warm welcome from a guest, or even from my coworkers. I love my job and the compliments I get. I work hard and am very proud of the job that I do.

What I least enjoy about being a bellman is when I go above and beyond the call of duty and do not feel appreciated. It's nice to have people recognize your hard work and extra effort.

7. Can you suggest a valuable "try this" for students considering a career in your profession?

Practice patience, because you will need to be patient with guests. Patience can be cultivated. And practice smiling. Hotel guests like to be greeted by a smiling face. Remember that you have to give people your time. Whatever you are doing at any given moment, do your best.

SELECTED SCHOOLS

Although some training in customer service in the hospitality and tourism industry may prove useful to the student interested in working as a bellhop or bell captain, the tried-and-true method of learning in this trade is that of apprenticeship, whereby a person starts out as an assistant baggage porter and learns the trade from an experienced bellhop or bell captain.

MORE INFORMATION

American Hotel & Lodging Association
1201 New York Avenue, NW
Suite 600
Washington, DC 20005-3931
202.289.3100
www.ahla.com

American Hotel & Lodging Educational Institute
800 N. Magnolia Avenue, Suite 300
Orlando, FL 32803
800.349.0299
www.ahlei.org

UNITE HERE! Headquarters
275 7th Avenue
New York, NY 10001-6709
212.265.7000
www.unitehere.org

Michael Auerbach/Editor

Bus Driver

Snapshot

Career Cluster: Hospitality & Tourism; Transportation

Interests: Driving, interacting with people, transportation

Earnings (Yearly Average): $38,470 (non-school bus); $29,150 (school bus)

Employment & Outlook: Average Growth Expected

OVERVIEW

Sphere of Work

Bus drivers transport commuters, travelers, students, special clients, and others to local and national destinations along specified routes. Perhaps the best-known type of bus driver is the transit and intercity bus driver, who transports passengers within a particular metropolitan area or between different cities or regions. There are also bus drivers who take travelers or other clients on chartered trips to specific destinations, including on guided tours. A third category of bus driver is the school bus driver, who transports students to and from school and school-related activities. Bus drivers usually

follow precise time schedules and mapped routes. They are always responsible for transporting passengers to their destinations safely and on time.

Work Environment

Bus drivers spend the majority of their day seated behind the wheel and may be subject to long driving hours. They work in all weather conditions and often experience heavy traffic, unruly passengers, and unexpected delays and obstacles. Transit bus drivers generally work a forty-hour week throughout the year, including nights and weekends, and also often work split shifts. Intercity, charter, and tour bus drivers may have more irregular schedules, and those who drive for larger companies often average less than forty hours per week. School bus drivers work only during the school year and normally work split shifts—that is, in the morning and the afternoon, with time off in between—sometimes for less than twenty hours a week, though they may also transport students to school-related activities on evenings and weekends. Most bus drivers, although employees of a company, work independently, without direct supervision.

Profile

Working Conditions: Work Indoors
Physical Strength: Medium Work
Education Needs: No High School Diploma, On-The-Job Training
Licensure/Certification: Required
Physical Abilities Not Required: No Heavy Labor
Opportunities For Experience: Military Service, Part-Time Work
Holland Interest Score*: RES

* See Appendix A

Occupation Interest

Individuals interested in becoming bus drivers should understand the rules of the road as well as the fundamentals of traffic rules and regulations. Bus drivers must always be pleasant, calm, and stoic, especially when dealing with unruly or volatile passengers. They should be organized, skilled at communicating and interacting with others, and able to juggle multiple tasks and shifting priorities. School bus drivers should find fulfillment in working with children and possess the patience necessary to adequately supervise them.

A Day in the Life—Duties and Responsibilities

Transit and charter bus drivers communicate with customers, collect tickets and cash fares, and answer questions regarding routes and schedules. They also help passengers needing special assistance, carry baggage, and make sure that passengers are properly seated. Occasionally, drivers handle onboard emergencies, fights, and other disruptions. Transit bus drivers usually travel the same route within one metropolitan area daily, making frequent stops throughout the day to pick up and drop off passengers, while intercity bus drivers may make very few stops along their route. Depending on the company they work for, transit and charter bus drivers may be required to inspect their vehicles for any maintenance problems or equipment failures and check fuel, oil, and other fluid levels before departing from any location. In some cases, bus drivers must also handle minor repairs. Most drivers use logbooks to record trip information, report delays, and note any problems or difficulties that may have occurred. Some of these same activities are carried out by tour bus drivers as well, along with the added responsibility of providing a commentary to passengers about the sites and scenes passed along the way or else having a tour guide onboard who handles this task.

School bus drivers follow a regular daily route, transporting students to and from school, to sporting events and field trips, and to other school-related activities. They follow strict safety and traffic regulations and do their best to ensure that students have a safe ride. School bus drivers and other bus drivers should be familiar with first aid procedures in the event of an emergency.

Duties and Responsibilities

- Driving the vehicle and complying with all local traffic regulations
- Inspecting the bus and checking gas, oil, tires, and water before departure
- Collecting and recording tickets or cash fares
- Loading and unloading baggage
- Providing schedule information and/or tour commentary as needed
- Ensuring the safety of passengers
- Regulating heating, lighting, and ventilating systems for passenger comfort
- Maintaining logs and reporting delays or accidents

OCCUPATION SPECIALTIES

Local and Intercity Drivers

Local and Intercity Drivers transport passengers within cities and towns or between them, usually following regular routes and schedules. Local Drivers stop frequently, often only a few blocks apart, and must navigate city and suburban streets. Intercity drivers often use interstate highways and may cross state lines, stopping at bus stations for passenger pick-up and drop-off along the way.

Motor-Coach (Charter and Tour) Drivers

Motor-Coach Drivers transport passengers on charted trips or sightseeing tours. Their schedule and route are generally arranged by a trip planner for the convenience of the passengers, who often are on vacation. Motor-Coach Drivers are usually away for long periods of time because they usually stay with vacationers for the length of the trip.

Mobile-Lounge DriversPhysical Environment

Mobile-Lounge Drivers drive mobile lounges to transport aircraft passengers between airport terminal buildings and aircraft on the runways.

School Bus Drivers

School Bus Drivers transport students between pick-up points and school. They may drive a bus on special trips as well.

WORK ENVIRONMENT

Physical Environment

Bus drivers spend most of their time in their vehicles, which they must keep clean and well maintained for passengers. Drivers are also responsible for regulating the temperature levels and other environmental conditions inside the bus. In addition, they must follow all local traffic regulations and drive safely in order to prevent accidents. Long-haul drivers are subject to fatigue and must guard against becoming drowsy at the wheel.

Human Environment

Bus drivers interact with numerous individuals on a daily basis. They communicate with passengers of all ages and ethnicities, and often assist disabled or impaired individuals. Bus drivers do not normally work with other drivers, but may coordinate with them via phone or radio throughout the day. Though they work independently, bus drivers occasionally meet with supervisors to deal with administrative, training, or scheduling issues. Charter and tour bus drivers often interact with foreign tourists and must anticipate some communication difficulties.

Technological Environment

Bus drivers must be familiar with a wide range of tools in order to operate their vehicles properly. They commonly utilize physical and electronic maps, two-way radios, and public address systems, and in some cases may also need to use first aid kits, emergency flares, fire extinguishers, tire pressure gauges, grease guns, snow chains, or wheelchair lifts and restraint systems.

Relevant Skills and Abilities

Communication Skills
- Speaking effectively

Interpersonal/Social Skills
- Being able to remain calm
- Cooperating with others
- Working as a member of a team

Organization & Management Skills
- Paying attention to and handling details
- Performing routine work

Work Environment Skills
- Driving a vehicle

EDUCATION, TRAINING, AND ADVANCEMENT

High School/Secondary

A high school diploma or its equivalent is sometimes required, though not always, to become a bus driver. High school students who are interested in working as bus drivers will benefit from classes in communications, basic mathematics, and health, as well as courses that deal with automotive applications, business operations, and mechanics. When they reach the age of sixteen, students should obtain a permit or driver's license and practice navigating local streets and following local bus routes. They should also travel locally by bus, paying close attention to the duties of the driver.

Suggested High School Subjects
- Auto Service Technology
- Diesel Maintenance Technology
- Driver Training
- English
- First Aid Training
- Mathematics

Famous First

The first night coach was placed in service between Los Angeles and San Francisco in 1929. The bus provided sleeping and seating accommodations for 26 people. It had two lavatories, a kitchen, and a pantry, and carried a crew of three: pilot (driver), steward, and porter.

Postsecondary

Bus drivers must have a driver's license and a clean driving record. Some employers require new bus drivers to pass a written test to demonstrate their understanding of complex bus schedules.

Most companies provide new drivers with two to eight weeks of instruction and training. Classroom instruction covers topics such as Department of Transportation rules, state and municipal driving regulations, schedule analysis, and record keeping; behind the wheel, drivers practice various maneuvers on set courses, in light traffic, and on crowded highways. After a period of time, they make mock trips along specified routes, without passengers, to simulate real driving. New bus drivers usually get help from an experienced driver who accompanies them along their routes, answering questions, giving advice, and noting their progress.

Related College Majors
- Truck, Bus & Other Commercial Vehicle Operation

Adult Job Seekers

Prospective bus drivers should contact local public and private schools or intercity and charter companies directly to inquire about openings. Bus driver unions and transportation authorities may also provide information about available jobs. Many new drivers start out by accepting part-time work and less desirable shifts and eventually work their way up to full-time employment.

Professional Certification and Licensure

Bus drivers are required to have a commercial driver's license (CDL) as well as appropriate endorsements in order to operate commercial vehicles. CDL requirements vary by state, but normally include both knowledge and skills tests. Transit and intercity bus drivers must have a P (passenger vehicle) endorsement on their CDL; school bus drivers must have a P as well as an S (school bus) endorsement. Candidates can obtain endorsements by passing additional knowledge and skills tests given by state licensing agencies. Bus drivers can contact the Federal Motor Carrier Safety Administration for more information on CDLs and endorsements.

Additional Requirements

Although some states allow bus drivers as young as eighteen to operate within their borders, federal regulations require interstate drivers to be at least twenty-one years old, and many companies prefer their drivers be at least twenty-four. Interstate bus drivers must also pass a physical examination every two years. Bus drivers should have good hearing and vision, normal blood pressure, and the ability to read and speak English. They must have no record of substance abuse and may be required to undergo periodic drug testing. Drivers may not be hired if ever convicted of a felony involving a motor vehicle or any such related crime. Some states require school bus drivers to pass a criminal and mental health background check.

EARNINGS AND ADVANCEMENT

Bus drivers are generally guaranteed a minimum number of miles or hours per pay period. Long-distance bus drivers are usually paid on a mileage basis with the time required for the trip and the seniority of the driver as factors. Hourly wages for local transit bus drivers are usually highest in the larger cities. School bus drivers' wages vary with the individual driver's experience and the specific school system.

Mean annual earnings of transit and intercity bus drivers were $38,470 in 2012. The lowest ten percent earned less than $21,320, and the highest ten percent earned more than $59,480.

Medial annual earnings of school bus drivers were $29,150 in 2012. The lowest ten percent earned less than $17,610, and the highest ten percent earned more than $43,560.

Bus drivers may receive paid vacations, holidays, and sick days; life and health insurance; and retirement benefits. These are usually paid by the employer. Some employers also provide uniforms.

Metropolitan Areas with the Highest
Employment Level in this Occupation

Metropolitan area	Employment[1]	Employment per thousand jobs	Hourly mean wage
New York-White Plains-Wayne, NY-NJ	18,660	3.62	$24.03
Chicago-Joliet-Naperville, IL	8,620	2.37	$22.39
Los Angeles-Long Beach-Glendale, CA	8,390	2.17	$19.47
Seattle-Bellevue-Everett, WA	4,310	3.06	$24.10
Orlando-Kissimmee-Sanford, FL	3,470	3.43	$11.79
Washington-Arlington-Alexandria, DC-VA-MD-WV	3,330	1.42	$19.58
San Francisco-San Mateo-Redwood City, CA	3,080	3.08	$23.94
Atlanta-Sandy Springs-Marietta, GA	2,890	1.28	$15.91

[1]Does not include school bus drivers. Source: Bureau of Labor Statistics

EMPLOYMENT AND OUTLOOK

There were approximately 163,000 bus and motor-coach drivers, not including school bus drivers, employed nationally in 2012. Another 490,000—i.e., the bulk of bus drivers—worked for school systems or companies that provide school bus services under contract. Most of the non-school bus drivers worked for private and local government transit systems; some also worked for intercity and charter bus lines.

Employment of bus drivers is expected to grow about as fast as the average for all occupations through the year 2022, which means employment is projected to increase 9 percent to 15 percent. This is due to the transportation needs of a growing general population and, in particular, a growing school-age population. Most openings will arise as experienced bus drivers transfer to other occupations or leave the labor force. Competition will be strong for higher paying inter-city and public transit bus driver positions. Most new jobs will be found in areas with a growing population, such as many communities in the Sunbelt states.

Employment Trend, Projected 2012–22

Total, All Occupations: 11%

Transit and Intercity Bus Drivers: 10%

All Bus Drivers: 9%

School and Charter Bus Drivers: 9%

Note: "All Occupations" includes all occupations in the U.S. Economy. Source: U.S. Bureau of Labor Statistics, Employment Projections Program

Related Occupations
- Taxi Driver & Chauffeur

Related Military Occupations
- Vehicle Driver
- Related Military Occupations
- Vehicle Driver

Conversation With . . .
DICK LEAHY
Tour Bus Operator, 8 years

1. What was your individual career path in terms of education/training, entry-level job, or other significant opportunity?

I worked for the phone company for quite a while, 25 years. I worked for Brigham & Women's Hospital and sold stereo equipment. I wanted to do something that was more fun, without the problems of email and meetings. I wanted to get away from the corporate world, a job that I could go home from and not think about. I like history and I like Boston.

2. What are the most important skills and/or qualities for someone in your profession?

Being able to connect with people and enjoy people. You have to be able to talk in front of people, which some people find very difficult. You hopefully establish some kind of connection. That can be hard, with people jumping on and off. And there can be a language barrier. Building a rapport with people is the number one thing. You have to be a good driver. You really can't be too aggressive. You don't want passengers thinking, "Oh, man, this is scary." You don't even want them thinking about the driving at all. You want to be slow, because it's sightseeing.

3. What do you wish you had known going into this profession?

I was sort of naive. I thought they'd put you on the bus and you'd be off on your own. There's a time schedule and script (Old Town Trolley) wants you to go on. As a customer, you don't realize it because you're not supposed to realize it. There's an overall script covering certain big historical things. For the rest you're sort of free to do different things. The multiple stops are a little frustrating, when a whole group gets off at, say, the *USS Constitution* and a whole new group gets on.

4. Are there many job opportunities in your profession? In what specific areas?

Yes, quite a few. There's a fairly high turnover. People do it for a year or a season, and then they move on. Or, someone like me who's getting to a point in life where I'm thinking about retirement might cut down to two days a week.

5. **How do you see your profession changing in the next five years? What role will technology play in those changes, and what skills will be required?**

There's always competition in this field. There are four companies doing this in Boston. Technology is changing, so you can plug in a foreign language and you can hear the tour in another language. I was in Dublin and the tour company had two tours—a recorded tour and a live tour. You're talking about retrofitting a lot of vehicles. In the next five years, I see that happening.

6. **What do you enjoy most about your job? What do you enjoy least?**

Making people laugh. Having fun with them. If you can connect with people and they get your sense of humor and you can make them laugh, I really enjoy that. Any time people are asking questions, then you can really go into the stories with more details. You can kind of tell who the people are who want to know more. Questions are good.

What I enjoy least is when you pull up to a stop and there are 20 people waiting and there are no seats and you have to tell them they can't get on. That's no fun. They've been waiting and they're angry and they might yell at you. I'm pretty tough-skinned at this point, but I still don't enjoy it. The other thing is people chatting on the tour and not paying attention. Sometimes it gets frustrating.

7. **Can you suggest a valuable "try this" for students considering a career in your profession?**

Try taking walking tours and watching carefully. I take tours when I go to another city. You have to be somewhat of a performer. I also watch comedians a lot. But it's a little bit different than a comedian, where people go there ready to laugh and be entertained. The people aren't getting onboard to see you; they're there to see the city. What you need to do to get good at this is do it a lot until you get comfortable and it becomes second nature.

SELECTED SCHOOLS

Most bus drivers train with the companies that have hired them (as trainees). It is also possible in some cases to train for a commercial operating license through a private agency. Interested students should check with local bus companies or examine area business listings for driving schools offering specialized training in bus operation.

MORE INFORMATION

Amalgamated Transit Union
5025 Wisconsin Avenue, NW
Washington, DC 20016
202.537.1645
www.atu.org

American Bus Association
700 13th Street NW
Suite 575
Washington, DC 20005-5923
202.842.1645
www.buses.org

American Public Transportation Association
1666 K Street NW, Suite 1100
Washington, DC 20006
202.496.4800
www.apta.com

Federal Motor Carrier Safety Administration
1200 New Jersey Avenue SE
Washington, DC 20590
800.832.5660
www.fmcsa.dot.gov

International Brotherhood of Teamsters
25 Louisiana Avenue, NW
Washington, DC 20001
202.624.6800
www.teamster.org

National School Transportation Association
113 South West Street, 4th Floor
Alexandria, VA 22314
800.222.6782
www.yellowbuses.org

United Motorcoach Association
113 South West Street, 4th Floor
Alexandria, VA 22314
800.424.8262
www.uma.org

United Transportation Union
24950 Country Club Boulevard
Suite 340
North Olmsted, OH 44070-5333
216.228.9400
www.utu.org

Briana Nadeau/Editor

Cook/Chef

Snapshot

Career Cluster: Hospitality & Tourism

Interests: Culinary arts, food, being independent, being creative

Earnings (Yearly Average): $32,272

Employment & Outlook: Average to Slower Than Average Growth Expected

OVERVIEW

Sphere of Work

Cooks and chefs prepare culinary dishes for restaurant clientele, private parties, and other customers. They also oversee kitchen activities and operation. Chefs and cooks design menus and dishes, order supplies and grocery items, prepare food, organize ingredients, set staff schedules, and direct other chefs and kitchen personnel. Chefs and cooks also ensure that kitchens are efficient, safe, and abide by health department standards. Cook and chef job descriptions vary based on their experience, the place of employment, and the staff size. In a large operation an executive chef or head cook oversees the kitchen while a variety of specialized chefs and line cooks prepare different parts of the dishes to be served.

Work Environment

The kitchen is the primary work environment for chefs and cooks. They work in restaurants, banquet halls, club houses, hospitals, school dining halls and cafeterias, and similar venues. Some work in smaller kitchens, including short-order restaurants and coffee shops. In most settings, chefs and cooks work in a complex and very busy environment, particularly during peak meal or event times. This environment may be stressful, as chefs and cooks are required to prepare many dishes simultaneously while coordinating with other kitchen and restaurant staff. Conditions are hot, and floors may be slippery and dangerous. New situations arise quickly, such as running out of certain items, problems with a guest or customer, or dealing with unique allergies. Hours may be long—chefs and cooks must arrive early to sign for orders and prepare foods, and they must stay late after hours to clean up and take inventory. Chefs and cooks must have physical stamina as they work on their feet and are active throughout the day.

Profile

Working Conditions: Work Indoors
Physical Strength: Medium Work
Education Needs: On-The-Job Training, High School Diploma Or G.E.D., Culinary Arts School Certificate, Apprenticeship
Licensure/Certification: Usually Not Required
Physical Abilities Not Required: No Heavy Labor
Opportunities For Experience: Apprenticeship, Military Service, Volunteer Work, Part-Time Work
Holland Interest Score*: ESR, RES, RSE

* See Appendix A

Occupation Interest

The best chefs and cooks are culinary artists. There are a wide range of venues in which chefs and cooks can express this artistry and love of food, including upscale and chain restaurants, cruise ships, local bistros, and corner delis. A wide range of positions is available, appealing to many different types of people. Although the work is very challenging, chefs and cooks take ownership of the dishes they prepare, which can be very empowering. Generally, individuals who become chefs and cooks simply love food and food preparation.

A Day in the Life—Duties and Responsibilities

The work of chefs and cooks varies based on the size of the kitchen staff as well as the professional level at which they work. Chefs meet with food suppliers to determine the quality and price of their food supplies, prepare vendor orders, and meet deliveries (inspecting them for quality). In the early morning, chefs organize food ingredients so that they are easily located during peak business hours and prepare certain food items (such as marinating meats, chopping vegetables, and preparing sauces). Chefs and cooks also design menu items, food displays, and individual plates, directing garnishment and food arrangement. Chefs and cooks are also accountable for managing food costs, balancing supply costs with labor costs and menu prices.

During meal times, cooks and chefs work at the stoves and ovens, cooking ingredients to order, arranging plates, and placing them where servers can easily find them. Additionally, head chefs direct the activities of other chefs and cooks at the facility, ensuring that all orders are being prepared quickly and properly. Between meal rushes, chefs and cooks work on daily accounting, staff schedules, new menus, and dish recipes. They also inspect equipment to ensure that it is working and has been cleaned properly.

Duties and Responsibilities

- Planning menus
- Selecting and developing recipes
- Preparing food items for cooking
- Weighing, measuring, and mixing ingredients
- Operating ovens, stoves, grills and other cooking equipment
- Cutting food portions and arranging food to be served
- Ordering supplies as needed

OCCUPATION SPECIALTIES

Executive Chefs and Head Cooks

Executive Chefs and Head Cooks are primarily responsible for overseeing the operation of a kitchen. They coordinate the work of sous chefs and other cooks, who prepare most of the meals. Executive chefs also have many duties beyond the kitchen. They design the menu, review food and beverage purchases, and often train employees. Some executive chefs are primarily occupied by administrative tasks and spend little time in the kitchen.

Sous Chefs

Sous Chefs are a kitchen's second-in-command. They supervise the restaurant's cooks, do some meal preparation tasks, and report results to the head chefs. In the absence of the head chef, sous chefs run the kitchen.

Restaurant Cooks

Restaurant Cooks usually prepare a wide selection of dishes and cook most orders individually. Some restaurant cooks may order supplies, set menu prices, and plan the daily menu.

Institutional Cooks

Institutional Cooks prepare soups, meats, vegetables, salads, dressings, and desserts in large quantities for schools, cafeterias, hospitals and other institutions.

Short-Order Cooks

Short-Order Cooks prepare foods in restaurants and coffee shops that emphasize fast service and quick food preparation. They usually prepare sandwiches, fry eggs, and cook french fries, often working on several orders at the same time.

Fast-Food Cooks

Fast-Food Cooks work in fast-food restaurants and prepare such foods as hamburgers, hot dogs, fish and chips, and tacos for window or counter service.

Bakers and Pastry Chefs

Bakers prepare bread, rolls, muffins, and biscuits and supervise other bakers in various institutions. Pastry Chefs specialize in sweet baked goods (e.g., cakes, pies, and tarts) and in the preparation of desserts.

Household and Personal Chefs and Cooks

Household and Personal Chefs and Cooks prepare meals in private homes, according to the client's taste's and dietary needs. They may also cater parties, holiday meals, luncheons, and other social events.

WORK ENVIRONMENT

Relevant Skills and Abilities

Communication Skills
- Generating ideas

Interpersonal/Social Skills
- Cooperating with others
- Working as a member of a team

Organization & Management Skills
- Organization & Management Skills
- Managing time
- Meeting goals and deadlines
- Organizing information or materials
- Paying attention to and handling details

Technical Skills
- Working with machines, tools, or other objects
- Working with your hands

Other Skills
- Performing work that produces tangible results
- Preparing food

Physical Environment

Chefs primarily work in the kitchens of restaurants, banquet halls, cafeterias, and other venues that cater to the public. Some chefs and cooks, such as personal chefs, work in settings that are more private. Kitchens are typically very busy, with many people working at a high pace, particularly during meal and event times. With stoves and other appliances running and frequent food spills, there are physical risks to chefs and cooks while on the job. Cuts on the hands and fingers from sharp knives are also a common hazard.

Human Environment

Chefs and cooks work with many other people, depending on the size and nature of the venue at which they work. Among those on the kitchen staff with whom chefs and cooks may interact are sous chefs, line and prep cooks, stewards, servers, bartenders and sommeliers (wine specialists), restaurant managers or owners, and dishwashers. In addition, chefs and cooks work with deliverymen, vendors, suppliers, and the public. Kitchens are often loud and boisterous places, and the chef often sets the tone for what happens in the back of the house.

Technological Environment

Chefs and cooks should be able to use stoves, fryers, ovens, grills, mixers, and other kitchen tools and appliances. Their knowledge of these kitchen tools should extend to legal rules on operation, cleaning, and maintenance, so that the facility complies with local, state and federal public health and workplace safety regulations. Chefs and cooks must also have skills in computers and office software to use for accounting, inventory, and supply orders.

EDUCATION, TRAINING, AND ADVANCEMENT

High School/Secondary

Interested high school students are encouraged to take food preparation and cooking courses. They may also benefit from health and nutrition classes. Higher-level cooks, such as head chefs and sous chefs, oversee the management of the kitchen – high school students seeking to reach such professional levels should take business courses as well. Most important, though, is on-the-job training. High school students interested in a culinary degree should find a job in food service to understand the atmosphere, the pace, and dynamics of a working kitchen.

Suggested High School Subjects
- Business
- Business Math
- English
- Family & Consumer Sciences
- First Aid Training
- Food Service & Management
- Foods & Nutrition
- Health Science Technology

Famous First

The first cyber café was the Electronic Café International, founded in Santa Monica, Calif., in 1988. Besides a coffeehouse menu and artistic events, it featured computers with modems and other telecommunications gear for use by patrons.

Postsecondary

Most cooks and chefs begin working in a kitchen right after high school, although many high-level chefs and cooks pursue a postsecondary degree. Many of these degrees can be earned at vocational schools, where students can receive culinary training. Two- and four-year colleges offer more extensive training for individuals seeking positions in fine dining and upscale restaurants.

Related College Majors
- Culinary Arts/Chef Training
- Food Services Operation

Adult Job Seekers

The most important qualification an aspiring chef or cook can have is experience. Adults seeking to become senior-level chefs and cooks must begin by pursuing jobs at lower levels, such as line or prep cook, which give them the experience and professional guidance they need to advance. Qualified chefs and cooks also find opportunities by networking through culinary and restaurant trade organizations, such as the National Restaurant Association and local affiliates of the American Culinary Federation.

Professional Certification and Licensure

While there are no licensure requirement for cooks and chefs, most states have food safety certification requirements for kitchen staff. This certification process addresses such subjects as food storage, preparation, and service. Interested individuals should research the food safety certification requirements of their home state.

Some cooks and chefs receive optional certification in specialized cooking skills, such as professional pastry-makers, personal chefs, and teachers of culinary arts. Such certification may enhance a job candidate's credentials.

Additional Requirements

Chefs and cooks are food lovers, knowledgeable about a wide range of different food styles and origins. They should know and have an appreciation for flavors, textures, techniques, and styles. Successful cooks often have a creative and artistic attitude, which helps in meal presentation. Cooks and chefs must have a tolerance for a busy and often chaotic atmosphere. Many chefs are enterprising, seeking to own and operate their own business or create their own unique style of dining experience. For those who seek this path, an understanding of business and management is essential, as many restaurants fail within the first three years of opening.

EARNINGS AND ADVANCEMENT

Earnings depend on the type, size, and geographic location of the employer, and the employee's experience and skill. Wages generally are highest in elegant restaurants and hotels, where many executive chefs are employed, and in major metropolitan areas. Median annual earnings of fast food, restaurant and short order cooks were $21,475 in 2012. The lowest ten percent earned less than $17,043, and the highest ten percent earned more than $32,344.

Median annual earnings of chefs and head cooks were $43,068 in 2012. The lowest ten percent earned less than $24,656, and the highest ten percent earned more than $75,218.

Cooks and chefs may receive paid vacations, holidays, and sick days; life and health insurance; and retirement benefits. These are usually paid by the employer. Cooks may also receive free meals and uniforms and laundry service.

Metropolitan Areas with the Highest
Employment Level in this Occupation

Metropolitan area	Employment[1]	Employment per thousand jobs	Hourly mean wage
*New York-White Plains-Wayne, NY-NJ	52,570	3.10	$18.31
*Chicago-Joliet-Naperville, IL	35,530	2.44	$14.00
*Los Angeles-Long Beach-Glendale, CA	37,5700	2.43	$15.61
*Atlanta-Sandy Springs-Marietta, GA	45,760	3.53	$12.63

[1]Does not include fast-food or household cooks. Source: Bureau of Labor Statistics

Fun Fact

Hey Chef, what's cooking? Among other things, strong feelings over the use of the term "chef" versus "cook." Some argue that to use the title of chef, one must have professional training, the ability to create menus and run a professional kitchen, creativity, and even knowledge of the history of cuisine. Baloney, say others. According to Chefpedia, "This is a fundamental and philosophical question." Now that's food for thought .

EMPLOYMENT AND OUTLOOK

Cooks and chefs held about 2 million jobs in2012. Employment of cooks and chefs is expected to grow slower than the average for all occupations through the year 2022, which means employment is projected to increase 5 percent to 10 percent. Employment growth will still continue because of the growing population's desire for the quickness and convenience of eating out and being prepared a ready-made meal. Employment of executive chefs and head cooks, however, is expected to fall slightly below the average as restaurants adjust to economic circumstances and make do with the staffs they have.

Employment Trend, Projected 2012–22

Total, All Occupations: 11%

Cooks: 10%

Chefs and Head Cooks: 5%

Note: "All Occupations" includes all occupations in the U.S. Economy. Source: U.S. Bureau of Labor Statistics, Employment Projections Program

Related Occupations
- Bartender
- Food & Beverage Service Worker
- Food Service Manager

Related Military Occupations
- Food Service Specialist

Conversation With . . . *PETER LAUFER*
Executive Chef
27 years in the industry

1. **What was your individual career path in terms of education/training, entry-level job, or other significant opportunity?**

   I started my career back in Germany with a three-year apprentice program working in a small hotel, working through all areas of the kitchen, while at the same time going to school at the Hotel Restaurant Bauer, where I graduated in 1986. Then my journey began. My goal was to get as much training as possible with the goal of moving up in position and title–commis de cuisine, chef de partie, sous chef, executive sous chef until, finally, executive chef.

   It was important to me to not to stay at the same place too long until I established myself. My first job, in Munich, was preparing cold appetizers and platters, with beautiful presentation using decorative pieces like mirrors, for a famous wine restaurant in Munich. I stayed there one year, and for each of the next seven years, I stayed just one year at each job: junior chef, first cook, chef entremetier, first assistant to the chef. I worked in Germany and Switzerland and for Norwegian Cruise Line out of Miami. I worked on cruise ships from 1993 to 2001. At 25 years old, I was one of the youngest executive chefs in the cruise industry. I worked on ships serving up to 2,400 guests and 1,000 crew members. I then worked at Sandals Resort in Montego Bay, followed by two years at a hotel in Miami. In 2012, I joined the Royal Sonesta in Houston.

2. **What are the most important skills and/or qualities for someone in your profession?**

   Creativity, an eye for color, and attention to the details are all important for a chef. You must be able to work long hours and be capable of handing stress. An executive chef will be responsible for menus, training and leading staff, purchasing, and more.

   If you enjoy cooking at home and for friends, you may be a candidate. If you love to be around food and like to spend time at a farmers market, butcher shop or produce row, you may be a candidate. If you like working with your hands and have an artistic drive, you may be a candidate. If you don't mind working long hours and like to be surrounded by an intense environment, you may be a candidate. If you would like to see the world and work in different places, you may be a candidate.

3. What do you wish you had known going into this profession?

This profession changes your personal life. It influences your circle of friends, as you work late nights, weekends and holidays.

4. Are there many job opportunities in your profession? In what specific areas?

The nice thing about this job is that you can work anywhere in the world. Working for a large company gives you the chance to branch out in different parts of the world. Restaurants, hotels and the cruise industry are always looking for talented chefs.

5. How do you see your profession changing in the next five years? What role will technology play in those changes, and what skills will be required?

Food trends are changing every year, with new things cropping up all the time: Peruvian Asian fusion, or farm to table, and tail to nose cooking (that is, eating the entire animal). A good chef needs to keep up with the trends and follow the patterns of his local customers.

With the implementation of low temperature cooking, re-thermo banquet cooking, and high tech smoking, a lot more skills are required in order to get the feeling for cooking with these techniques.

Also, the demand for nutritional value is getting more important, so some of the training needs to be geared to the whole healthy living aspect of food.

6. What do you enjoy most about your job? What do you enjoy least?

No day is the same. During my time working on cruise ships, I enjoyed being able to see the world and working with different cultures. What I enjoy least about this job is dealing with paperwork.

7. Can you suggest a valuable "try this" for students considering a career in your profession?

Ask your favorite restaurant, bakery or hotel if you can stay in the kitchen for a couple of days and see what it's like to work as a chef.

Try to copy a dish from a fine dining restaurant that you frequent and serve it to your friends.

Take a whole fish or chicken and try to de-bone it.

Attend a local American Culinary Federation (ACF) Chefs chapter meeting and get information about pros and cons in the industry.

SELECTED SCHOOLS

Many large urban centers have culinary/food service training schools. The student may also gain training at a technical/vocational or community college. Another tried-and-true method is that of apprenticeship, whereby a person starts out as a dishwasher or kitchen assistant and learns the trade from an experienced cook or chef.

MORE INFORMATION

American Culinary Federation
180 Center Place Way
St. Augustine, FL 32095
800.624.9458
www.acfchefs.org

Asian Chef Association
3145 Geary Boulevard, #112
San Francisco, CA 94118
408.634.9462
www.acasf.com

International Association of Culinary Professionals
1100 Johnson Ferry Road
Suite 300
Atlanta, GA 30342
404.252.3663
www.iacp.com

James Beard Foundation
167 West 12th Street
New York, NY 10011
212.675.4984
www.jamesbeard.org

National Restaurant Association Educational Foundation
175 West Jackson Boulevard
Suite 1500
Chicago, IL 60604-2814
800.765.2122
www.nraef.org

UNITE HERE! Headquarters
275 7th Avenue
New York, NY 10001-6709
212.265.7000
www.unitehere.org

United States Personal Chef Association
5728 Major Boulevard
Suite 750
Orlando, FL 32819
800.995.2138
www.uspca.com

Michael Auerbach/Editor

Cosmetologist

Snapshot

Career Cluster: Beauty & Fashion; Hospitality & Tourism; Personal Services

Interests: Fashion, beauty care, design, people

Earnings (Yearly Average): $26,790

Employment & Outlook: Average Growth Expected

OVERVIEW

Sphere of Work

Cosmetologists work in the beauty industry and provide customers with a wide variety of services, including hair care and maintenance, facial care and grooming, nail care, removal of unwanted body hair, and fitting of wigs. A cosmetologist usually works out of a salon or beauty shop, spa, resort, or film set, and caters to regular clients or first-time customers. While cosmetologists should be knowledgeable about a wide array of personal grooming services, some cosmetologists have enough clients and work to be able to specialize in a certain area of expertise, such as styling hair or providing manicures and pedicures.

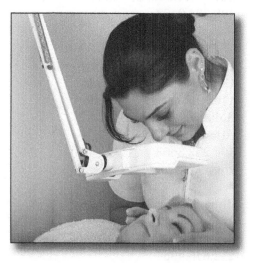

Work Environment

Cosmetologists usually operate independently out of clean, well-lit, owner-run salons. Some cosmetologists choose to rent their own booths within salons, work independently, and keep all of their earnings. In this scenario, the cosmetologist must pay a rental fee to the salon owner for the use of the work space. Cosmetologists may also travel to clients' homes to provide beauty care. They usually work a forty-hour week that often includes weekends and evenings, since many customers prefer to schedule appointments at those times. Sometimes, cosmetologists are required to work additional hours during holiday seasons or before special events like weddings.

Profile

Working Conditions: Work Indoors
Physical Strength: Light Work
Education Needs: No High School Diploma, High School Diploma with Technical Education, Apprenticeship
Licensure/Certification: Required
Physical Abilities Not Required: No Heavy Labor
Opportunities For Experience: Internship, Apprenticeship
Holland Interest Score*: SEA

* See Appendix A

Occupation Interest

People looking to pursue a career in cosmetology must be able to grasp practical concepts related to hair and the body. They must be able to understand and translate ideas into practical hair, skin, or nail designs, while offering advice to clients. Cosmetologists must enjoy working with and listening to people. They should be innately creative and passionate about fashion, design, and beauty care, and should follow current fashion trends. Cosmetologists who possess excellent people skills and listening skills generally attract a more loyal clientele and can expect more stable and successful careers.

A Day in the Life—Duties and Responsibilities

Most cosmetologists work in a comfortable, well-ventilated salon or beauty shop. They spend the majority of the day on their feet, working with their hands and arms at shoulder- or waist-level. Cosmetologists cut and style hair, provide manicures, pedicures, and skin care treatments, or offer other beauty services.

Hair stylists receive multiple clients per day. They must analyze, wash, cut, style, straighten, wave, and dye hair according to customer instructions. They typically also engage in discussions with the client to confirm the appropriateness of the desired hair color or style. Nail technicians, or manicurists, are cosmetologists who are usually work exclusively with clients' hands and nails. Nail technicians cut, style, polish, and treat nails.

Estheticians are cosmetologists who normally care for the skin. Estheticians provide customers with facials, body treatments, make-up application, upper-body massages, and hair removal. Cosmetologists clean their workspaces after each appointment. They must keep work tools, such as scissors, combs, or needles, clean and sanitary at all times. Hair stylists also sweep their work space floor between appointments.

Many cosmetologists must also perform administrative and managerial tasks. These activities may include opening and closing the shop, ordering supplies, keeping detailed records, scheduling client appointments, receiving incoming calls, handling financial transactions, and hiring, supervising, or firing other workers.

Duties and Responsibilities

- Analyzing hair to determine its condition
- Shampooing, cutting, and styling hair
- Waving or straightening hair
- Applying bleach, dye, or tint to hair
- Keeping records of hair color or permanent wave formulas used on regular customers
- Cleaning, cutting, and styling wigs
- Giving scalp and facial treatments
- Providing make-up analysis for customers
- Giving manicures and pedicures
- Keeping the work area clean and sterilizing all work aids
- Ordering supplies

OCCUPATION SPECIALTIES

Hair Stylists

Hair Stylists shampoo, cut, color, and style hair according to the customer's instructions. They serve both male and female clients, keeping records of all products and services provided.

Electrologists

Electrologists remove hair from the skin by using a round-tipped needle.

Manicurists

Manicurists clean, shape, and polish customers' fingernails and toenails. They may apply false nails, wrap nails, and provide other beauty services.

Estheticians and Makeup Artists

Estheticians and Makeup Artists provide facial and skin treatments and makeup analysis. Some also sell and apply skin care products and makeup.

Barbers

Barbers cut, trim, and style hair for male clients. They also provide shaves and trim facial hair

WORK ENVIRONMENT

Physical Environment

Cosmetologists usually operate within a clean, air-conditioned, and well-lit salon, shop, or spa. They work at designated booths or tables where clients sit while receiving treatments. They clean the workspace after each appointment as needed.

Cosmetologists must possess the energy and endurance to withstand long hours of sustained movement, which may make them vulnerable to repetitive stress-related injuries. They are also frequently exposed to chemical formulas, creams, nail polishes, and other treatments that may irritate the skin or nose, so they should limit exposure to and protect against harmful toxins.

Relevant Skills and Abilities

Creative Skills
- Creating ideas

Communication Skills
- Speaking effectively

Interpersonal/Social Skills
- Cooperating with others
- Working as a member of a team

Organization & Management Skills
- Making decisions
- Paying attention to and handling details
- Performing duties which change frequently

Other Skills
- Performing work that produces tangible results

Human Environment

Cosmetologists' jobs involve a high level of customer service and interaction with others. Cosmetologists work with fellow employees, salon managers or owners, and new and existing clients.

Technological Environment

Cosmetologists use a wide range of equipment and treatments in their daily activities. Hair stylists practice complex techniques with hair accessories like combs, brushes, pins, scissors, clips and clippers, curling irons, and hair dryers. They also must learn to use infrared or ultraviolet lamps; to apply bleaches, tints, and highlighting foils; and to appropriately use shampoos, conditioners, and other chemical treatments, such as a permanent wave. Cosmetologists who provide skin care and nail services use makeup, electric needles, lotions, oils, creams, and nail polish. Some cosmetologists are trained to provide electrolysis or laser treatments, which use needles or lasers to remove hair.

EDUCATION, TRAINING, AND ADVANCEMENT

High School/Secondary

High school students looking to become cosmetologists should study business, communications, science, technology, fashion, and economics. Interested students should also experiment at home with beauty products and accessories to familiarize themselves with the various processes involved in hair, skin, and nail maintenance. They can also learn about secondary vocational education programs in cosmetology by talking with their high school guidance or career counselors.

Suggested High School Subjects
- Applied Biology/Chemistry
- Applied Math
- Bookkeeping
- Business
- Cosmetology
- English
- Health Science Technology

Famous First

The first shampoo to be commercially produced and widely distributed was Breck shampoo, originated by John Breck of Springfield, Mass., in 1930. Breck, a fire chief, suffered hair loss at an early age and began experimenting with scalp treatments. From his experiments came a variety of shampoos and massage oils. By 1940 Breck shampoo was a nationwide best seller, known especially for its ads featuring attractive (and often famous) "Breck Girls."

Postsecondary

After high school, potential cosmetologists usually attend a public or private postsecondary vocational school in cosmetology. Some programs lead to an associate's degree in cosmetology and can take approximately nine to twenty-four months to complete. Cosmetologists planning to specialize in a specific area may be able to complete their programs in less time. Full-time programs in cosmetology teach students about the various aspects of the beauty industry, including anatomy and physiology, hairstyling, electrology, wiggery, hair coloring, manicures, facials, salon management, and cosmetology law. Trends in cosmetology are constantly shifting, and as a result, many professional cosmetologists take advanced courses in their specialized fields.

Related College Majors
- Barbering/Hairstyling
- Cosmetology

Adult Job Seekers

In some states, cosmetologists are required to obtain a high school diploma or the equivalent in order to work in the field. Most states also require cosmetologists to have successfully completed a state-licensed cosmetology program before beginning work. Job seekers can apply for work directly with a salon or spa. They can also inquire at skill centers and cosmetology school placement offices.

Professional Certification and Licensure

Cosmetologists must be licensed before going to work in a salon or beauty shop. In order to receive a license, prospective cosmetologists must have graduated from a state-licensed cosmetology program, and must possess a high school diploma. To obtain a license, cosmetologists must pass a written examination, and in some states, an oral examination or practical skills test. Cosmetologists who specialize in a specific area are usually required to complete additional examinations in their areas of expertise. Those interested in becoming cosmetologists should check the licensure requirements of their home state.

Additional Requirements

Cosmetologists should possess a deep passion for and understanding of the fashion design and beauty industries. A cosmetologist's appearance should reflect his or her knowledge of current trends in the cosmetology industry, and they must maintain an outwardly positive attitude that will make their clients feel comfortable and confident in their abilities.

EARNINGS AND ADVANCEMENT

Earnings depend on the size and geographic location of the employer, the number of hours worked, the quality and speed of the work and the ability to keep regular customers. Mean annual earnings of cosmetologists were $26,790 in 2012. The lowest ten percent earned less than $16,850, and the highest ten percent earned more than $42,360.

Cosmetologists may receive paid vacations, holidays, and sick days; life and health insurance; and retirement benefits. These are usually paid by the employer.

Fun Fact

Wigs were the fashion of the day until the reign of France's Louis XV, whose mistress was Madame de Pompadour, (yes, the woman for whom the hairstyle is named.) Theme parties were all the rage back then, and well tressed ladies hired artists to create elaborate hairstyles incorporating the party's theme: live birds in cages, naval battles with ships – IN THEIR HAIR! This talent of dressing the hair with ornamentation led to the word "hairdresser." The number of hairdressers in Paris went from none to 1,200 in 1767.

Metropolitan Areas with the Highest Employment Level in this Occupation

Metropolitan area	Employment[1]	Employment per thousand jobs	Hourly mean wage
New York-White Plains-Wayne, NY-NJ	14,280	2.77	$14.84
Chicago-Joliet-Naperville, IL	12,530	3.44	$13.94
Minneapolis-St. Paul-Bloomington, MN-WI	7,610	4.35	$13.48
Philadelphia, PA	7,270	3.99	$13.45
Washington-Arlington-Alexandria, DC-VA-MD-WV	6,850	2.92	$16.04
Atlanta-Sandy Springs-Marietta, GA	6,510	2.88	$11.41
Houston-Sugar Land-Baytown, TX	6,470	2.45	$14.65
Boston-Cambridge-Quincy, MA	5,810	3.40	$13.79

(1)Does not include self-employed. Source: Bureau of Labor Statistics

EMPLOYMENT AND OUTLOOK

There were approximately 635,000 cosmetologists employed nationally in 2012. About half of all cosmetologists are self-employed. Employment is expected to grow about as fast as the average for all occupations through the year 2022, which means employment is projected to increase 8 percent to 14 percent. Job growth is due to an increase in population, incomes and the demand for personal appearance services.

Employment Trend, Projected 2012–22

Hairdressers, Hairstylists, and Cosmetologists: 13%

Total, All Occupations: 11%

Barbers: 10%

Note: "All Occupations" includes all occupations in the U.S. Economy. Source: U.S. Bureau of Labor Statistics, Employment Projections Program

Conversation With . . . LISA PĒNA

Hair and Makeup Stylist, 30 years

1. What was your individual career path in terms of education/training, entry-level job, or other significant opportunity?

I knew at 15 what I wanted to do. It's always been a part of me, hairdressing. I was always using my mother as a guinea pig when I was a little girl. I went to Grace Beauty School in Brooklyn and after I graduated, I worked part-time teaching. Once I got married and had kids, I worked part-time in a salon for a while. For about 10 years, I had my own salon. I decided to learn high styling and went to Robert Fiance Beauty School n the city, on Park Ave. After I moved to Florida in 1990, I started working for Disney. I went and auditioned and I got the job. I continued growing because Disney is such a great company to work for. I was styling wigs for the princesses, I did a lot of backstage work, I worked with celebrities and did shows on the road.

Disney opened the Wedding Pavilion in 1995 and the wedding business just exploded. Because I'm so good with people, they asked me to work on weddings and I absolutely loved it. Eventually, Disney decided to outsource. They told me that if I opened my own business, they would refer people to me. So I did it.

2. What are the most important skills and/or qualities for someone in your profession?

The best qualities and skills are being able to deal with impossible people! You have to learn how to smile and keep your cool. It's very important that you dress well. Customers are going to look at your appearance.

You need to be creative, definitely. I've never been able to explain to someone what I'm going to do. I create as I go. I go according to what the hair is telling me to do.

Never rush. If they don't like what I've done, I will take it down and do it over. I will never let someone go away unhappy. If they want a style that I don't think is right, I tell them, "I will do it if you want me to," but I am honest with them.

3. What do you wish you had known going into this profession?

You know what? Nothing, really. I've been very, very happy. I have no regrets. Disney taught me how to deal with difficult people. I have diplomas! They made you take classes. We have bridezillas. We have groomzillas, too. We've seen it all.

4. Are there many job opportunities in your profession? In what specific areas?

There are plenty of jobs. The problem is, all the people who come out of school want to do is cut hair and blow dry. They don't know how to do updos and styling. They can't do a French twist. Maybe that would be a good opportunity, schools training them to do these things. You can specialize in many areas: haircuts, extensions, color, styling, on-stage makeup, films.

5. How do you see your profession changing in the next five years? What role will technology play in those changes, and what skills will be required?

Every day there's something new. I like going to hair shows. I like experimenting with new products. If you don't do those things, you get stale. The products are changing. Technology is changing the tools, like curling irons, but you have to use them and see if they work for you. You need to know how to use a computer for scheduling and billing.

6. What do you enjoy most about your job? What do you enjoy least?

I most enjoy looking at clients' faces when they see themselves in the mirror! They say, "Wow, is that me? I didn't know I could look so beautiful." I love it. It's a great thing to see people so happy.

What I like least are the difficult people. I just try to deal with them. I tell them, "It's not brain surgery, honey. If you don't like it, it can be reversed. We'll just take it down and try something else."

7. Can you suggest a valuable "try this" for students considering a career in your profession?

Work on hair. Work on your friends and family. I always tell young people who want to become hairdressers: go to the salon of your choice, offer to wash hair a couple of days a week for free, and keep your eyes open. Learn everything you possibly can.

SELECTED SCHOOLS

Many cities and large towns have privately run cosmetology schools. The student may also acquire training at a technical community college. Another method is that of apprenticeship, whereby a person starts out as a salon assistant and learns the trade from an experienced cosmetologist.

MORE INFORMATION

American Association of Cosmetology Schools
9927 E. Bell Road, Suite 110
Scottsdale, AZ 85260
800.831.1086
www.beautyschools.org

Beauty Schools Directory
www.beautyschoolsdirectory.com

National-Interstate Council of State Boards of Cosmetology, Inc.
7622 Briarwood Circle
Little Rock, AR 72205
www.nictesting.org

National Accrediting Commission of Cosmetology Arts & Sciences
4401 Ford Avenue, Suite 1300
Alexandria, VA 22302-1432
703.600.7600
www.naccas.org

National Beauty Culturists League
25 Logan Circle, NW
Washington, DC 20005
202.332.2695
www.nbcl.org

Professional Beauty Association/National Cosmetology Association (PBA/NCA)
15825 N. 71st Street, Suite 100
Scottsdale, AZ 85254
800.468.2274
www.probeauty.org

United Food and Commercial Workers Union
1775 K Street NW
Washington, DC 20006-1598
202.223.3111
www.ufcw.org

Briana Nadeau/Editor

Counter & Rental Clerk

Snapshot

Career Cluster: Business Administration; Sales & Service; Hospitality & Tourism

Interests: Customer service, communicating with others, data entry & record keeping

Earnings (Yearly Average): $24,430

Employment & Outlook: Slower Than Average Growth Expected

OVERVIEW

Sphere of Work

Counter and rental clerks act as both customer service representatives and retail associates. They are employed by companies that rent equipment and machines, including car and truck rental companies, general equipment rental firms, and various tourist rental outlets, including airports, hotels and motels, and clubhouses. Rental clerks are responsible for collecting and recording customer data, maintaining transaction records and payment information, and explaining relevant rules, policies, and fees. Counter and rental clerks also answer phones, take orders and reservations for rental items, and inspect rented items upon their return.

Work Environment

Rental clerks work in retail locations and private businesses. Many national car rental agencies have retail counters or offices at airports, bus stations, and other major transportation hubs. Companies renting heavy construction equipment may operate as independent businesses or as facets of larger retailers. Holiday, tourism, and leisure rentals offering rooms and temporary use of equipment such as paddleboats, canoes, golf carts, and even horses traditionally operate out of or adjacent to resorts, theme parks, or wildlife and nature sanctuaries. Counter and rental clerks interact extensively with the public and may work nights, weekends, and holidays to meet the needs of their customers.

Profile

Working Conditions: Work Indoors
Physical Strength: Light Work
Education Needs: On-The-Job High School Diploma Or G.E.D.
Licensure/Certification: Usually Not Required
Physical Abilities Not Required: No Heavy Labor
Opportunities For Experience: Part-Time Work
Holland Interest Score*: CRE, CSE

* See Appendix A

Occupation Interest

Counter and rental clerks are a diverse group of professionals. Many are young workers eager to gain administrative and customer service experience, while some are seasonal employees seeking to earn extra income. Much of the training for rental clerk positions can be acquired on the job, which is another factor that contributes to the diversity of those employed in the rental industry.

A Day in the Life—Duties and Responsibilities

The duties and responsibilities of counter and rental clerks are intensely focused on customer service. In addition to greeting customers with prior rental reservations and interacting with individuals calling or visiting to make new rental reservations, counter and rental clerks must also verify renters' identities, process payments, and complete liability paperwork for all renters.

Rental clerks must be well versed in the rental options available to customers, such as make and model of vehicles and size and capacity of trucks or sporting equipment. Counter staff must also explain the risks, damage policies, and other rules related to renting equipment.

Additionally, any policies regarding how or where the rented equipment may be used must be made clear. Rental clerks must also inform clients of return policies, expected return dates, and return location options.

When not interacting with customers, counter and rental clerks are often responsible for cleaning or maintaining rented equipment. Ski or skate rental clerks, for example, may be responsible for waxing or sharpening the equipment, and car and truck rental clerks may need to refuel, clean, or perform routine maintenance on their companies' vehicles.

In addition to providing information and recording data for outbound equipment and vehicle rentals, counter clerks are also responsible for the data entry and relevant administrative tasks involved in returns. Return tasks may include asking clients about the quality of their experience, offering payment receipts, and inspecting equipment to ensure it is being returned in the same condition in which it was rented.

Duties and Responsibilities

- Greeting customers
- Determining service needs of customers
- Providing information to customers about available items and services
- Calculating and explaining rate charges
- Receiving payment from customers for services and making change
- Keeping records of transactions
- Preparing customer order forms or work tickets
- Answering the telephone and taking orders over the telephone

OCCUPATION SPECIALTIES

Hotel and Motel Clerks

Hotel and Motel Clerks greet and register customers, issue keys, transmit and receive messages, keep records, compute bills, collect payments, and make and confirm reservations.

Tool and Equipment Rental Clerks

Tool and Equipment Rental Clerks rent tools and equipment to customers and clean, lubricate, and adjust rental items.

Automobile Rental Clerks

Automobile Rental Clerks rent automobiles to customers at airports, hotels, marinas, and other locations by preparing a rental contract and informing customers about policies and procedures.

Customer Service Clerks

Customer Service Clerks arrange for gift-wrapping, monogramming and printing of items, take and prepare orders for goods and services, and keep records of services.

WORK ENVIRONMENT

Physical Environment

Counter and rental clerks work primarily at indoor rental counters, which are often located near or within large urban areas. Resorts, theme parks, and airports also employ counter and rental clerks. Clerks must often spend much of the workday on their feet.

Relevant Skills and Abilities

Communication Skills
- Listening carefully
- Speaking effectively

Interpersonal/Social Skills
- Cooperating with others
- Providing support to others
- Working as a member of a team

Organization & Management Skills
- Following instructions
- Paying attention to and handling details
- Performing duties that change frequently
- Performing routine work

Technical Skills
- Performing mechanical or technical work

Human Environment

Counter and rental clerks work primarily with the public, communicating either face-to-face or over the phone. Counter and rental clerks also interact with outside vendors and fellow staff members. Courtesy is a paramount quality for counter and rental clerks, and it must be displayed even in the face of customer complaints.

Technological Environment

Counter and rental clerks use traditional retail technologies such as cash registers and telephone systems. They must be comfortable with computers and printers as well as database, point-of-sale, and word processing software. Bar code scanners and related equipment are also common.

EDUCATION, TRAINING, AND ADVANCEMENT

High School/Secondary

High school students can best prepare for the position of counter or rental clerk by taking courses in basic business administration and introductory computing. The communication and problem-solving skills that are needed to succeed in this field can be honed in English and composition courses. Participation in school-oriented activities, such as school stores or event information booths, may help prepare students for the team-oriented nature of the position.

Suggested High School Subjects
- Accounting
- Business & Computer Technology
- Business English
- Business Math
- Computer Science
- English
- Foreign Languages
- Mathematics
- Speech

Famous First

The first automobile rental company was established by Joe Saunders of Omaha, Neb., in 1916. Saunders started out with a single Model T Ford but within ten years had expanded his operations to fifty-six cities. One of Saunders' early competitors was Walter Jacobs of Chicago, who founded his car rental business in 1918. In the 1920s Jacobs' company was bought by John D. Hertz, who later reorganized and rebranded the business as the Hertz Corporation. Saunders' company was bought in the 1950s by a third competitor, Avis (founded 1946). Today Hertz and Avis remain the largest auto rental agencies in the world.

Postsecondary

Postsecondary education is not traditionally a requirement for counter or rental clerks. However, those interested in advancing to managerial or supervisory positions or opening their own rental establishments may benefit tremendously from exposure to postsecondary coursework in business management, finance, or administration.

Adult Job Seekers

As nearly all training occurs on the job, eliminating the need for extensive experience or education, the position may be a good fit for adults seeking temporary or seasonal employment. Rental clerks may have the opportunity to advance to managerial or supervisory roles after accumulating several years of experience. However, advancement opportunities are limited, and temporary positions in the rental industry rarely offer employee benefits.

Professional Certification and Licensure

No specific certification or licensure is required, although a valid driver's license may be required for counter and rental clerks who are involved in vehicular rentals.

Additional Requirements

Counter and rental clerks must possess considerable patience as well as the ability to handle many duties and responsibilities simultaneously. As the rental industry is very competitive, customer service is often the major factor that separates successful firms from their competitors.

EARNINGS AND ADVANCEMENT

Counter and rental clerks usually start at minimum wage. In addition to their wages, some counter and rental clerks receive commissions based on the number of contracts they complete or services they sell. Mean annual earnings of counter and rental clerks were $26,900 in 2012. The comparable figure for motel, hotel, and resort desk clerks was $21,960.

Counter and rental clerks may receive paid vacations, holidays, and sick days; life and health insurance; and retirement benefits. These are usually paid by the employer. When uniforms are required, they are generally provided by the employer.

Metropolitan Areas with the Highest Employment Level in this Occupation (Counter & Rental Clerk)

Metropolitan area	Employment	Employment per thousand jobs	Hourly mean wage
Los Angeles-Long Beach-Glendale, CA	23,620	6.10	$13.66
Chicago-Joliet-Naperville, IL	10,410	2.86	$13.24
Houston-Sugar Land-Baytown, TX	9,530	3.61	$13.19
New York-White Plains-Wayne, NY-NJ	8,510	1.65	$13.98
San Diego-Carlsbad-San Marcos, CA	7,640	6.06	$14.75

Source: Bureau of Labor Statistics

Metropolitan Areas with the Highest Employment Level in this Occupation (Hotel, Motel & Resort Clerk)

Metropolitan area	Employment	Employment per thousand jobs	Hourly mean wage
New York-White Plains-Wayne, NY-NJ	4,450	0.86	$16.96
Atlanta-Sandy Springs-Marietta, GA	4,030	1.78	$9.34
Los Angeles-Long Beach-Glendale, CA	4,000	1.03	$11.30
Chicago-Joliet-Naperville, IL	3,970	1.09	$11.26
Orlando-Kissimmee-Sanford, FL	3,700	3.66	$10.38

Source: Bureau of Labor Statistics

EMPLOYMENT AND OUTLOOK

Counter and rental clerks held about 433,000 jobs in 2012. Most were employed by the real estate industry, automotive rental and leasing services, and the consumer goods and recreation rental industries. Another 230,000 were employed as hotel, motel, and resort desk clerks in 2012. In both of these areas employment is expected to grow slightly less than the average for all occupations through the year 2022, which means it is projected to increase 4 percent to 12 percent. Most openings will occur as workers transfer to other occupations or leave the work force.

Employment Trend, Projected 2012–22

Total, All Occupations: 11%

Counter & Rental Clerks: 9%

Hotel, Motel & Resort Desk Clerks: 7%

Note: "All Occupations" includes all occupations in the U.S. Economy. Source: U.S. Bureau of Labor Statistics, Employment Projections Program

Related Occupations
- Gaming Services Operator
- Reservation & Ticket Agent

Conversation With . . .
JOSEPH EMORY
Rental Company Owner
5 years in industry

1. What was your individual career path in terms of education/training, entry-level job, or other significant opportunity?

I'm a retired school teacher. I taught physics in Atlanta, and vacationed here on Tybee for years. Once I retired, I felt like I wanted to have something to do that was easy, but good money. We have four different places on the island.

2. What are the most important skills and/or qualities for someone in your profession?

People skills. Whether you're having a miserable day or a great day, you have to have a smile on your face. You have to make your customers feel that you want them there and you're glad to see them, that you want them to enjoy your product, and enjoy themselves. People skills are better than any other skill you can have in this business.

3. What do you wish you had known going into this profession?

What I wish I had known, really, is how much work it is. It's a lot of work taking care of the bikes, getting them ready for the next season, keeping them in good condition. But I like working with my hands, so that's one good thing about it.

4. Are there many job opportunities in your profession? In what specific areas?

Not here, no. The equipment rental business is really tied up. We've got beach chair rentals, lawn chairs, umbrellas, bicycles. This place has been here 40 years. It used to be called Pack Rat Bicycle Shop. But in general, tourist areas and resort areas will always have a need for equipment rentals. We've been here at the bottom of the economy and we've been here at the top of the economy. It's a seasonal business, but luckily we have a long season.

5. How do you see your profession changing in the next five years? What role will technology play in those changes, and what skills will be required?

I think the business will remain steady. I don't see a major increase in it. I've been coming here since the 1960s. The only thing that has changed since then, really, are the prices. A bike is a bike. I don't have any geared bikes. I have cruising bikes and baby trailers to pull behind the bikes. In terms of GPS or technology like that, it won't impact us. This is a tiny island. It's only two and three-quarter miles long. You take a bike, ride out to one end of the island, have a beer and ride back.

6. What do you enjoy most about your job? What do you enjoy least?

What I enjoy most is meeting the tourists and associating with them, helping them have a good time. Making sure they enjoy their time with my product and their time here. I'm a talker. I've had people from as far away as Lichtenstein and from as close by as the City of Savannah 20 miles away. What I enjoy least are the winters. We do nothing. From November to the end of February, it's dead. Again, it's a seasonal business.

7. Can you suggest a valuable "try this" for students considering a career in your profession?

I tell people this all the time: if you're a people person, you can learn anything. Being a people person is the most important thing. Start with that. You can open up a bike shop pretty easily. Open up a small stand at a bike trail; in Atlanta, we have extensive bike trails. Get a little place and hang your hat. Start off with 20 bikes and you can build up from there. It's not expensive. You can buy 20 bikes for $4,000. If business is good, start expanding.

SELECTED SCHOOLS

Although training beyond high school is not necessarily expected of counter and rental clerks, interested parties may obtain training in general business practices at a community college or privately run vocational school. Work experience remains one of the most important qualifications, however, particularly for those dealing directly with customers.

MORE INFORMATION

American Hotel & Lodging Association
1201 New York Avenue, NW
Suite 600
Washington, DC 20005
202.289.3100
www.ahla.com

American Rental Association
1900 19th Street
Moline, IL 61265
800.334.2177
www.ararental.org

Global Rental Alliance
1900 19th Street
Moline, IL 61265
www.theglobalrentalalliance.com

John Pritchard/Editor

Event Planner

Snapshot

Career Cluster: Business Administration; Hospitality & Tourism

Interests: Working with people, coordinating activities, planning and scheduling

Earnings (Yearly Average): $49,830

Employment & Outlook: Faster Than Average Growth

OVERVIEW

Sphere of Work

Event planners coordinate all aspects of professional and social meetings, gatherings, and events. Working with clients, they choose event locations, organize the invitation process, arrange for food and beverages, and coordinate all other details, including transportation and lodging. They may work as employees of a service organization specializing in events and event planning, such as a convention bureau or resort center, or they may work inside a business corporation or nonprofit organization, where they work with departmental heads or managers to plan important meetings, fundraisers, or other special events. They may also work independently. Their work encompasses planning for such occasions as weddings, reunions, and other private celebrations as well as for functions such as trade shows, conventions, and fundraisers.

Work Environment

Event planners work in office environments most of the time, although they also work onsite at hotels, convention centers, and similar venues. They often travel to visit prospective meeting sites and attend events. During meetings or conventions, event planners may work very long hours. They interact with many different individuals, from musicians and food caterers to facilities managers and technical services personnel, in the course of setting up a large event.

Profile

Physical Strength: Light Work
Education Needs: Technical/
  Community College, Bachelor's Degree
Licensure/Certification: Usually Not
  Required
Physical Abilities Not Required: No
  Heavy Labor
Opportunities for Experience:
  Volunteer Work, Part-Time Work
Holland Interest Score: CES

* See Appendix A

Occupation Interest

This occupation suits people who combine administrative and organizational capabilities with the ability to work with others and satisfy their needs. Event planners have generally proven their administrative capabilities by first excelling in an entry-level administrative position. Successful event planners enjoy working with people and have strong oral communication skills, allowing them to dialogue with clients and provide suggestions with tact and confidence. Although they work largely independently in the role of "broker" or "agent" on behalf of their clients, event planners must also be comfortable collaborating with members of their own team.

A Day in the Life—Duties and Responsibilities

An event planner's day is likely to involve a combination of personal interaction and business administration. This is a job in which success usually requires a blend of skills in several areas, including management, creative awareness, technology, the ability to coordinate with other service organizations, and communication skills.

During a typical day, event planners may meet with clients to understand the purpose of a meeting or event. They may help plan the scope of the event, including time, location, and cost. They might solicit bids from venues and service providers (for example, florists or photographers), inspect venues to ensure that they meet the client's requirements, coordinate event services such as rooms, transportation, and food service, and monitor event activities to ensure the client and event attendees are satisfied.

Whether it is a wedding, educational conference, or business convention, meetings and events bring people together for a common purpose. Event planners work to ensure that this purpose is achieved efficiently and seamlessly. They coordinate every detail of events, from beginning to end. Before a meeting, for example, planners will meet with clients to estimate attendance and determine the meeting's purpose. During the meeting, they handle meeting logistics, such as registering guests and organizing audio/visual equipment for speakers. After the meeting, they may survey attendees to find out how the event was received. They may also review event bills and approve payment to vendors.

In many cases, they organize speakers, entertainment, or activities. They must also ensure that services such as wheelchair accessibility, interpreters, and other accommodations are in place.

Duties and Responsibilities

- Identifying client needs and interests, including scheduling requirements and budget limitations
- Recommending venues, activities, design elements, food items, and logistics arrangements
- Renting rooms or facilities as needed to accommodate planned events
- Inviting attendees or helping client to do so
- Lining up and contracting with outside vendors and suppliers
- Attending events as needed to coordinate efforts and ensure success
- Reviewing post-event data and/or comments for lessons to be learned
- Handling contractor invoices and making payments

OCCUPATION SPECIALTIES

Association Planners

Association Planners organize annual conferences and trade shows for professional associations. Because member attendance is often voluntary, marketing the meeting's value is an important aspect of their work.

Convention Service Managers

Convention Service Managers help organize major events, as employees of hotels and convention centers. They act as liaisons between the meeting facility and the planners who work for associations, businesses, and governments. They present food service options to outside planners, coordinate special requests, and suggest hotel services depending on a planner's budget.

Corporate & Government Meeting Planners

Corporate Planners organize internal business meetings and meetings between businesses. Government Meeting Planners organize meetings for government officials and agencies; being familiar with government regulations, such as procedures for buying materials and booking hotels, is vital to their work.

Nonprofit Event Planners

Nonprofit Event Planners plan large events with the goal of raising donations for a charity or advocacy organization. Events may include banquets, charity races, and food drives.

Wedding & Party Planners

Wedding and Party Planners arrange the details of celebratory events, including weddings, reunions, and large birthday parties.

WORK ENVIRONMENT

Physical Environment

Event planners spend much of their time in comfortable indoor settings such as offices or similar facilities. During meetings and events, they usually work on-site at hotels or convention centers. They travel regularly to attend the events they organize and to visit prospective meeting sites, sometimes in exotic locations around the world. Some events are held outdoors—typically under tents—and event planners should be prepared for weather changes and uneven ground. Planners may have very long workdays, and sometimes work on weekends.

Relevant Skills and Abilities

Communication Skills
- Expressing thoughts and ideas clearly
- Speaking and writing effectively

Interpersonal/Social Skills
- Cooperating with others
- Inspiring confidence in others
- Listening well
- Working both independently and as a member of a team

Organization & Management Skills
- Managing time
- Meeting goals and deadlines
- Paying attention to and handling details

Research & Planning Skills
- Investigating resources
- Laying out a plan

Human Environment

Event planners regularly collaborate with clients, hospitality workers, and event attendees. The work of event planners can be fast-paced and demanding. Planners oversee many aspects of an event at the same time and face numerous deadlines. They must sometimes deal with anxious clients or vendors and try to calm them while ensuring the success of the event.

Technological Environment

Event planners make use of standard office technologies, including computers, telephones, e-mail, photocopiers, and the Internet. They should be proficient in the use of basic office software such as word processing programs, contact management software, spreadsheets, and presentation programs. More recently, planners also consider whether an online meeting can achieve the same objectives as a face-to-face meeting in certain cases; therefore they need to be familiar with online conferencing tools.

EDUCATION, TRAINING, AND ADVANCEMENT

High School/Secondary

High school students can best prepare for a career as an event planner by taking courses in English, composition, and business writing. Courses that develop general business skills may include accounting, entrepreneurship, bookkeeping, business management, and applied mathematics. Administrative and clerical skills may be developed by taking subjects such as business computing, typing, and shorthand. Subjects such as history and social studies help the student to develop his or her general research and analytical skills. Studies in psychology may be beneficial for developing understanding about human behavior and motivation.

Becoming involved in volunteer work at fundraising events while still in high school is an excellent way to gain entry-level experience in the profession. High school students may also gain part-time administrative experience with local business organizations as well as with scholastic clubs and societies. A wide variety of extracurricular activities provide opportunities for enhancing social skills.

Suggested High School Subjects
- Applied Communication
- Bookkeeping
- Business
- Business & Computer Technology
- Business Data Processing
- Business English
- Business Math
- English
- Keyboarding
- Social Studies
- Psychology

Famous First

The first manufacturers' fair was held in Masonic Hall, New York City, in 1828, under the auspices of the American Institute. The purpose of the event was to publicize, encourage, and promote domestic industry. Other organizations soon began hosting similar fairs and expositions, in agriculture, commerce, and the arts. Together they formed the early context for the eventual rise of the profession of event planning.

College/Postsecondary

Many employers prefer applicants who have a bachelor's degree and some work experience in hotels or planning. The proportion of planners with a bachelor's degree is increasing because work responsibilities are becoming more complex and because there are more college degree programs related to hospitality or tourism management. If an applicant's degree is not related to these fields, employers are likely to require at least one to two years of related experience.

Event planners often come from a variety of academic disciplines. Some related undergraduate majors include marketing, public relations, communications, and business. Planners who have studied hospitality management may start out with greater responsibilities than those from other academic disciplines. College students may also gain experience by planning meetings for a university club. In addition, some colleges offer continuing education courses in meeting and event planning.

Related College Majors
- Business Administration & Management
- Hospitality Management
- Meeting & Event Planning

Adult Job Seekers

Adults seeking a career transition or returning to an event planner role are advised to refresh their skills and update their resume. Any relevant administrative skills, project management, or supervisory experience should be highlighted in the candidate's resume and application letter. Networking, job searching, and interviewing are critical, and those without prior experience may find it helpful to obtain specialized training. Aspiring event planners may also find it beneficial to consider related roles, such as office manager, administrative assistant, and any position involving special events.

Professional Certification and Licensure

The Convention Industry Council offers the Certified Meeting Professional (CMP) credential, a voluntary certification for meeting and convention planners. Although the CMP is not required, it is widely recognized in the industry and may help in career advancement. To qualify, candidates must have a minimum of 36 months of meeting management experience, recent employment in a meeting management job, and proof of continuing education credits. Those who qualify must then pass an exam that covers topics such as adult learning, financial management, facilities and services, logistics, and meeting programs.

The Society of Government Meeting Professionals (SGMP) offers the Certified Government Meeting Professional (CGMP) designation for meeting planners who work for, or contract with, federal, state, or local government. This certification is not required to work as a government meeting planner; however, it may be helpful for those who want to show that they know government buying policies and travel regulations. To qualify, candidates must have worked as a meeting planner for at least one year and have been a member of SGMP for six months. To become a certified planner, members must take a three-day course and pass an exam.

Additional Requirements

Event planners are often under pressure to work quickly and efficiently, while at the same time making clients feel that their needs are being attended to. Beyond such business basics, however, the best event planners cultivate an awareness of how not only to satisfy clients but to "wow" them, or exceed their expectations. It is by their reputations that independent event planners, and planning/catering agencies, are known, and it is by their reputations that they will thrive or fail to grow.

EARNINGS AND ADVANCEMENT

Entry-level planners tend to focus on meeting logistics, such as registering guests and organizing audio/visual equipment. Experienced planners manage interpersonal tasks, such as client relations and contract negotiations. With significant experience, event planners can become independent consultants.

Event planners earned mean annual salaries of $49,830 in 2012. The lowest 10 percent had salaries of less than $26,560, and the highest 10 percent had salaries of over $79,270.

Event planners may receive paid vacations, holidays, and sick days; life and health insurance; and retirement benefits. These are usually paid by the employer.

Metropolitan Areas with the Highest Employment Level in this Occupation

Metropolitan area	Employment[1]	Employment per thousand jobs	Hourly mean wage
New York-White Plains-Wayne, NY-NJ	5,680	1.10	$28.45
Washington-Arlington-Alexandria, DC-VA-MD-WV	5,100	2.18	$30.33
Chicago-Joliet-Naperville, IL	2,300	0.63	$22.90
Los Angeles-Long Beach-Glendale, CA	1,840	0.47	$25.49
Atlanta-Sandy Springs-Marietta, GA	1,690	0.75	$22.68
Dallas-Plano-Irving, TX	1,480	0.70	$25.52
Boston-Cambridge-Quincy, MA	1,270	0.74	$29.22
Philadelphia, PA	1,270	0.69	$24.66

[1]Does not include self-employed. Source: Bureau of Labor Statistics

EMPLOYMENT AND OUTLOOK

There were approximately 70,000 event planners employed nationally in 2012. Employment is expected to grow much faster than the average for all occupations through the year 2022, which means employment is projected to increase by over 30 percent. Growth will occur in most all areas, including the business/professional sector, the travel and tourism industry, the nonprofit sector (including colleges and universities), and the arts and entertainment industry.

Employment Trend, Projected 2012–22

Event Planners: 33%

Business and Financial Operations Occupations: 13%

Total, all occupations: 11%

Note: "All Occupations" includes all occupations in the U.S. Economy. Source: U.S. Bureau of Labor Statistics, Employment Projections Program

Related Occupations
- Food Services Manager
- Hotel /Motel Manager
- Property & Real Estate Manager

Fun Fact

The top five states with the largest number of meeting and event planners are California, New York, Texas, Florida and Virginia.

Source: Froomz, from BLS.gov.

Conversation With . . .
ALYSSA BURSTYN
Corporate Event Coordinator, 3 years

1. What was your individual career path in terms of education/training, entry-level job, or other significant opportunity?

I have always loved being around food and people, so the hospitality field was the perfect fit. All of my jobs have been in various facets of the hospitality industry. My first job at age 14 was as a bakery associate for a local grocery store. I spent a few summers as catering wait staff for both on and offsite events at both a local country club and a function hall.

I had an internship with a local Chamber of Commerce as an administrative and event coordinator, where I helped market upcoming events as well as check members in at events.

I pursued my college degree in hospitality and tourism management from the University of Massachusetts – Amherst, ranked fourth in the county for hospitality schools. I applied and was selected to be a part of "SOMTAP – School of Management Talent Advancement Program" as an incoming freshman – a selective program of 50 incoming freshman business students who would live and take classes together. I decided to pursue food and beverage management and travel tourism and event management as a dual track within the Hospitality and Tourism Management program.

I am serv-safe certified, food allergen safety certified and I am in the process of attaining my CMP certification (certified meeting planner). I have attended a few professional groups in my field – National Association of Catering Executives (NACE) and International Special Events Society (ISES).

2. What are the most important skills and/or qualities for someone in your profession?

The most important skills are time management and good communication skills. The most important qualities are being a people person, working well under pressure, having a sense of humor, working well with others, adaptability and dependability.

3. What do you wish you had known going into this profession?

Having had a pretty good sense of the hospitality industry prior to this role, I knew what I was getting into. If I had to pick one thing that I wish I has known, that would probably be that corporate events happen quickly, most of the time with a week or two lead time, so you have to stay on top of your priorities in order to have successful events.

4. Are there many job opportunities in your profession? In what specific areas?

Yes! There will always be occasions in which people hold events and because of that, there will always be a need for people to plan/coordinate those events! With the economy picking up and both social and corporate clients having more disposable income, the number of events will continue to grow. I have read a few articles that state that a meeting planner is one of the top growing jobs between 2010-2020.

5. How do you see your profession changing in the next five years? What role will technology play in those changes, and what skills will be required?

I see a lot more growth for this profession in the next five years. Technology will play a large role in streamlining the way events are produced to make it easier for all the working parts (planner, client, vendors, staff). Expert knowledge of event software may be required as well as certifications in the field.

6. What do you enjoy most about your job? What do you enjoy least?

I love the creativity that my job brings. I get to come up with the décor and setup of the events and make fun food signs to tie in the theme. That really makes it fun for me! I also like how my job allows me to work on different types of events, from plated dinners to casual open houses.

If I had to pick something I liked least about my job, it's that corporate events tend to come with little lead time. Sometimes when we receive an inquiry from a client, they expect an event in a week or less. That causes last-minute running around, but the job always gets accomplished even with the extra bit of last minute stress!

7. Can you suggest a valuable "try this" for students considering a career in your profession?

I would suggest to anyone interested in this field to be an active participant in hospitality related clubs. Volunteering to be on a food and beverage committee or event committee will really give people a taste of what it is like to work within a budget to accomplish a goal.

SELECTED SCHOOLS

Most colleges and universities offer bachelor's degrees in business administration and management; some have programs specifically in hospitality and tourism. The student may also gain initial training at a technical or community college. Below are listed some of the more prominent four-year institutions in this field.

Fairleigh Dickinson University
International School of Hospitality and Tourism Management
285 Madison Avenue
Madison, NJ 07940
973.443.8500
www.fdu.edu

Iowa State University
Apparel, Events, and Hospitality Management
31 MacKay Hall
Ames, IA 50011
515.294.7474
www.aeshm.hs.iastate.edu

Michigan State University
School of Hospitality Business
345 N. Shaw Lane, Rm. 232
East Lansing, MI 48824
517.353.9211
hospitalitybusiness.broad.msu.edu

Penn State University
School of Hospitality Management
201 Mateer Building
University Park, PA 16802
814.865.1853
www.hhd.psu.edu/shm

Purdue University
School of Hospitality and Tourism Management
900 W. State Street
West Lafayette, IN 47907
765.494.4643
www.purdue.edu/hhs/htm

University of Central Florida
Rosen College of Hospitality Management
9907 Universal Boulevard
Orlando, FL 32819
407.903.8000
hospitality.ucf.edu

University of Massachusetts, Amherst
Isenberg School of Management
Department of Hospitality and Tourism Management
121 Presidents Drive
Amherst, MA 01003
413.545.5610
www.isenberg.umass.edu/htm

University of Nevada, Las Vegas
William F. Harrah College of Hotel Administration
4505 S. Maryland Parkway
Las Vegas, NV 89154
702.895.3011
www.unlv.edu/hotel

Virginia Tech
Pamplin College of Business
Department of Hospitality and
Tourism Management
362 Wallace Hall
295 W. Campus Drive
Blacksburg, VA 24061
540.231.1515
www.htm.pamplin.vt.edu

Washington State University
School of Hospitality Business
Management
PO Box 644750
Pullman, WA 99164
509.335.4750
www.business.wsu.edu/academics/
hospitality

MORE INFORMATION

Convention Industry Council
700 N. Fairfax Street
Suite 510
Alexandria, VA 22314
571.527.3116
www.conventionindustry.org

Event Planners Association
25432 Trabuco
Suite 207
Lake Forest, CA 92630
866.380.3372
eventplannersassociation.com

**Meeting Professionals
International**
3030 Lyndon B. Johnson Freeway
Suite 1700
Dallas, TX 75234
972.702.3000
www.mpiweb.org

**Professional Convention
Management Association**
35 E. Wacker Drive
Suite 500
Chicago, IL 60601
312.423.7262
www.pcma.org

**Society of Government Meeting
Professionals**
908 King Street
Suite 200
Alexandria, VA 22314
703.549.0892
www.sgmp.org

Michael Shally-Jensen

Fitness Trainer & Instructor

Snapshot

Career Cluster: Sport & Athletics; Hospitality & Tourism; Personal Services

Interests: Exercise, being active, motivating others

Earnings (Yearly Average): $36,900

Employment & Outlook: Average Growth Expected

OVERVIEW

Sphere of Work

Fitness trainers and instructors design, organize, and lead exercise and sports programs that allow individuals to improve their health through cardiovascular activity, strength training, and stretching exercises. They usually offer private lessons as well as group instruction. They teach the fundamentals of fitness by presenting clients with various techniques, helping them set individually tailored fitness goals, and motivating them physically and mentally to reach those goals. Fitness trainers and instructors often focus on one or more areas of fitness, such as aerobics, weight lifting, yoga, or Pilates.

Work Environment

Fitness trainers and instructors work in a variety of settings, from health clubs and exercise studios to resorts and universities. Some travel to clients' homes to provide regular instruction, while others organize fitness programs for large businesses. The majority of fitness trainers and instructors work indoors in cool climates; however, some offer instruction in pleasant outdoor environments. Most fitness trainers and instructors work full time with irregular hours, as they must cater to the schedules of their clients. They often work early in the morning, at night, on weekends, and during holidays. Fitness trainers and instructors spend most of their time standing, walking, and participating in physical activities.

Profile

Working Conditions: Work both Indoors and Outdoors
Physical Strength: Medium Work
Education Needs: High School Diploma, Technical/Community College, Bachelor's Degree
Licensure/Certification: Recommended
Physical Abilities Not Required: No Heavy Labor
Opportunities For Experience: Internship, Volunteer Work
Holland Interest Score*: ESR

* See Appendix A

Occupation Interest

Those looking to become fitness trainers and instructors must be in excellent physical condition and have natural athletic ability. They should have a passion for instructing and motivating individuals. Sometimes clients are reluctant or unwilling to participate in specified activities, so fitness trainers and instructors should be firm, persuasive, and encouraging. Creativity and patience are also valuable traits. Fitness trainers and instructors must have strong customer service skills in order to find and maintain their clientele.

A Day in the Life—Duties and Responsibilities

Fitness trainers and instructors spend most of their day working with clients to achieve and build upon specified fitness goals. They begin by evaluating the physical strengths and weaknesses of each individual and providing corrective feedback for improvement. Fitness trainers and instructors design appropriate exercise programs based on the skill level, strength, and endurance of each client. They keep detailed records of clients' progress and advancement, noting accomplishments as well as areas that need improvement. Many fitness trainers and instructors have a background in nutrition and often advise clients on suitable diets, weight control techniques, and lifestyle modifications. They are responsible for informing clients of safety procedures and regulations related to sports and aerobic activities, as well as the proper use of exercise machines and other equipment.

When instructing large groups of people, fitness trainers and instructors plan lessons and routines, select music, and create innovative exercise programs. They must keep lessons and classes exciting, challenging, and safe for all participants. Because the skill levels of participants vary greatly, fitness trainers and instructors must offer alternative fitness regimens to accommodate all individuals within the group. They usually demonstrate a particular exercise method or sequence, observe participants in action, and correct any mistakes in order to prevent injury. Fitness trainers and instructors must also treat minor injuries, administer first aid, and refer clients to specialty physicians as needed.

Duties and Responsibilities

- Developing fitness programs for individuals or groups
- Conducting fitness training either one-on-one or before a group
- Making dietary and nutritional suggestions
- Recommending and purchasing equipment
- Monitoring exercise programs and making changes as necessary
- Hiring additional staff members

OCCUPATION SPECIALTIES

Group Fitness Instructors

Group Fitness Instructors organize and lead group exercise sessions, which can include aerobic exercise, stretching, muscle conditioning, or meditation. Some classes are set to music. In these classes, instructors may select the music and choreograph an exercise sequence.

Personal Fitness Instructors

Personal Fitness Instructors work with a single client or a small group. They may train in a gym or in the clients' homes. Personal fitness trainers assess the clients' level of physical fitness and help them set and reach their fitness goals.

Specialized Fitness Instructors

Specialized Fitness Instructors teach popular conditioning methods such as Pilates or yoga. In these classes, instructors show the different moves and positions of the particular method. They also watch students and correct those who are doing the exercises improperly.

Fitness Directors

Fitness Directors oversee the fitness-related aspects of a gym or other type of health club. They often handle administrative duties, such as scheduling personal training sessions for clients or creating workout incentive programs. They often select and order fitness equipment for their facility.

WORK ENVIRONMENT

Physical Environment

Most fitness trainers and instructors work indoors at fitness centers, health clubs, and exercise studios. Others work in hospitals, country clubs, resorts, and clients' homes. Gym environments are generally cool, clean, and well ventilated. Fitness trainers and instructors who lead outdoor fitness classes tend to work in warm weather conditions.

Human Environment

Fitness trainers and instructors mostly interact with their clients, regularly seeing individuals at least once a week and often more. Many are self-employed; however, those who work in fitness or health clubs typically report to fitness directors or gym managers.

Relevant Skills and Abilities

Communication Skills
- Speaking effectively

Interpersonal/Social Skills
- Being sensitive to others
- Cooperating with others
- Motivating others
- Providing support to others
- Working as a member of a team

Organization & Management Skills
- Coordinating tasks
- Managing people/groups
- Organizing information or materials

Technical Skills
- Working with your hands

Other Skills
- Being physically active

Technological Environment

Fitness trainers and instructors commonly use balance boards and discs, exercise balls, fitness weights, pedometers, and first aid kits in their daily activities. In order to track sessions and schedule clientele, they may use accounting, calendar, and project management software.

EDUCATION, TRAINING, AND ADVANCEMENT

High School/Secondary

High school students who are interested in becoming fitness trainers and instructors can prepare by taking courses not only in physical education but also in sciences such as biology, physiology, and chemistry. They should study business, English, nutrition, psychology, and basic math. Interested students can join school sports teams, participate in local sports leagues, or take individual lessons to learn the fundamentals of physical activity. Aspiring fitness trainers and instructors can gain experience by volunteering or working part time for a private gym, resort, or health club, or the gym of a local hospital, country club, or university.

Suggested High School Subjects
- Applied Math
- Biology
- Business
- Chemistry
- English
- First Aid Training
- Foods & Nutrition
- Health Science Technology
- Physics
- Physiology
- Psychology

Famous First

The first sport and fitness trainer to work full-time at an athletic facility was Bob Rogers of the New York Athletic Club, starting in 1883. Rogers had previously been a trainer with the London Athletic Club. Both organizations were exclusive "gentlemen's clubs" specializing in such activities as fencing, rowing, platform tennis, squash, and water polo. Eventually they diversified, in terms of both their sports programs and their clientele. New York Athletic Club members have won over 230 Olympic medals, more than 120 of which have been gold.

Postsecondary

After high school, prospective fitness trainers and instructors may pursue various modes of training for their area of desired specialization. They often enroll in classes that will qualify them for professional certification. Once certified, many fitness trainers and instructors work with or shadow an experienced trainer to better understand the practical applications of fitness instruction. After a period of time, new fitness trainers and instructors begin to establish their own clientele. Instructors looking to teach group classes must usually audition to teach at a particular gym or club. Those specializing in a certain method of exercise may need additional training or specialty certification.

An associate's or bachelor's degree in physical education, kinesiology, health, or exercise science is sometimes beneficial for new fitness trainers and instructors. In some cases, employers allow fitness trainers and instructors to substitute a postsecondary degree for professional licensure. Those looking to advance to management positions at health clubs or fitness centers should study exercise science, kinesiology, business administration, and accounting.

Related College Majors
- Exercise Science/Physiology/Movement Studies
- Health & Physical Education
- Parks, Recreation & Leisure Studies
- Physical Education Teaching & Coaching
- Sport & Fitness Administration/Management
- Sports Medicine & Athletic Training

Adult Job Seekers

Fitness trainers and instructors entering the job market should begin by contacting local health centers and other potential employers to determine their various needs. They are expected to be able to fulfill all of the job functions at the time of employment, without the need for on-the-job training. Many fitness trainers and instructors participate in part-time internships, apprenticeships, and job shadowing opportunities with experienced instructors at local health and fitness centers to gain necessary skills before beginning full-time work.

Professional Certification and Licensure

Certification in the fitness field is not always required; however, many employers prefer to hire fitness trainers and instructors who are certified. Candidates must have a high school diploma, maintain cardiopulmonary resuscitation (CPR) certification, and successfully complete an exam comprising both written and practical components related to physiology and exercise programs. Fitness trainers and instructors must be recertified every two years. Because there are many certifying organizations within the fitness field, candidates should first verify an organization's validity with the National Association for Certifying Agencies.

Additional Requirements

Employers in the fitness industry look for outgoing, dynamic, and confident staff. Communication is one of the most important aspects of the job, so fitness trainers and instructors should be comfortable addressing, leading, and motivating individuals and larger groups. They should also be sensitive to the needs and concerns of their clients while inspiring them to challenge themselves and improve their physical health.

EARNINGS AND ADVANCEMENT

Individuals can advance by locating jobs in more prestigious settings and by obtaining jobs with more responsibilities. Those who continually improve their skills by attending workshops, seminars, training sessions and classes will advance more quickly.

Mean annual earnings of fitness trainers and instructors were $36,900 in 2012. The lowest ten percent earned less than $18,094, and the highest ten percent earned more than $67,204. Persons in charge of large fitness programs and those who work in business environments earned the most.

Fitness trainers and instructors may receive paid vacations, holidays, and sick days; life and health insurance; and retirement benefits. These are usually paid by the employer.

Metropolitan Areas with the Highest
Employment Level in this Occupation

Metropolitan area	Employment	Employment per thousand jobs	Hourly mean wage
Chicago-Joliet-Naperville, IL	11,900	3.27	$15.21
New York-White Plains-Wayne, NY-NJ	9,510	1.84	$31.64
Los Angeles-Long Beach-Glendale, CA	5,790	1.49	$22.84
Boston-Cambridge-Quincy, MA	5,630	3.29	$21.92
Washington-Arlington-Alexandria, DC-VA-MD-WV	5,540	2.36	$19.85
Philadelphia, PA	4,490	2.46	$14.26
Seattle-Bellevue-Everett, WA	3,950	2.80	$21.03
Baltimore-Towson, MD	3,550	2.82	$15.77

Source: Bureau of Labor Statistics

EMPLOYMENT AND OUTLOOK

Fitness trainers and instructors held about 235,000 jobs nationally in 2012. About ten percent were self-employed, mostly as personal trainers. Employment is expected to grow faster than the average for all occupations through the year 2022, which means employment is projected to increase 12 percent to 22 percent. An increasing number of people spend more time and money on fitness to remain active, lose weight and have healthy lifestyles. This trend is seen in young people, baby boomers and the elderly alike. In addition, more businesses are recognizing the benefits of recreation and fitness programs and other services, such as wellness programs, for their employees.

Employment Trend, Projected 2012–22

Personal Care and Service Occupations: 21%

Fitness Trainers & Instructors: 13%

All Bus Drivers: 11%

Note: "All Occupations" includes all occupations in the U.S. Economy. Source: U.S. Bureau of Labor Statistics, Employment Projections Program

Related Occupations
- Health & Fitness Center Manager
- Recreation Program Director

> ## *Conversation With . . .*
> ## *BRIAN JOHNSON*
> ### Fitness Trainer, 3 years

1. What was your individual career path in terms of education/training, entry-level job, or other significant opportunity?

I was in corporate America for almost 20 years. I became unemployable because I topped out on the rate scale. My last job was running a Safeway distribution center. I asked myself: what's the one thing I've always done? And that's go to the gym. So I got my certification and started training people. I had enough money saved up so I was living off my savings, but the motivating piece was, I didn't want to work for anybody else ever again. I did a 12-week online course to get my certification in 8 weeks. I joined networking groups, which is how I got my clients.

I have my own gym. I trained my first client outside at the park across the street. I used an eight foot chain TRX and a five dollar fitness map. I migrated from individual clients into boot camps, which just makes sense because you're leveraging your time and working with 20 people for $15 each, as opposed to one person at $80.

Through all my marketing and networking, I got hooked up with a couple of wedding vendors. The clients walk in there, see my business cards, and the next thing you know I'll have a bridal party boot camp that usually lasts about two months. I also am starting a two-hour ultimate boot camp challenge, that also has a 5K mudrun, live music, vendors…a fitness festival. We have one coming up in May in Annapolis, and I'm talking about doing one with a guy on Long Island, NY, and a guy in Raleigh, NC. My goal is to do one a month across the nation.

2. What are the most important skills and/or qualities for someone in your profession?

The ability to inspire, motivate and hold people accountable, that´s the most important piece. Without that, whether you're working in a gym or doing your own gig, you´re never going to retain people.

3. What do you wish you had known going into this profession?

How difficult it would be to get clients. I thought it would be easy. In the fitness industry, word of mouth is everything, networking and social media. You've got to get your name out there. I do Business Networking International and other local area mixers. You have to identify the best social media for your industry. For mine, it's Facebook. For a banker, it's LinkedIn. At the end of the day, I have a very extensive and elaborate website but the majority of my clients come from word of mouth.

Also, in hindsight, I would have trained at a gym for two or three months to gain that confidence level to train people. I only charged my first client $30 a session. Now, I charge $80 for a private session. You need to research what other people are charging. You don't want to devalue yourself, or overprice yourself out of business. You've got to find that balance and test the market.

4. Are there many job opportunities in your profession? In what specific areas?

Yes. I say that because I've seen constant turnover at the gyms. They're always looking for quality instructors.

5. How do you see your profession changing in the next five years? What role will technology play in those changes, and what skills will be required?

I think a lot of it's going to go online. I can already see that shift happening. My vision is, you have this ten-by-ten room, you have a nice camera in there, people log in every day, and I instruct them for an hour. For $1, I have 1,000 people logging in for an hour.

6. What do you enjoy most about your job? What do you enjoy least?

Getting people to their goals, whether somebody is morbidly obese or somebody is already fit and training for a tough event. At my gym, we have a whiteboard where everybody writes their goals. I have a 61-year-old lady flipping a 200-pound tractor tire. It helps to motivate everyone.

What I like least is that you're always on. It's hard to shut it off. Not that I ever would, but God forbid if I ever wanted to go to McDonalds and have a cheeseburger. Too many people in this town know me! But it's a blessing. If I was working for a gym training someone, I would leave there at the end of the day and be done.

7. Can you suggest a valuable "try this" for students considering a career in your profession?

Try it at a gym first. Don't try it on your own. Write out all the pros and cons and make sure it's right for you, because it's not right for everybody.

SELECTED SCHOOLS

Although training beyond high school is not necessarily expected of beginning fitness trainers and instructors, interested parties may obtain training in fitness and exercise science at selected technical/community colleges or at privately run programs designed to prepare students for certification. Selected four-year college programs, too, offer degrees in this field.

MORE INFORMATION

American Alliance for Health, Physical Education, Recreation & Dance
1900 Association Drive
Reston, VA 20192-1598
800.213.7193
www.aahperd.org

American Council on Exercise
4851 Paramount Drive
San Diego, CA 92123
888.825.3636
www.acefitness.org

American Fitness Professionals and Associates
1601 Long Beach Boulevard
P.O. Box 214
Ship Bottom, NJ 08008
800.494.7782
www.afpafitness.com

International Fitness Professionals Association
14509 University Point Place
Tampa, FL 33613
www.ifpa-fitness.com

International Health, Racquet, and Sportsclub Association
70 Fargo Street
Boston, MA 02210
617.951.0055
www.ihrsa.org

National Board of Fitness Examiners
1650 Margaret Street
Suite 302-342
Jacksonville, FL 32204
www.nbfe.org

National Gym Association
P.O. Box 970579
Coconut Creek, FL 33097
954.344.8410
www.nationalgym.com

National Strength and Conditioning Association
1885 Bob Johnson Drive
Colorado Springs, CO 80906
800.815.6826
www.nsca.com

**Society of State Directors
of Health, Physical Educ. &
Recreation**
1900 Association Drive, Suite 100
Reston, VA 20191-1599
703.390.4599
www.thesociety.org

United States Pilates Association
1500 E. Broward Boulevard
Suite 250
Fort Lauderdale, FL 33301
888.484.8771
unitedstatespilatesassociation.com

Yoga Alliance
1701 Clarendon Boulevard
Suite 100
Arlington, VA 22209
571.482.3355
www.yogaalliance.org

Briana Nadeau/Editor

Flight Attendant

Snapshot

Career Cluster: Hospitality & Tourism; Transportation

Interests: Aviation, travel, communicating with others, handling emergency situations

Earnings (Yearly Average): $42,340

Employment & Outlook: Slower Than Average Growth Expected

OVERVIEW

Sphere of Work

A flight attendant is an airline professional who ensures the overall safety and security of the passengers aboard a flight, as well as their comfort and satisfaction. Flight attendants attend to passenger's needs, and are responsible for serving food and beverages to the passengers and crew. A flight attendant guarantees successful compliance with standard aviation safety regulations and protocols, and must thoroughly understand the ways in which airplanes operate. Flight attendants report to a flight supervisor and also to the captain of the aircraft on which he or she is working.

Work Environment

Flight attendants spend most of their time aboard an aircraft, and are assigned a home base location from which they generally operate. Generally, they are away from their home base location for at least one third of their working time, per month. Most flight attendants are expected to work nights, holidays, and weekends, in addition to regular hours during the week. They usually spend sixty-five to eighty-five hours per month in flight (with shifts lasting up to fourteen hours), with the ability to request additional hours, and another fifty hours per month on the ground performing tasks such as flight and report preparation.

Profile

Working Conditions: Work Indoors
Physical Strength: Light Work
Education Needs: High School Diploma Or G.E.D., Technical/Community College
Licensure/Certification: Required
Physical Abilities Not Required: No Heavy Labor
Opportunities For Experience: Military Service, Part-Time Work
Holland Interest Score*: ESA

* See Appendix A

Occupation Interest

Potential flight attendants should be interested in learning about aviation, national and international travel, and safety and emergency regulations. They should also possess outstanding communication skills. Flight attendants must interact with diverse and, at times, difficult passengers, and must project a pleasant and personable attitude, regardless of the circumstances. Individuals interested in becoming flight attendants should possess poise as well as strength of character, as these qualities will help them remain calm and effective during crisis or emergency situations aboard an aircraft.

A Day in the Life—Duties and Responsibilities

When a flight attendant reports for duty, he or she will typically meet with the captain and other crew members one hour before take-off to discuss evacuation procedures, airline crew coordination, flight duration, relevant passenger information (such as health or mobility issues), and anticipated weather conditions. Before passengers board the airplane, flight attendants take inventory of and prepare food and beverages and check first aid kits and emergency equipment. Once passengers begin boarding, flight attendants are responsible for greeting them, helping them find their seats, and assisting with the storage of carry-on luggage. Before take-off, flight attendants check the aircraft for any dangerous materials and note any passengers exhibiting odd or potentially threatening behavior. They welcome passengers aboard the flight, and provide information regarding safety procedures and emergency escape routes.

A flight attendant ensures the safety and security of the passengers and attends to their comfort and satisfaction from the time they board the aircraft until they depart. This includes assisting sick or injured passengers, providing food and beverages, answering any questions passengers might have, and preparing the passengers and plane for a safe landing. To further ensure passenger satisfaction, a flight attendant might also calm the nerves of anxious passengers and supervise small children. Prior to departure, flight attendants also collect audio headsets and trash, as well as take inventory. Once the plane is on the ground, flight attendants assist passengers exiting the aircraft and report the condition of cabin equipment. The lead flight attendant supervises crewmembers aboard the airplane in addition to performing his or her own regular duties.

Duties and Responsibilities

- Attending briefing sessions with crew members on weather conditions, number of passengers, and route
- Checking the cabin for supplies, emergency equipment, and food and beverages
- Greeting passengers and assisting them with carry-on luggage and personal items
- Verifying passengers' tickets
- Recording destinations
- Explaining and demonstrating the use of emergency equipment
- Providing passengers with newspapers, magazines, pillows and blankets
- Heating and serving cooked meals, sandwiches, or other light refreshments and beverages
- Observing passengers and enforcing in-flight rules and regulations
- Assisting passengers in any emergency situation

WORK ENVIRONMENT

Physical Environment

The majority of a flight attendant's work takes place inside the cabin of a clean, well-ventilated airplane. He or she is required to wear a uniform representing the airline for which he or she works, and must stand for long periods of time. A flight attendant also spends time in or around airline terminals. Constant exposure to re-circulated air, repetitive lifting and pushing motions, and the lack of safety restraints as the airplane encounters turbulence all contribute to a higher than average rate of job-related illness and injury.

Relevant Skills and Abilities

Communication Skills
- Speaking effectively

Interpersonal/Social Skills
- Cooperating with others
- Working as a member of a team

Organization & Management Skills
- Managing time and resources
- Meeting goals and deadlines
- Performing duties that change frequently
- Performing routine work

Work Environment Skills
- Being comfortable with air travel

Human Environment

Flight attendants work and deal with large groups of passengers, as well as other crewmembers. They report to flight supervisors and captains. Because they interact with so many people on a daily basis, flight attendants are susceptible to airborne illnesses and other sicknesses. In spite of work-related stressors, they must maintain a visibly positive attitude when in public situations, and must address passenger requests in a cordial yet authoritative manner. They must be adept at handling passenger needs, including the needs of elders, the disabled, and children.

Technological Environment

In addition to learning and understanding the basic functions of an airplane, flight attendants must use intercoms and public address systems, compact food and beverage carts, movie and music systems, first aid kits, microwave ovens, seating charts, and demonstration equipment, emergency survival equipment and systems, and other new technology as it becomes available.

EDUCATION, TRAINING, AND ADVANCEMENT

High School/Secondary

High school students who wish to become flight attendants can prepare by studying foreign languages, foods and nutrition, psychology, and public speaking. They should also take a basic first aid training and certification course. An understanding of the fundamentals of aviation, emergency procedures, and airplane operation and maintenance is useful. They should also participate in social clubs or volunteer groups that allow them to interact with peers and the public.

Suggested High School Subjects
- English
- First Aid Training
- Food Service & Management
- Foreign Languages
- Psychology
- Speech

Famous First

The first female flight attendant, or stewardess, was Ellen Church, a nurse from Iowa. She made her first flight between San Francisco, Calif., and Cheyenne, Wy. on Boeing Air Transport, a forerunner of United Airlines, in 1930. Prior to that time the job of flight attendant was done exclusively by male "stewards" or "cabin boys." Within a few years of Church's flight, however, women came to dominate the position. For decades flight attendants were required to be unmarried. That began to change in the late 1960s, when attendants challenged the practice as discriminatory.

Postsecondary

Potential flight attendants are required to have earned a high school diploma or its equivalent. Certain schools and colleges also offer flight attendant training, but a postsecondary degree is generally not required; however, increasingly often, some airlines give preference to those candidates with some college or a college degree and who have already completed some kind of related training. Flight attendants may find it helpful to study postsecondary subjects related to the hospitality industry, such as communications and travel and tourism. Flight attendants who wish to work for an international airline are usually proficient in at least one foreign language.

Related College Majors
- Flight Attendant Training
- Hospitality & Tourism

Adult Job Seekers

Potential flight attendants should have extensive experience working with the public and should demonstrate the ability to think on their feet and remain calm during a dispute or crisis. Most airlines require that flight attendants be at least eighteen to twenty-one years of age, undergo thorough background checks, and pass stringent medical evaluations.

Professional Certification and Licensure

To become eligible to work aboard aircraft carriers, flight attendants must complete a training program that covers a wide variety of duties. He or she then receives a flight attendant certificate from the Federal Aviation Administration (FAA). Successful certification depends on a flight attendant's ability to fulfill specific training requirements, set forth by the FAA and the Transportation Security Administration, including safety procedures, evacuations, and medical emergencies.

Additional Requirements

Some flight attendants are constantly traveling to and from fun and exotic destinations; others may be just making a run between regional airports. Due to their schedule, flight attendants and other members of the aircrew are often away from home for long periods of time. Therefore, potential flight attendants should consider that they may never experience a "normal" schedule, and will have to leave family members and loved ones for extended periods.

Successful flight attendants possess an interest in working with people and a willingness to learn about other cultures. Flight attendants, above all else, must display calm under pressure and patience for difficult people and situations. Though air travel is not usually dangerous, some flights may be incredibly unpleasant because of turbulence, mechanical failure, or other mishaps. Because of this, flight attendants must handle themselves with poise and confidence under severe pressure or duress. Most airlines require that applicants be physically fit in proportion to their height, and stay within a certain weight range throughout their years of service. Most flight attendants pay union dues and belong to the Association of Flight Attendants, the Transport Workers Union of America, or the International Brotherhood of Teamsters.

EARNINGS AND ADVANCEMENT

Earnings depend on the size of the airline company and the type of aircraft. Flight attendants are usually paid guaranteed monthly salaries based on a minimum number of flight hours (75-90). For time flown above the minimum guarantee or for night and international flights, they receive extra compensation.

According to data from the Association of Flight Attendants, beginning flight attendants had median annual earnings of $17,095 in 2012. Mean annual earnings of flight attendants, as a group, were $42,340 in 2012. The lowest ten percent earned less than $26,426, and the highest ten percent earned more than $67,829. Flight attendants also receive an allowance for meal expenses while on duty away from home.

Flight attendants may receive paid vacations, holidays, and sick days; life and health insurance; and retirement benefits. These are usually paid by the employer. Flight attendants may also receive free or reduced air fares for themselves and their families. Flight attendants are required to purchase uniforms and wear them while on duty. The airlines usually pay for uniform replacement items and may provide a small allowance to cover cleaning and upkeep of the uniforms.

Metropolitan Areas with the Highest Employment Level in this Occupation

Metropolitan area	Employment	Employment per thousand jobs	Annual mean wage
New York-White Plains-Wayne, NY-NJ	9,100	1.76	$39,900
Chicago-Joliet-Naperville, IL	8,560	2.35	$37,240
Atlanta-Sandy Springs-Marietta, GA	8,310	3.67	n/a
Los Angeles-Long Beach-Glendale, CA	4,540	1.17	$35,380
San Francisco-San Mateo-Redwood City, CA	3,490	3.49	$37,530
Denver-Aurora-Broomfield, CO	2,270	1.84	$34,280
Dallas-Plano-Irving, TX	2,040	0.97	$60,050
Las Vegas-Paradise, NV	1,970	2.41	n/a

Fun Fact

It may surprise you to learn that the first flight attendant was a man. Heinrich Kubis was hired as "steward" on a German passenger zeppelin in 1912. It wasn't until 18 years later that United Airlines hired the first female flight attendant. Soon women had all but taken over the profession, a trend that continued for decades. Today, an estimated 30 percent of flight attendants are men.

EMPLOYMENT AND OUTLOOK

Flight attendants held about 85,000 jobs nationally in 2012. Employment is expected to decrease compared with the average for all occupations through the year 2022, which means employment is projected to fall by 5 percent to 10 percent. A leveling off in air travel and a slowly improving economy, combined with increased efficiency in the airline industry, means that slightly fewer flight attendants will be needed.

Competition for jobs as flight attendants is expected to remain very strong because the number of applicants is expected to greatly exceed the number of job openings. As more career-minded people enter this occupation, job turnover will decline. Nevertheless, most job openings are expected from the need to replace flight attendants who stop working or transfer to other occupations. Employment of flight attendants is sensitive to cyclical swings in the economy.

Employment Trend, Projected 2012–22

Total, All Occupations: 11%

Transportation and Material Moving Occupations: 9%

Flight Attendants: -7%

Note: "All Occupations" includes all occupations in the U.S. Economy. Source: U.S. Bureau of Labor Statistics, Employment Projections Program

Related Occupations
- Bellhop/Bell Captain
- Food & Beverage Service Worker
- Waiter/Waitress

Related Military Occupations
- Transportation Specialist

Conversation With . . .
PAULA McCAULEY
Flight Attendant, 22 years

1. What was your individual career path in terms of education/training, entry-level job, or other significant opportunity?

When I graduated from college, a lot of my friends did the whole backpacking through Europe thing, but I never really traveled. I had a job at a software company for about a year. After church one Sunday, I saw an ad for what they called "a cattle call" back then. I was living in DC and drove to Baltimore. It was a whole day and there were hundreds of people, and you did interview after interview. I got hired on the spot. I never even thought about it until I saw the ad. I thought I would do it for a year. But my mom calls it "the golden handcuffs"– I'll never leave because there are so many perks!

2. What are the most important skills and/or qualities for someone in your profession?

You have to have patience. Just being patient and being kind goes a long way. And, honestly, you have to have some level of physical fitness. If you have an aborted landing, say, you have to open the door and the doors are heavy. That hardly ever happens, but it could.

My philosophy is being kind is not that hard. You have to be assertive and there are angry and drunk passengers. People get kicked off planes more often than you would think. Recently, we were flying to Madrid and had a woman, who was a New Yorker with an edge. She was forced to check her bag and took all kinds of stuff out of the bag and she had all these magazines on her lap. I went over and said, "What can I do to make your day better? Do you want me to store some of these magazines for you? You've had a rough time," and she said, "That's all I wanted. I just wanted to hear someone say that."

3. What do you wish you had known going into this profession?

What I didn't know at the beginning is that seniority is everything. The first couple of years you have to be on reserve. I had to carry a pager with me everywhere–this was before cell phones. It's almost like being a pledge in a sorority. You have to put in your time.

4. Are there many job opportunities in your profession? In what specific areas?

It's on and off. Right now we're not hiring flight attendants. But there's always somebody hiring, Jet Blue or Southwest. If you get on with the smaller companies like Express Jet and get experience, you'll get in with the bigger ones—American, Delta, United—eventually. The bigger the airlines, the more flight options. I have three kids, my husband, my parents—we all fly for free all over the world. It's standby. And we're paid better at the bigger airlines.

5. How do you see your profession changing in the next five years? What role will technology play in those changes, and what skills will be required?

I don't see it changing that much. People can be replaced by technology in some fields, but with flight attendants, we need to be there for security reasons. And it's all about the smiling flight attendant.

I'm not allowed to talk much about our training, but it has changed so much since 9/11. It used to focus on customer service. Now a large percentage of our training is about self-defense and how to spot certain things. I never thought I'd be learning tae kwon do as part of my training.

6. What do you enjoy most about your job? What do you enjoy least?

I love the flexibility. It is so unbelievably flexible for a mom. And I love being able to get away. Sunday I'm home and Monday I'm in a hotel in Miami. It's always great to be in the sun.

I love the travel and I love the people. I meet such fascinating people, crews included. Every day is different, and I don't take my work home with me.

Sometimes I think about the danger, just because I have three kids. In Billings, Montana, we had a flight attendant in critical condition; they hit a pocket of air and she hit the ceiling and broke her spine. But I try not to think about those things. Also, dealing with delays and irate passengers.

7. Can you suggest a valuable "try this" for students considering a career in your profession?

Every time you fly, just pay attention and watch and learn. Customer service is what it is—whether you're waitressing, or bar tending, or working behind the counter at Macy's. Having any sort of customer service job will help you decide if this is right for you.

SELECTED SCHOOLS

Training beyond high school is not generally expected of beginning flight attendants. However, such training can prove beneficial. Interested parties may find relevant programs at selected technical/community colleges or at privately run vocational schools designed to lay the basis for later certification.

MORE INFORMATION

Air Transport Association of America
Office of Communications
1301 Pennsylvania Avenue, NW
Suite 1100
Washington, DC 20004-1707
202.626.4000
www.air-transport.org

Association of Flight Attendants
501 3rd Street, NW
Washington, DC 20001
202.434.1300
www.afanet.org

U.S. Department of Transportation
Federal Aviation Administration
800 Independence Avenue SW
Washington, DC 20591
866.835.5322
www.faa.gov

Briana Nadeau/Editor

Florist

Snapshot

Career Cluster: Art & Design; Hospitality & Tourism; Sales & Service
Interests: Horticulture, flowers, plants, creative tasks
Earnings (Yearly Average): $25,550
Employment & Outlook: Decline Expected

OVERVIEW

Sphere of Work

Florists, also called floral designers, work with flowers, plants, and greenery to fashion and assemble arrangements and bouquets according to customer needs. Florists are responsible for the configuration of each arrangement, from conception to completion. They are creative individuals who use their talents to produce attractive arrangements for various occasions, including weddings and funerals, parties, holidays, corporate and school functions, and other special events. Some florists may have long-term agreements with hotels and restaurants or the owners of office buildings and private homes to replace old flowers with new

flower arrangements on a recurring schedule—usually daily, weekly, or monthly—to keep areas looking fresh and appealing. Some work with interior designers in creating these displays.

Work Environment

Most florists work out of retail florist shops under the supervision of a store manager or owner. Increasingly, however, many work in grocery stores with floral departments. Some florists own their own businesses and may work out of a small shop or within a home environment. Others are employed by wholesale floral companies and nurseries. Florists should expect to work in varying temperatures, as certain flowers are kept in refrigerated or humid storage areas, which florists must access regularly. They usually work a standard eight-hour day during the week and often work on weekends, especially during periods when flowers are in high demand.

Profile

Working Conditions: Work Indoors
Physical Strength: Light Work
Education Needs: On-The-Job Training, High School Diploma Or G.E.D.
Licensure/Certification: Recommended
Physical Abilities Not Required: No Heavy Labor
Opportunities For Experience: Part-Time Work
Holland Interest Score*: RAE

* See Appendix A

Occupation Interest

Those who are interested in pursuing a career in floral design must be passionate about horticulture and the history of plants and flowers. They should be able to create emotionally meaningful arrangements in various settings and with different plant materials. Florists must also interpret and translate the ideas of customers into unique floral arrangements. They must also have an interest in the concepts of business, as many florists are also shop managers or owners.

A Day in the Life—Duties and Responsibilities

Florists normally spend the majority of the workday in a flower shop or retail setting, cutting and clipping flowers, and designing various floral arrangements for private clients and large events. The frequency of customer orders may vary by season, and before or during popular holidays, a florist may be required to work overtime or longer hours to accommodate customer demands.

Florists are generally responsible for most daily back-end operations of a flower business. When a client requests an arrangement, the florist must evaluate the client's idea and choose the appropriate floral arrangement or bouquet for the occasion. A florist's clients may include private individuals, hotels, restaurants, museums and libraries, banks, retail stores, religious institutions, and corporations. A large part of the day is spent trimming and cutting flowers and materials, planning and preparing floral arrangements, and working with wreaths, terrariums, and related items. Some florists decorate store windows and travel to various locations to prepare large-scale floral arrangements or landscapes.

Florists commonly perform administrative duties in order to keep the business running smoothly. They track financial transactions and orders, take messages via phone and the Internet, and often purchase and maintain the inventory of flowers and plants. Depending on the type of floral business, they may also be responsible for the sale of items, including plant food, gardening equipment, storage containers, and decorative accessories. They may also spend a good deal of time interacting with customers and advising them on how to care for various kinds of plants and flowers.

Duties and Responsibilities

- Talking with customers regarding the price and type of arrangement desired
- Planning the arrangement according to the customer's requirements and costs, using knowledge of design and properties of materials or an appropriate standard design pattern
- Choosing the flora and foliage necessary for the arrangement
- Trimming material and arranging bouquets, sprays, wreaths, dish gardens, terrariums and other items
- Packing and wrapping completed arrangements
- Decorating buildings, churches, halls or other facilities where events are planned

WORK ENVIRONMENT

Physical Environment

Most florists work in clean, comfortable, and well-ventilated settings. In some cases, they may be required to gather and harvest flowers and plants in outdoor environments. Storage areas for collected flowers and plants are typically cool and humid. Some florists travel to various locations to deliver floral arrangements.

Human Environment

Florists generally work with a small number of other employees or administrative personnel. Some florists report to a shop manager or owner, while others hold supervisory positions themselves. Florists who have home-based businesses usually work alone. Most florists frequently interact with clients who place orders for bouquets and arrangements. Some florists also collaborate with interior designers and other design professionals for residential or corporate projects.

Relevant Skills and Abilities

Creative/Artistic Skills
- Being skilled in art and design

Interpersonal/Social Skills
- Cooperating with others
- Perceiving others' feelings
- Working as a member of a team

Organization & Management Skills
- Meeting goals and deadlines
- Selling ideas or products
- Working quickly when necessary
- Paying attention to and handling details

Research & Planning Skills
- Gathering information
- Creating ideas

Technological Environment

Florists work with various tools and materials to produce their floral creations. They regularly use pruners, wires and wire cutters, shears, pins, foams, spray paints, knives, and other sharp tools. They also work with many different kinds of flowers and plants. Florists must also be familiar with office equipment and cash registers.

EDUCATION, TRAINING, AND ADVANCEMENT

High School/Secondary

High school students who wish to become florists should concentrate on subjects related to the sciences, agriculture, and botany. In addition to these core subjects, students should also take courses that emphasize creative art design, communications, and business. Interested students should familiarize themselves with flower and plant growing, harvesting, and arranging by visiting public gardens or local farms or by experimenting with plants and flowers in their own private gardens. Students are also encouraged to participate in apprenticeships or summer internships that allow them to work with flowers and plants.

Suggested High School Subjects
- Agricultural Education
- Applied Math
- Arts
- Bookkeeping
- Crafts
- English
- Ornamental Horticulture

Famous First

The first flowers to be dispensed in a vending machine were placed in New York City's Grand Central Station in 1961 by the Automated Flowers Company of Greenwich, Conn. The machine was six feet high, by three feet wide, and two feet deep. It was a self-contained refrigerated unit that required no plumbing. Since that time floral vending machines have grown steadily in use in large public facilities and now offer everything from small lapel decorations to substantial floral arrangements.

Postsecondary

Though florists are not required to earn an undergraduate degree to begin working in their field, many choose to study floral design or basic design and color concepts at vocational schools, community colleges, or universities. Postsecondary programs in floral design teach students the fundamentals of preparing, designing, and packaging flowers and floral arrangements. They also cover sales and business approaches, customer service, garden construction, and horticulture and greenhouse management. Students work with fresh, dry, and artificial flowers. In addition to practical approaches to floral design, students gain an understanding of the philosophical ideas behind designing flowers. They also learn about current trends in the industry. Training in general horticulture or botany is also useful.

Adult Job Seekers

Many florists start out by gaining experience in the floral industry as cashiers, delivery people, or assistants in retail floral shops. These jobs provide opportunities to develop skills related to floral design like drawing and sketching, molding clay, and creating displays and exhibits.

Job seekers commonly apply directly to floral shops or private employers. Those who complete a formal floral design program often have learned how to manage a floral shop or start their own business. Some floral design programs also provide job placement services. Membership in professional floral design associations may provide networking opportunities and job listings for adults seeking employment as florists.

Professional Certification and Licensure

Certification in floral design is not generally required. However, some florists find it helpful to become accredited by a professional association, such as The American Institute of Floral Designers (AIFD), as a demonstration of their expertise in the field. For the AIFD examination, test-takers should expect to complete a written portion that covers basic principles and terminology of floral design and pass a practical section that demonstrates their proficiency in creating displays and arrangements. Continuing education is often a requirement for certification renewal. As with any voluntary certification program, it is useful to consult credible professional associations within the field, and follow professional debate as to the relevancy and value of the certification program.

Additional Requirements

Because floral design is a highly creative and interpretive line of work, prospective florists should be able to process and translate the customer's artistic concepts and general feelings into an evocative floral product. Florists rely on their senses to make informed decisions; therefore, potential florists should be able to recognize differences in color, scents, and textures. As customers often need arrangements at the last minute, florists should be organized, possess a sense of urgency, and have great time-management skills.

EARNINGS AND ADVANCEMENT

Earnings of florists depend on the geographic location of the employer and the individual's level of skill and years of experience. Mean annual earnings of florists were $25,550 in 2012. The lowest ten percent earned less than $17,956, and the highest ten percent earned more than $37,990.

Florists may receive paid vacations, holidays, and sick days. Because most floral shops are small, other fringe benefits are limited. Some employers pay part of the cost of life and health insurance, but few contribute to retirement plans other than Social Security.

Metropolitan Areas with the Highest Employment Level in this Occupation

Metropolitan area	Employment[1]	Employment per thousand jobs	Hourly mean wage[1]
New York-White Plains-Wayne, NY-NJ	1,540	0.30	$16.00
Chicago-Joliet-Naperville, IL	1,330	0.37	$13.12
Philadelphia, PA	950	0.52	$12.47
Houston-Sugar Land-Baytown, TX	650	0.25	$12.22
Los Angeles-Long Beach-Glendale, CA	650	0.17	$14.14
Dallas-Plano-Irving, TX	650	0.31	$12.36
Boston-Cambridge-Quincy, MA	650	0.38	$13.26
Miami-Miami Beach-Kendall, FL	600	0.60	$12.23

[1]Does not include self-employed. Source: Bureau of Labor Statistics

Fun Fact

It took 20 florists and a small contingent of engineers and builders to create the world's tallest floral arrangement: a tower of pompon flowers reaching more than 89 feet (about seven stories) skyward. According to Guinness World Records, the arrangement of 65,000 yellow, blue, green and white flowers was organized by the Mexican beer maker Cerveza Modelo Especial in Mexico City on May 10, 2013 in honor of Mother's Day.

EMPLOYMENT AND OUTLOOK

Florists held about 62,400 jobs nationally in 2012. About one-half worked in florist shops, and many others worked in the floral departments of grocery stores. Employment is expected to decline through the year 2022.

Opportunities should be available in grocery store and Internet floral shops as sales of floral arrangements from these outlets grow. The prearranged displays and gifts available in these stores appeal to consumers because of the convenience and because of prices that are lower than can be found in independent floral shops.

Employment Trend, Projected 2012–22

Total, All Occupations: 11%

Arts, Design, Entertainment, Sports, and Media Occupations: 7%

Florists: -8%

Note: "All Occupations" includes all occupations in the U.S. Economy. Source: U.S. Bureau of Labor Statistics, Employment Projections Program

Related Occupations
- Gardener & Groundskeeper
- Interior Designer

Conversation With . . .
TIMI HUSKINSON
Florist, 19 years

1. What was your individual career path in terms of education/training, entry-level job, or other significant opportunity?

While volunteering as a Master Gardener as part of the Cooperative Extension in Las Vegas, I became aware of an Ornamental Horticulture Program at College of Southern Nevada. I began taking classes in Floral Design and in Urban Horticulture, thinking the two areas would benefit me in floral design. Armed with beginning classes and training from the Master Gardener program, I stepped out in faith and opened my business offering xeriscape maintenance, horticulture management and floral design, as I continued with my education.

Right now corporate events and convention events are probably 40 percent of my business. I'll get a call from, let's just say IBM, saying "We need 220 centerpieces because we'll be in town for a convention." Generally for a corporate event, they don't want as many flowers; they want something with a more modern, streamlined look to it.

2. What are the most important skills and/or qualities for someone in your profession?

I'd say hands-on training through a college that offers specific instruction in floral design is invaluable. An art, interior design, or horticulture background are natural for the skills and creativity required to be a top-rated floral designer. Qualities should include a passion for nature in order to work with fresh-cut flowers and plants and unusual textures from the horticultural world. You must be self-motivated to keep up with ever-changing design styles and continue your education.

3. What do you wish you had known going into this profession?

I felt lucky to have a background in management. I would encourage anyone entering the profession to continue with a balance of design and management classes. An internship in a flower shop, event company or floral design studio will help you learn about the profession before getting into it.

4. Are there many job opportunities in your profession? In what specific areas?

The opportunities in floral design are endless. Every city, county and state has flower shops. You can take the skills you acquire from classes in floral design anywhere. Resorts and hotels have their own floral departments, as do cruise ships. Upscale couture floral design studios are in great demand, as are opportunities in the Event Design end of the industry. If you have a passion for teaching, there's also a need for trained, qualified educators and instructors.

5. How do you see your profession changing in the next five years? What role will technology play in those changes, and what skills will be required?

Floral designers are leaving cookie cutter membership services that dictate the exact style of floral design offered to consumers. With mobile technology and Internet mapping, consumers are searching the zip code of the person receiving flowers, then selecting a florist from an actual small business to custom design their order. Consumers want to send flowers that convey their emotions and prefer to have an original design. Owners of florist shops are quickly adapting to these changes. In the next five years, we will need to continue to acquire social media skills, including joining conversations and circles. The Internet will continue to be the best source for consumers to find reliable service companies, florists included. Social networking skills, such as posting images of your most current designs instantly and spontaneously, are technology skills we will be need to perfect.

6. What do you enjoy most about your job? What do you enjoy least?

I love flowers! I enjoy using my flower shop and the original designs we feature as a ministry to connect the good word of the Gospel to our clients, especially on occasions when they are at a loss for words. Flowers speak a language of comfort at times of grief and loss. I have a passion for designing with unusual and original elements found in nature. I like to be inspired by other professionals who also keep up with the newest design styles. Attending national symposiums, like those offered by the American Institute of Floral Designers (AIFD), is an exciting way to see what's happening around the world.

My least favorite thing about this industry? Easy: clients trying to place last minute orders at the end of the workday and weekend, and on major holidays when we are closed.

7. Can you suggest a valuable "try this" for students considering a career in your profession?

Get to know your local florist. They are the eyes and ears of the industry, and are in the know about classes and opportunities. Ask your local florist to put together a mixed bunch of flowers for you to take home and arrange, to see if this is a skill that comes naturally to you and makes you happy. Volunteer organizations frequently have events where all hands are needed, with instructors there to oversee and give some hands-on training.

SELECTED SCHOOLS

Training beyond high school is not necessarily expected of beginning florists. However, such training can prove beneficial. Interested parties may find relevant programs at selected technical/community colleges or at privately run vocational schools with floral design programs or programs in horticulture.

MORE INFORMATION

American Floral Endowment
1601 Duke Street
Alexandria, VA 22314
703.838.5211
www.endowment.org

American Institute of Floral Designers
720 Light Street
Baltimore, MD 21230
410.752.3318
www.aifd.org

Association of Specialty Cut Flower Growers
PO Box 268
17½ West College Street
Oberlin, OH, 44074
440.774.2887
www.ascfg.org

Master Florists Association
1171 Broadway Street
San Francisco, CA 94109
415.298.1943
www.masterfloristsassn.org

National Garden Clubs, Inc.
4401 Magnolia Avenue
St. Louis, MO 63110
314.776.7574
www.gardenclub.org

Society of American Florists
1601 Duke Street
Alexandria, VA 22314
800.336.4743
www.safnow.org

Briana Nadeau/Editor

Food Service Manager

Snapshot

Career Cluster: Business Administration; Hospitality & Tourism
Interests: Restaurants, customer service, managing others
Earnings (Yearly Average): $52,580
Employment & Outlook: Slower Growth Than Average

OVERVIEW

Sphere of Work

Food service managers are responsible for overseeing the daily operations of various establishments that serve food and beverages to patrons. They recruit, hire, and train restaurant employees and commonly supervise assistant managers, waitstaff, cooks, and other administrative personnel.

They make decisions regarding pricing and selection of menu items, order food and supplies, and ensure the proper upkeep of the establishments they run. In addition to their managerial tasks, food service managers usually handle most administrative and human resource-related activities of the business.

Work Environment

Most food service managers work indoors and spend a good deal of time on their feet, moving from the dining room to the kitchen, the bar, and other areas. They usually have their own office within the establishment. Working environments range from small, independent restaurants to large resorts, country clubs, or nightclubs. Food service managers generally work long and irregular hours that include weekends and holidays, especially those in fine dining, and rarely follow a standard forty-hour work week. Those who work in schools, cafeterias, or hospitals usually hold a more regular schedule.

Profile

Working Conditions: Work Indoors
Physical Strength: Light Work
Education Needs: High School Diploma Or G.E.D., Technical/Community College, Apprenticeship
Licensure/Certification: Recommended
Physical Abilities Not Required: No Heavy Labor
Opportunities For Experience: Apprenticeship, Military Service Volunteer Work, Part-Time Work
Holland Interest Score*: ESR

* See Appendix A

Occupation Interest

Food service managers constantly deal with customers, and therefore must demonstrate a pleasant, positive attitude at all times. Those interested in becoming food service managers must be highly motivated, as the job can be all-consuming, often requiring managers to work seven days a week with little time off. Restaurant environments can be stressful and unpredictable, so potential managers should be calm, resilient, and able to work well under pressure.

A Day in the Life—Duties and Responsibilities

Food service managers rely heavily on their waitstaff to provide excellent service and to present and maintain a satisfactory dining experience for customers. To this end, managers put a significant amount of energy into finding reliable, hardworking waiters and waitresses. They interview and hire dining room staff, whom they then must instruct in their particular establishment's policies and procedures, as well as the fundamentals of working in a restaurant if necessary. Occasionally, food service managers must lay off or fire employees, then replace them on short notice. Managers create work schedules for staff members, plan menus with cooks or chefs, and prepare the restaurant for service. They also explain performance and customer service standards to the waitstaff and other personnel.

During service, food service managers ensure the satisfaction of patrons and respond to any questions, complaints, or comments customers may have. During busy shifts or special events, managers often take orders, clear tables, serve drinks, and assist in the kitchen. They also review and approve food preparation, portion sizes, and presentation. At the end of service, managers tally and report earnings and often make bank deposits on behalf of the establishment.

During non-service hours or the off season, food service managers handle numerous administrative details. They continuously evaluate the amount and cost of food and beverages needed, calculate budgets and payroll records, monitor inventory, and make equipment and food purchases. They also oversee the cleaning of the kitchen, dining room, and other areas, and report any maintenance problems that arise.

Duties and Responsibilities

- Estimating food and beverage amounts and costs
- Purchasing food, supplies, and equipment
- Keeping records of inventory and employees' work schedules
- Consulting with the cook or chef to plan and evaluate menus
- Inspecting the dining room, the kitchen, and equipment for cleanliness
- Interviewing, hiring, training, and discharging employees
- Settling customer complaints about food or service

OCCUPATION SPECIALTIES

Caterers

Caterers plan and supervise the preparation and serving of food and beverages at social affairs, business functions, and other special events.

Liquor Establishment Managers

Liquor Establishment Managers coordinate the activities of workers who sell and serve alcoholic beverages to patrons in taverns, cocktail lounges, and night clubs.

WORK ENVIRONMENT

Physical Environment

Food service managers work in both small and large restaurants, usually indoors. Work environments can be noisy and hectic. Dining rooms are normally clean, well lit, and well ventilated, while kitchens and other back-of-house sections can be hot, dark, and cluttered. Catering service managers work in a variety of environments, from private homes and banquet rooms inside hotels to outdoor venues such as tented lawns and urban plazas.

Human Environment

Food service managers work with and supervise a wide array of restaurant personnel, including assistant managers, purchasing agents, cashiers, waitstaff, cooks, bartenders, dishwashers, bus people, and office administrators. They often report to restaurant or club owners, or in some cases a panel of trustees, and regularly interact with customers.

Relevant Skills and Abilities

Communication Skills
- Speaking effectively

Interpersonal/Social Skills
- Cooperating with others
- Working as a member of a team

Organization & Management Skills
- Coordinating tasks
- Demonstrating leadership
- Managing people/groups
- Paying attention to and handling details
- Performing duties that change frequently

Research & Planning Skills
- Developing evaluation strategies
- Laying out a plan

Technological Environment

Food service managers use computers on a daily basis to place orders, monitor inventory, schedule events, and coordinate staff hours. They commonly handle large- and small-scale kitchen equipment, as well as cash registers and point-of-sale software.

EDUCATION, TRAINING, AND ADVANCEMENT

High School/Secondary

High school students who are interested in becoming food service managers should begin by taking courses in foods and nutrition, economics, and communications. In addition, they should enroll in classes that focus on business management and administration. During summer and holiday vacations, students can apply for part-time employment at local restaurants, country clubs, or resorts. Students normally start out working as bus people, hosts, dishwashers, or waitstaff, and quickly become familiar with the daily operations of a food and beverage establishment. In this setting, they can observe food service managers in action.

Suggested High School Subjects
- Bookkeeping
- Business
- Business Math
- College Preparatory
- English
- Food Service & Management
- Foods & Nutrition
- Mathematics

Famous First

The first cafeteria was opened in Chicago in 1895. Created by Ernest Kimball, it stood on Adams Street between Clark and La Salle streets. In 1899 Kimball moved the entire operation to the basement of the New York Life Building on Madison Avenue in New York City, where it remained until 1925. Another noted cafeteria opened around that time in the Time-Life Building. It still exists today, although it has been eclipsed in terms of its menu and setting by the cafeterias of the Condé Nast Building and Hearst Tower.

Postsecondary

Many food service managers have a high school diploma or its equivalent, and are not required to possess a bachelor's degree in order to run a restaurant—as long as they have the experience. However, an increasing number of employers expect prospective managers to have some kind of postsecondary training, if not a bachelor's degree. Many colleges and universities across the country offer four-year programs in restaurant or food service management. Alternatively, many community colleges, junior colleges, and technical institutes offer two-year associate's degree programs in hospitality. All postsecondary programs in hospitality teach students the fundamentals of food preparation, nutrition, sanitation, management, computer science, and accounting.

Related College Majors
- Culinary Arts/Chef Training
- Enterprise Management & Operation
- Hospitality & Recreation Marketing Operations
- Hotel/Motel & Restaurant Management
- Institutional Food Workers & Administration

Adult Job Seekers

Restaurant chains and management companies often find new employees through hospitality education programs that offer internships and work-study opportunities. Restaurant owners and managers also attend career fairs and advertise on the Internet and in local newspapers to recruit new workers. Job seekers with experience in the service industry generally have a greater chance of securing assistant manager and food service manager positions. Many managers have a background in cooking and the culinary arts, which can prove helpful when looking to advance.

Professional Certification and Licensure

Though not required for employment, many food service managers voluntarily become certified as Foodservice Management Professionals (FMP), a title awarded by the National Restaurant Association Educational Foundation. This designation is helpful in demonstrating the professional competence of experienced managers. In order to obtain licensure, managers must pass a written examination and complete several courses covering a variety of food service management topics.

Additional Requirements

Ultimately, food service managers must demonstrate unquestionable leadership skills, as the successful operation of an establishment depends on their ability to motivate others, solve problems, and communicate well with clientele. Food service managers should also have an eye for detail and great taste, as they are responsible for the general appearance of the restaurant they manage.

EARNINGS AND ADVANCEMENT

Earnings of food service managers depend on the type, size, and geographic location of the establishment and the manager's particular duties. Mean annual earnings of food service managers were $52,580 in 2012. The lowest ten percent earned less than $30,820, and the highest ten percent earned more than $81,030.

Food service managers may receive paid vacations, holidays, and sick days; life and health insurance; and retirement benefits. These are usually paid by the employer. Most employers also provide free meals.

Metropolitan Areas with the Highest Employment Level in this Occupation

Metropolitan area	Employment	Employment per thousand jobs	Hourly mean wage
Los Angeles-Long Beach-Glendale, CA	6,910	1.78	$24.73
New York-White Plains-Wayne, NY-NJ	4,960	0.96	$33.32
Chicago-Joliet-Naperville, IL	4,510	1.24	$23.43
Dallas-Plano-Irving, TX	3,490	1.66	$22.61
Washington-Arlington-Alexandria, DC-VA-MD-WV	3,460	1.48	$31.44
Minneapolis-St. Paul-Bloomington, MN-WI	3,440	1.97	$24.39
San Diego-Carlsbad-San Marcos, CA	3,340	2.65	$26.90
Santa Ana-Anaheim-Irvine, CA	3,010	2.13	$26.53

Source: Bureau of Labor Statistics

EMPLOYMENT AND OUTLOOK

Food service managers held about 321,000 jobs nationally in 2012. Employment is expected to hold more or less steady through 2022. The number of new restaurants opening is expected to decline slightly from the previous decade. Food service managers will be needed to manage not only restaurants but also grocery and convenience stores and other retail and recreation establishments that are known for being able to provide food to consumers quickly. Job opportunities are expected to be best for persons with bachelor's or associate's degrees in restaurant and institutional food service management, or with solid experience in the trade (such as having worked as an assistant manager).

Employment Trend, Projected 2012–22

Total, All Occupations: 11%

Management Occupations: 7%

Food Service Managers: 2%

Note: "All Occupations" includes all occupations in the U.S. Economy. Source: U.S. Bureau of Labor Statistics, Employment Projections Program

Related Occupations
- Cook/Chef
- Hotel/Motel Manager
- Waiter/Waitress

Related Military Occupations
- Food Service Manager
- Food Service Specialist
- Store Manager

Conversation With . . .
CARL CITRON
Food Service Manager
44 years in the industry

1. What was your individual career path in terms of education/training, entry-level job, or other significant opportunity?

My degree is a bachelor's of science in technology. I majored in food and nutrition in college. Afterward, I went through restaurant management training.

2. What are the most important skills and/or qualities for someone in your profession?

Communication, leadership and financial acumen. I manage food services operations at colleges and universities. Because I deal with people from a college president right down to a utility worker in a dish room, I need to be able to communicate with people from different socioeconomic levels and different ethnic backgrounds. It's important to maintain relationships. So, if I'm talking with a college president, I need to be able to speak about college and university business. I need to know what keeps them awake at night so that I can offer solutions to those issues. I also need to be able to motivate employees at many levels, many of whom don't speak English.

From a leadership perspective, nothing that I can do to be successful involves anything that I have direct control or input over. If I want to be successful, I have to build teams who are going to understand the company's vision and the tools at their disposal. That's what will guide them through the maze of bringing solutions to our clients.

I have 48 food service managers in my district at all levels, from general managers, to operations mangers, to retail managers, to registered dieticians. All of those managers cross four generations. There are baby boomers, Generation Xers, Generation Ys and millennials. I have to understand the most effective way to communicate to people from each of those generations, how they interact with one another and how they see their jobs, because each viewpoint is different depending on when they grew up.

As for financial acumen, it's very important to understand profit- and-loss statements, balance sheets, assets, accounting work. You need to understand how business works and how to come out with win-win situations with clients.

3. What do you wish you had known going into this profession?

I wish I had a broader business background. In terms of negotiating finances with a client, if I have an understanding of how their company is doing and look at their financial report, I can draw conclusions about challenges they might have. That puts me in a good position to offer them solutions in the services that we negotiate.

4. Are there many job opportunities in your profession? In what specific areas?

There are tons of job opportunities in this profession. In food services, there are jobs in facilities management, food management. There are opportunities for chefs, financial controllers, marketing people, IT people. My company is even hiring marketing people who specialize in social media.

5. How do you see your profession changing in the next five years? What role will technology play in those changes, and what skills will be required?

There's a greater emphasis on nutrition and health, specifically gluten-free and providing choices for people with peanut allergies and celiac disease. Also, locally-sourced food and sustainable farming is becoming more important.

Social media is also changing things. Information is just passed along so fast, both positive and negative. So, getting ahead of the chats that are out there and being aware of what people are saying and being able to turn on a dime and respond is much more of a priority than ever before. I'm hiring people to administer multiple Facebook accounts, Instagram accounts and to tweet on a regular basis because that's how young people want to communicate these days.

6. What do you enjoy most about your job? What do you enjoy least?

I like developing my managers. Probably the most satisfaction I get is being able to see my managers grow and move their careers in a positive direction. What I like least about my job is negotiating. I'm not really great at it and I like to be very direct. When you get into negotiations, whether they're financial negotiations or collective bargaining agreements, there's so much nonsense that goes into negotiation, I just want to cut to the chase and get it done. You have to deal with process and consensus. That's the part I don't like, but it's one of the most important parts of my job that I do.

7. Can you suggest a valuable "try this" for students considering a career in your profession?

Seek out internships. Ask to shadow a manager somewhere for a day to get a sense of what they do. Go to career fairs where companies are set up to answer questions for people seeking information.

SELECTED SCHOOLS

It is not necessary in all cases to have a college degree in order to work as a food services manager. However, in many cases employers do prefer candidates with some college; at large, high-end establishments a college degree is generally expected. Interested students can gain initial training at a community college or vocational school. For those interested in a bachelor's degree, below are listed some of the more prominent institutions in this field.

California State Polytechnic University, Pomona
Collins College of Hospitality Management
3801 W. Temple Avenue 79B
Pomona, CA 91768
909.869.2275
www.csupomona.edu/~collins

Drexel University
Center for Hospitality and Sport Management
101 N. 33rd Street
Philadelphia, PA 19104
215.895.2411
drexel.edu/hsm

Georgia State University
Cecil B. Day School of Hospitality Administration
Robinson College of Business
35 Broad Street, Suite 220
Atlanta, GA 30303
404.413.7615
hospitality.robinson.gsu.edu

Johnson & Wales University
The Hospitality College
8 Abbot Park Place
Providence, RI 02903
401.598.1000
www.jwu.edu/hospitality

Kansas State University
Department of Hospitality Management and Dietetics
119 Justin Hall
Manhattan, KS 66506
785.532.5500
www.he.k-state.edu/hmd

Northern Arizona University
W.A. Franke College of Business
Hotel and Restaurant Management
20 W. McConnell Drive
Flagstaff, AZ 86011
928.523.5232
franke.nau.edu/hrm

Oklahoma State University
School of Hotel and Restaurant Administration
210 Human Sciences W
Stillwater, OK 74078
405.744.6713
humansciences.okstate.edu/hrad

University of Denver
Fritz Knoebel School of Hospitality Management
Daniels College of Business
2101 S. University Boulevard
Denver, CO 80208
303.871.3411

University of Houston
Conrad N. Hilton College of Hotel
and Restaurant Management
4800 Calhoun Road
Houston, TX 77004
713.743.2255
www.hrm.uh.edu

**University of Massachusetts,
Amherst**
Isenberg School of Management
Department of Hospitality and
Tourism Management
121 Presidents Drive
Amherst, MA 01003
413.545.5610
www.isenberg.umass.edu/htm

MORE INFORMATION

**Association of Nutrition and
Food Service Professionals**
406 Surrey Woods Drive
St. Charles, IL 60174
800.323.1908
www.anfponline.org

**International Council on Hotel,
Restaurant, and Institutional
Education**
2810 North Parham Rd.
Suite 230
Richmond, VA 23294
804.346.4800
www.chrie.org

National Restaurant Association
1200 17th St. NW
Washington, DC 20036
202.331.5900
www.restaurant.org

**National Restaurant Association
Educational Foundation**
175 West Jackson Boulevard
Suite 1500
Chicago, IL 60604
800.765.2122
www.nraef.org

**Society for Hospitality and
Foodservice Management**
455 S. 4th Street, Suite 650
Louisville, KY 40202
502.574.9931
www.sfhm-online.org

Briana Nadeau/Editor

Gaming Services Operator

Snapshot

Career Cluster: Hospitality & Tourism; Sports & Gaming

Interests: Gambling, gaming, entertainment, customer service

Earnings (Yearly Average): $26,500 (all); $49,290 (supervisors)

Employment & Outlook: Average Growth Expected

OVERVIEW

Sphere of Work

Gaming services operators serve customers in gambling establishments, such as casinos or racetracks. Some operators tend slot machines or deal cards. Others take bets or pay out winnings. Still others supervise or manage gaming workers and operations. The principal occupations consist of gaming dealers, who operate table games such as blackjack (twenty-one) and craps; slot supervisors, who oversee the operation of slot machines; gaming managers and supervisors, who direct operations and personnel in assigned areas;

and sports book writers and runners, who handle bets on sporting events.

Work Environment

Most of the jobs in the gaming industry are in commercial casinos, riverboat casinos, casino hotels, Native American casinos, and racetracks with casinos. These establishments are not legal in every state. Because most such establishments are open 24 hours a day, 7 days a week, employees work nights, weekends, and holidays—on shifts. Many gaming environments are windowless and can become quite crowded and noisy. Gaming services operators spend much of the time on their feet.

Profile

Working Conditions: Work Indoors
Physical Strength: Light Work
Education Needs: On-The-Job Training, High School Diploma Or G.E.D.
Licensure/Certification: Recommended
Physical Abilities Not Required: No Heavy Labor
Opportunities For Experience: Part-Time Work
Holland Interest Score*: RAE
* See Appendix A

Occupation Interest

People who are interested in gaming occupations enjoy interacting with people. Successful gaming services operators must be able to explain the rules of the game to customers and answer any questions they have, so a natural interest in gaming is useful. Because they deal with large amounts of money, they must be good at math. Gaming managers and supervisors oversee other gaming services workers and must be able to guide them in doing their jobs and developing their skills. All gaming services operators have to be able to keep their composure when handling a customer who becomes upset or breaks a rule. They must also be patient in dealing with equipment failure or malfunction.

A Day in the Life—Duties and Responsibilities

Gaming services operators typically start their shift by setting up their assigned area or taking it over from the operator on the previous shift. During a game they interact with customers and ensure that they have a pleasant experience. They must keep the flow of the game going, monitor customers for violations of gaming regulations or casino policies, and inform their supervisor or a security employee of any irregularities they observe. They may handle money, dice, chips, cards, sports betting tickets, and other gaming paraphernalia in the course of performing their duties. At all times, too, they must enforce safety rules and report any hazards.

Some gaming services occupations are relatively demanding physically. Gaming dealers spend most of their shift standing behind a table. Managers and supervisors are constantly walking up and down the casino floor. Most of the work takes place in large, enclosed spaces with artificial light and ventilation. Because alcoholic beverages are commonly served to customers throughout the day and night, gaming operators must sometimes deal with rowdy guests and be prepared to call for assistance when needed.

Although the work can often be repetitive, gaming service operators perform a sufficient variety of tasks to keep them busy. As a game unfolds, they must keep track of the amount of money that customers bet, determine winners, calculate and pay off winning bets, and collect on losing bets. They must continually inspect cards, dice, or other game objects to ensure their proper functioning. They must exchange paper money for gaming chips, refill slot machines as needed, respond to customer questions or complaints, consult with supervisors and managers, and in general make sure that the game for which they are responsible runs smoothly.

Duties and Responsibilities

- Preparing and maintaining assigned gaming area
- Interacting with customers, explaining the rules as necessary and advising them of any breaches of rules
- Handling money, chips, dice, cards, and other gaming paraphernalia in the course of conducting a game
- Keeping track of bets and determining winners and losers, making payouts on wins and collecting losing bets as required
- Coordinating with supervisors or managers as needed
- Operating a safe and customer-friendly game and gaming area

OCCUPATION SPECIALTIES

Gaming Dealers

Gaming Dealers operate table games such as craps, blackjack, and roulette. They stand or sit behind tables while serving customers. Dealers control the pace and action of the game. They announce each player's move to the rest of the table and let players know when it is their turn. Most dealers can work with at least two games, usually blackjack or craps.

Gaming Managers and Supervisors

Gaming Managers and Supervisors direct and oversee the gaming operations and personnel in their assigned area. Supervisors circulate among the tables to make sure that everything is running smoothly and that all areas are properly staffed. Managers work in the back office as well as on the floor at times.

Slot Supervisors

Slot Supervisors oversee the activities of the slot department. Because most casinos use video slot machines that give out tickets instead of cash and thus require very little oversight, workers in this occupation spend most of their time providing customer service to slot players.

Sports Book Writers and Runners

Sports Book Writers and Runners handle bets on sporting events and take and record bets for customers. Sports book writers and runners also verify tickets and pay out winning tickets. In addition, they help run games such as bingo and keno. Some gaming runners collect winning tickets from customers in a casino.

WORK ENVIRONMENT

Physical Environment

Most gaming services operators are employed in casino hotels or other gambling facilities. A casino atmosphere may expose gaming services workers to hazards such as secondhand smoke from cigarettes, cigars, and pipes. Noise from slot machines, gaming tables, and loud customers may be distracting to some, although workers wear protective headgear in areas where machinery is used to count money. An absence of windows and the use of artificial lighting and indoor ventilation are factors to consider as well.

Relevant Skills and Abilities

Communication Skills
- Speaking clearly

Interpersonal Skills
- Cooperating with others
- Interacting professionally

Organization & Management Skills
- Following instructions
- Paying attention to and handling details
- Performing routine work

Technical Skills
- Keeping track of an unfolding process
- Using set methods and standards
- Working with your hands

Human Environment

All gaming jobs involve a lot of interaction with customers. The success or failure of a casino depends on how customers view the casino, making customer service important for all gaming services occupations. Simple misunderstandings can cost a customer a lot of money and damage the reputation of the casino. Gaming managers and supervisors oversee other gaming services operators and must be able to guide them in doing their jobs and developing their skills.

Technological Environment

Gaming services operators use a variety of manual gaming objects, such as cards, dice, and chips in carrying out their work, along with selected mechanical gaming devices such as the roulette wheel. They must have good hand-eye coordination and manual dexterity. Managers and supervisors operate standard office equipment, such as computers and phones, along with video recording equipment designed to monitor action on the floor.

EDUCATION, TRAINING, AND ADVANCEMENT

High School/Secondary

A high school diploma or its equivalent is usually required for gaming services jobs; in many cases, employers require postsecondary training at a gaming school as well. High school courses of prime importance include English, mathematics, and social studies. Training in a foreign language can be beneficial too. Those hoping eventually to become supervisors or managers should have a background in business administration.

Suggested High School Subjects
- Applied Math
- Business Administration
- Computers
- English
- Foreign Language
- Social Studies

Famous First

The first Las Vegas casino was the Flamingo Hotel, built in 1946 by mobster Bugsy Siegel. Financing was provided by crime syndicate chieftain Meyer Lansky. Siegel was thought to be skimming from the profits owed to the syndicate, and was found shot dead in 1947. The Flamingo was acquired by Hilton Hotels Corp. in 1972. In 1993 a major expansion destroyed Siegel's former quarters and added such amenities as an outdoor habitat with live Chilean flamingos and African penguins. Today the property is owned by Caesars Entertainment.

Postsecondary

Individual casinos or other gaming establishments have their own training requirements. Usually, new gaming dealers are sent to gaming school for a few weeks to learn a casino game, such as blackjack or craps. These schools teach the rules and procedures of the game, as well as state and local laws and regulations related to the game. Although gaming school is primarily for new employees, some experienced dealers have to go to gaming school if they want to be trained in a new casino game.

Gaming and sports book writers and runners usually do not have to go to gaming school. They can be trained by the casino in less than one month. The casino teaches them state and local laws and regulations related to the game, as well the particulars of their job, such as keno calling.

Educational requirements for gaming managers likewise differ by casino. Although some casinos may only require a high school diploma or equivalent, others require gaming managers to have a college degree. Those who choose to pursue a degree may study hotel management, hospitality, or accounting in addition to taking formal management classes.

Related College Majors
- Accounting
- Business Administration
- Gaming Services Management
- Hotel Management
- Hospitality
- Management Science

Adult Job Seekers

Strong competition is expected for jobs at casinos. Those with work experience in customer service at a hotel or resort should have better job prospects than most because of the importance of customer service in casinos. Completing gaming school before being hired may increase a prospective dealer's chances of being hired, but it does not guarantee a job. Casinos usually audition prospective dealers for open positions to assess their personal qualities.

Professional Certification and Licensure

Gaming services workers must be licensed by a state regulatory agency, such as a state casino control board or gaming commission. Licensing requirements for supervisory or managerial positions may differ from those for gaming dealers, gaming and sports book writers and runners, and all other gaming workers. However, all applicants for a license must provide photo identification and pay a fee. They must also typically pass a background check and drug test. Age requirements, too, vary by state. For specific licensing requirements, interested parties should visit a state's gaming commission website.

Additional Requirements

Gaming services operators must be decisive and able to follow tactical moves in a game situation. They must be careful observers and have an ability to preserve rules and procedures in their heads and act accordingly. They should have good communication skills and manual dexterity, and should be adept at arithmetic calculations. Previous work experience in customer service is helpful but not necessary in all cases.

EARNINGS AND ADVANCEMENT

Earnings depend on the location of the employer and the particular job. Earnings are higher in major resort centers than in smaller, more remote gambling facilities. The mean annual wage for gaming services operators was $26,500 in 2012. The lowest 10 percent earned less than $16,530, and the top 10 percent earned more than $54,830.

The median annual wages for individual gaming occupations in 2012 were as follows:
- $65,220 for gaming managers
- $49,290 for gaming supervisors
- $32,390 for slot supervisors
- $23,490 for all other gaming services workers
- $21,810 for sports book writers and runners
- $18,630 for gaming dealers

Gaming services operators may receive paid vacations, holidays, and sick days; life and health insurance; and retirement benefits. These are usually paid by the employer.

Metropolitan Areas with the Highest Employment Level in this Occupation (Gaming Services Operators)

Metropolitan area	Employmenthttp	Employment per thousand jobs	Hourly mean wage
Las Vegas-Paradise, NV	2,610	3.18	$13.21
San Diego-Carlsbad-San Marcos, CA	750	0.60	$9.86
Reno-Sparks, NV	430	2.29	$10.46
Fort Worth-Arlington, TX	240	0.28	$21.38
Chicago-Joliet-Naperville, IL	180	0.05	$12.83
Atlantic City-Hammonton, NJ	180	1.29	$13.38

Source: Bureau of Labor Statistics

Metropolitan Areas with the Highest Employment Level in this Occupation (Gaming Services Supervisors)

Metropolitan area	Employmenthttp	Employment per thousand jobs	Hourly mean wage
Las Vegas-Paradise, NV	6,110	7.46	$26.32
Atlantic City-Hammonton, NJ	1,850	13.61	$27.37
Detroit-Livonia-Dearborn, MI	640	0.92	$27.88
Reno-Sparks, NV	610	3.26	$21.05
Los Angeles-Long Beach-Glendale, CA	500	0.13	$20.11
Phoenix-Mesa-Glendale, AZ	490	0.28	$23.48

Source: Bureau of Labor Statistics

EMPLOYMENT AND OUTLOOK

Gaming services operators held about 182,200 jobs nationally in 2012. Employment in gaming services occupations is projected to grow 10 percent from 2012 to 2022, about as fast as the average for all occupations. Employment growth of gaming managers and supervisors is projected to be 7 and 8 percent, respectively. Employment of sports book writers and runners is projected to grow 8 percent.

These occupations will be driven by the increasing popularity of gambling establishments such as Native American casinos and regional casinos. However, as more states approve the development of gaming establishments over the next decade, the competition for customers will increase and some casinos may be at risk of oversaturation. Those establishments that fail to keep or attract customers may be forced to close.

Employment Trend, Projected 2012–22

Total, All Occupations: 11%

Gaming Services Operators: 7%

Note: "All Occupations" includes all occupations in the U.S. Economy. Source: U.S. Bureau of Labor Statistics, Employment Projections Program

Related Occupations
- Bartender
- Hotel & Motel Manager
- Waiter/Waitress

Conversation With . . .
RANDALL ENSLEY
Training School Coordinator, Table Games

22 years in the industry

1. What was your individual career path in terms of education/training, entry-level job, or other significant opportunity?

Most people are drawn to careers in table games because the entry level salary is about the same as you would earn after graduating college with a bachelor's or master's degree. That's why I explored becoming a table games dealer. After a relocation, I was looking for a job in my "real" field of expertise, human services, and coincidentally Foxwoods Resort Casino opened at the same time. There was an ad in the paper for dealers and the salary mentioned was about the same as what I was making as a manager in the human services field. Once I entered the Table Games department, it became clear that there were opportunities for advancement. I worked my way up from dealing table games to running the table games and our poker dealer school.

2. What are the most important skills and/or qualities for someone in your profession?

The most important qualities are customer service skills, a willingness to learn, comfort working in a highly regulated environment and an ability to leave your problems at home. Furthermore, you should also be willing to do shift work. Shift changes usually come with a job promotion.

Additionally, one should have good ethics and character. In this, as well as in many other careers, hiring managers look for candidates who have a good character. That's very important because people can always be trained with the skills they need to do the job. You can't train someone to have good ethics and a solid character.

3. What do you wish you had known going into this profession?

Technology, technology and technology. Although I did not have a lot of computer skills when Foxwoods Casino opened, I did have the opportunity to learn technology skills when asked to perform human resources functions, casino scheduling and customer tracking. Further, I am often involved in software implementation whenever we introduce new payroll or scheduling technology to our department.

4. **Are there many job opportunities in your profession? In what specific areas?**

The casino industry is growing, so there are many opportunities. States and regions are introducing gaming almost every time there's an election. In this region alone, there are new casinos being planned for Massachusetts and New York. Across the country, and internationally, new casinos are being planned and legislation introduced geared toward new gaming, including online gaming.

Fields that are popular in the gaming industry include marketing, IT, hotel operations, engineering, security, surveillance, food and beverage, compliance and more. Growing fields within the casino industry are database marketing and financial analysis. Working in a casino can prepare you for many opportunities because the skills often translate easily to other public and private industries and the non-profit world.

5. **How do you see your profession changing in the next five years? What role will technology play in those changes, and what skills will be required?**

While there will likely always be customers who want to interact with a live dealer, the trend is towards slot operations and online gaming. As the cost of operations rises, casinos are looking to having a more lean and efficient workforce.

At the same time, the world of casino marketing is becoming much more personalized. Targeted marketing, using electronic readers to identify customers, and other location- specific marketing tools are making it easier to design an almost individualized marketing plan based on who is in your property or area at a given time. We can reach customers with special incentives. And we can even predict what promotions will appeal to a particular patron based on their past play, where they live, what restaurants they visit, etc. This technology has found its way to table games and will only become stronger as time goes on. Certainly, training and education in marketing and hotel operations will be dealing with these trends in our industry.

6. **What do you enjoy most about your job? What do you enjoy least?**

One has to enjoy working with others and being comfortable with performing, much as an actor or other entertainment personality would. When you are dealing table games you are the focus of the players' attention and there is rarely an empty seat at your table.

I can honestly say that I enjoy my job greatly and don't have any complaints. It is a fun, mentally engaging environment and there is certainly something new every day.

7. Can you suggest a valuable "try this" for students considering a career in your profession?

Go visit a casino (if you are of legal gambling age) to see if this is an environment which looks fun. Be open to working with others, particularly those who work in other areas. Always remember the basics of appropriate human interaction, i.e., use good manners, say hello and goodbye to your peers, the people who work for you, and to your managers. Most importantly, lead by example and be a good role model!

SELECTED SCHOOLS

Training beyond high school is not necessarily expected of beginning gaming services operators. However, enrolling in a gaming school can prove beneficial. A list of such schools is available on the website of Casino Careers. com (see below). Students interested in eventually supervising or managing gaming operations may acquire initial training through hospitality programs at community colleges or at four-year collegiate institutions, many of which are also listed at casinocareers.com.

MORE INFORMATION

American Gaming Association
1299 Pennsylvania Avenue NW
Suite 1175
Washington, DC 20004
202.552.2676
www.americangaming.org

Casino Careers
2327 Ridgewood Plaza
Suite 205, New Road
Northfield, NJ 08225
609.813.2333
www.casinocareers.com

Michael Shally-Jensen

Gardener & Groundskeeper

Snapshot

Career Cluster: Agriculture & Natural Resources; Architecture & Construction; Hospitality & Tourism

Interests: Environment, working outdoors, working with your hands

Earnings (Yearly Average): $25,870

Employment & Outlook: Faster Than Average Growth Expected

OVERVIEW

Sphere of Work

As outdoor maintenance specialists, gardeners and groundskeepers usually perform similar tasks, such as pruning trees and shrubs, maintaining flowerbeds, and picking up litter. These titles are often interchangeable; however, some employers distinguish between their responsibilities. Groundskeepers tend to be responsible for the overall maintenance of a property, which means they might shovel snow, sweep tennis courts, clean swimming pools, or, if employed by an athletic organization, maintain

synthetic turf. Gardeners might focus strictly on caring for plants and maintaining a variety of different types of gardens, including above-ground gardens (e.g., patios and decks) with potted plants.

Work Environment

Gardeners and groundskeepers are employed in residential, government, commercial, and industrial settings, including college campuses, golf courses, apartment complexes, museums and public gardens, amusement parks, resorts, and cemeteries. They work alone, with assistants, or with a large crew. Many of these jobs are seasonal or part-time, with hours that depend on weather conditions.

Profile

Working Conditions: Work Outdoors
Physical Strength: Medium to Heavy Work
Education Needs: On-The-Job Training, High School Diploma Or G.E.D.
Licensure/Certification: Recommended
Physical Abilities Not Required: No Strenuous Labor
Opportunities For Experience: Apprenticeship, Part-Time Work
Holland Interest Score*: CRS, RCE, RCI

* See Appendix A

Occupation Interest

People who are interested in gardening and groundskeeping enjoy being outside and value a well-manicured environment. They are physically fit and able to handle many different responsibilities. Successful gardeners and groundskeepers have the ability to follow a schedule, solve problems, and attend to details as well as the larger landscape.

A Day in the Life—Duties and Responsibilities

The outdoor work performed by gardeners and groundskeepers usually depends greatly on the regional climate of their place of employment. Cold-weather tasks might involve shoveling snow and plowing parking lots, tending to plants in a privately owned greenhouse, and performing indoor jobs, such as sharpening and cleaning tools or building wooden trellises.

Springtime tends to be a busy time. During these months, groundskeepers commonly paint and repair outdoor furniture, edge sidewalks and flower beds, lay sod, clean fountains, and maintain lawns, including fertilizing, aerating, and mowing. Gardening responsibilities include weeding, raking debris from flowerbeds, pruning shrubs and trees, adding compost to soil, and planting bushes, trees, and flowers.

During hot periods, gardeners and groundskeepers usually give special attention to irrigation or watering systems. Weeding, mowing, deadheading flowers, transplanting plants, and applying fertilizer and insecticides occupy much of the time for many workers. Winter preparations may include raking leaves, putting away outdoor furniture, cleaning gardens, and additional weeding and pruning.

Gardeners and groundskeepers also handle a variety of paperwork, maintain inventories, purchase supplies and tools, and study gardening catalogues and manuals. Some employers may require additional tasks. Groundskeepers employed by cemeteries also dig graves and prepare for funerals. Those responsible for athletic stadiums also spray paint lines, names, and numbers on the turf in preparation for games.

Duties and Responsibilities

- Cutting lawns and pruning trees and shrubs
- Trimming and edging around walks, flower beds, and walls
- Raking and removing leaves and cleaning up litter
- Repairing concrete or asphalt walks and driveways
- Maintaining small equipment
- Planting, fertilizing, mulching, and watering flowers, grass, trees, and shrubs
- Hauling in dirt, rock, and other material to improve or alter the landscape

OCCUPATION SPECIALTIES

Arborists

Arborists, or Tree Service Specialists, cut away dead or excess branches from trees or shrubs to clear utility lines, roads, and sidewalks. Although many workers strive to improve the appearance and health of trees and plants, some specialize in diagnosing and treating tree diseases. Others specialize in pruning, trimming, and shaping ornamental trees and shrubs. Tree trimmers and pruners use chain saws, chippers, and stump grinders while on the job. When trimming near power lines, they usually work on truck-mounted lifts and use power pruners.

Groundskeepers and Greenskeepers

Groundskeepers maintain existing grounds. They care for plants and trees, rake and mulch leaves, and clear snow from walkways. They also see to the proper upkeep of sidewalks, parking lots, groundskeeping equipment, fountains, fences, planters, and benches. A special type of groundskeeper known as a greenskeeper maintains golf courses.

Landscapers

Landscapers, or Landscape Specialists, create new outdoor spaces or upgrade existing ones by planting trees, flowers, and shrubs. They also trim, fertilize, mulch, and water plants. Some grade and install lawns or construct hardscapes such as walkways, patios, and decks. Others help install lighting or sprinkler systems. Landscaping workers are employed in a variety of residential and commercial settings, such as homes, apartment buildings, office buildings, shopping malls, and hotels and motels. Landscape laborers assist landscape specialists by moving soil, equipment, and materials, digging holes, and performing related duties.

Pesticide Application Specialists

Pesticide Application Specialists apply herbicides, fungicides, or insecticides on plants or the soil to prevent or control weeds, insects, and diseases. Those who work for chemical lawn or tree service firms are more specialized, inspecting lawns for problems and applying fertilizers, pesticides, and other chemicals to stimulate growth and prevent or control weeds, diseases, or insect infestations.

WORK ENVIRONMENT

Physical Environment

The work performed by gardeners and groundskeepers is physically demanding, as it involves much walking, bending, pushing, and heavy lifting. It is especially hard on the back, hands, and knees. The use of ladders and power tools puts workers at risk for injuries. Other occupational hazards are related to sun exposure, insects, pesticides, and herbicides. Gardeners and groundskeepers are also exposed to variable weather conditions throughout the year.

Relevant Skills and Abilities

Organization & Management Skills
- Following instructions
- Paying attention to and handling details
- Performing routine work

Technical Skills
- Working with machines, tools, or other objects

Other Skills
- Using set methods and standards in your work

Work Environment Skills
- Working outdoors
- Working with plants

Human Environment

Unless self-employed, a gardener or groundskeeper usually reports to a supervisor and may work closely with that person until he or she gains enough experience to work independently. Some gardeners and groundskeepers might supervise part-time or temporary workers. While some work alone, others interact regularly with horticulturalists, botanists, landscape architects, and other professionals.

Technological Environment

Gardeners and groundskeepers use many hand and power tools, including electric clippers, chain saws, and lawnmowers. They may drive riding mowers, golf carts, tractors, or trucks. Landscapers may use backhoes, borers, and other heavy equipment, while tree trimmers must be adept at maneuvering through the crowns of trees, either manually (rope and tackle) or by means of a basket crane ("cherry picker"). Most gardeners or groundskeepers use cell phones and may use two-way radios to communicate with coworkers.

EDUCATION, TRAINING, AND ADVANCEMENT

High School/Secondary

A high school diploma is usually sufficient for gardening and groundskeeping jobs; however, some employers require postsecondary training as well. A vocational program in agriculture, horticulture, or landscaping can prepare students for directly after high school, but might limit advancement possibilities. Courses of prime importance include botany, biology, chemistry, and earth sciences. Art courses may help future gardeners design pleasing flowerbeds. Students should also consider volunteer or part-time jobs in horticultural or agricultural businesses as well as participating in relevant extracurricular programs, such as 4-H clubs.

Suggested High School Subjects
- Agricultural Education
- Applied Biology/Chemistry
- Applied Math
- Building & Grounds Maintenance
- English
- Landscaping
- Mathematics
- Ornamental Horticulture

Famous First

The first Japanese cherry trees in North America were a gift to the United States from the people of Tokyo, Japan. The first shipment arrived in 1909 but had to be destroyed because of insect infestation. A second shipment was planted along the waterway in Potomac Park, Washington, DC, where they remain today and serve as an annual springtime tourist attraction.

Postsecondary

While gardeners and groundskeepers traditionally learn their skills on the job, a postsecondary certificate or an associate's or bachelor's degree can give job seekers an advantage, allow for more flexibility in job duties, and provide a foundation for future advancement. Relevant programs include landscaping, botany, horticulture, ecology, agriculture, and turfgrass science. Those who envision establishing their own businesses might want to consider a degree in business as well.

Related College Majors
- Horticulture Services Operations & Management

Adult Job Seekers

On-the-job training is typically available for those who wish to become gardeners or groundskeepers. Adults who have personal garden or property management experience or have worked in a nursery or related business will find professional gardening or groundskeeping to be a rewarding occupation and easy career transition. The long summer and weekend hours required may prove challenging for those who have personal responsibilities.

Advancement depends on experience and education. Advancement opportunities include supervisory positions, responsibility for larger or more complicated properties, or specializing in one particular area, such as turfgrass management or rose gardens.

Professional Certification and Licensure

There are no required licenses or certificates for most gardeners and groundskeepers. State licensure may be required for those who work with pesticides. Interested individuals should check the requirements of their home state.

Some colleges, professional associations, and trade schools offer their own voluntary certifications. The American Society for Horticultural Science (ASHS) certifies horticulturists, and the Professional Grounds Management Society (PGMS) offers the Certified Grounds Manager (CGM) and Certified Grounds Technician (CGT) certification programs. These certification programs require specified amounts of education or work experience or both as well as satisfactory completion of a written exam.

Additional Requirements

A driver's license and clean driving record is usually required. Some employees might have to pass drug tests and background checks. Those who intend to establish their own business must have strong business and marketing skills. As the wages in this occupation tend to be low, prospective gardeners and groundskeepers should appreciate and find satisfaction in the work itself.

EARNINGS AND ADVANCEMENT

Earnings depend on the geographic location of the employer and the particular job. Earnings are higher in urban areas than in small rural areas. Gardeners and groundskeepers are often employed on a part-time, seasonal basis. Mean annual earnings for gardeners and groundskeepers were $25,870 in 2012. The lowest ten percent earned less than $17,730, and the highest ten percent earned more than $37,770.

Gardeners and groundskeepers may receive paid vacations, holidays, and sick days; life and health insurance; and retirement benefits. These are usually paid by the employer.

Metropolitan Areas with the Highest Employment Level in this Occupation

Metropolitan area	Employment[1]	Employment per thousand jobs	Hourly mean wage
Chicago-Joliet-Naperville, IL	20,060	5.51	$12.32
Los Angeles-Long Beach-Glendale, CA	19,090	4.93	$13.40
New York-White Plains-Wayne, NY-NJ	16,980	3.29	$15.57
Dallas-Plano-Irving, TX	13,540	6.45	$11.13
Santa Ana-Anaheim-Irvine, CA	13,300	9.42	$12.37
Houston-Sugar Land-Baytown, TX	13,230	5.01	$10.93
Phoenix-Mesa-Glendale, AZ	13,140	7.60	$10.96
Riverside-San Bernardino-Ontario, CA	12,900	11.12	$11.89

[1]Does not include self-employed. Source: Bureau of Labor Statistics

EMPLOYMENT AND OUTLOOK

Gardeners and groundskeepers held about 1.2 million jobs nationally in 2012. About one-third worked for landscaping services companies. Others worked for firms operating and building real estate; amusement and recreation facilities, such as golf courses and race tracks; educational institutions; and local governments. About one-fourth were self-employed.

Employment is expected to grow slightly faster than the average for all occupations through the year 2022, which means employment is projected to increase about 13 percent. Expected growth in the construction of all types of buildings requiring lawn care and maintenance, plus more highways and parks, will contribute to demand for gardeners and groundskeepers. In addition, owners of many buildings recognize the importance of landscaping in attracting business and maintaining the value of the property, and they are expected to use gardeners and groundskeepers more extensively to maintain and upgrade their properties. Homeowners are also a growing source of demand for gardeners and groundkeepers. Because many two-income households lack the time to take care of the lawn, they are increasingly hiring people to maintain it for them. As the population ages, more elderly homeowners will require lawn care services to help maintain their yards.

Employment Trend, Projected 2012–22

Building and Grounds Maintenance Occupations: 13%

Gardeners and Groundskeepers: 13%

Total, All Occupations: 11%

Note: "All Occupations" includes all occupations in the U.S. Economy. Source: U.S. Bureau of Labor Statistics, Employment Projections Program

Related Occupations
• Florist

Cnversation With . . .
NED CABE
Assistant Greenhouse Manager

8 years in the industry

1. What was your individual career path in terms of education/training, entry-level job, or other significant opportunity?

I was a field engineer for Xerox for 33 years. When I retired from Xerox, I started volunteering at the Elizabethan Gardens. I did maintenance, pruning, anything that they needed. I found I loved the work, so I took the Master Gardener program run by North Carolina State University. It's a three-month program that meets once a week. After about a year of volunteering, I was hired to work here.

2. What are the most important skills and/or qualities for someone in your profession?

You have to love plants, first of all. But you also have to be able to visualize what a garden bed will look like once the flowers bloom. That way, you'll be able to create a planting design for an area and plant flowers that will bloom at different times of the year so you'll always have color. We continually have color year round. Another important quality is that you can't be scared of getting dirty. Most of all, you have to be someone who's interested in botany and in school. The first several weeks of the Master Gardener program is all about learning or refreshing your knowledge of botany.

3. What do you wish you had known going into this profession?

I wish I had known how much fun it is! It's something you really get into. I come from a family of farmers, but I left that field to become an engineer. But it gets in your blood and it's been great to get back to the basics.

4. Are there many job opportunities in your profession? In what specific areas?

There are quite a few job opportunities in this area of North Carolina. The only unfortunate part of them is they're mostly seasonal. However, at Elizabethan

Gardens, we tend the gardens year-round. There are a lot of things we do in the winter that you can't do in the summer when we have lots of tourists. In the winter we do things like pruning the trees and planting. We plant twice a year, winter annuals and summer annuals.

5.   How do you see your profession changing in the next five years? What role will technology play in those changes, and what skills will be required?

We're going to continue to see new plants developed. The major seed companies that do plant research are constantly coming out with new types of plants, new colors, plants that will survive in different temperate zones. The seed companies patent these plants. When the new items come out, we can buy them and put them in the garden, but we can't propagate them to sell in our greenhouse until the patent expires.

6.   What do you enjoy most about your job? What do you enjoy least?

Probably, what I most enjoy about my job is being out and bonding with nature because I spent most of my life in computer rooms looking out windows and wishing I could be outside. We're 100 yards or so from the [Roanoke] Sound, so when I'm outside and hear the waves lapping, it's just about the best. About the closest you can get to heaven is working at a garden.

What I enjoy least about my job is also being outside -- when the weather is bad. When we get a nor'easter and the wind is whipping and its 28 degrees, that's not fun. We've had several hurricanes since I've been here. I don't enjoy cleaning up after hurricanes.

7.   Can you suggest a valuable "try this" for students considering a career in your profession?

The best thing you can do is look for a community garden in the area where you live. They're always looking for volunteers. We get lots of kids here who volunteer and who do internships. Some find they're not suited for the job. Some find that this is what they want to do. If you can't get your hands dirty, you don't want to do this.

SELECTED SCHOOLS

It is generally not expected that gardeners and groundskeepers receive training beyond high school. However, obtaining college credits in horticulture or landscaping from a technical/community college program can prove beneficial, particularly for those interested in operating their own business or becoming managers. Experience in the trade continues to be one of the most important qualifications.

MORE INFORMATION

American Hort
2130 Stella Court
Columbus, OH 43215
614.487.1117
americanhort.org

American Society for Horticultural Science
1018 Duke Street
Alexandria, VA 22314
703.836.4606
www.ashs.org

Garden Club of America
14 East 60th Street, 3rd Floor
New York, NY 10022
212.753.8287
www.gcamerica.org

National Garden Clubs, Inc.
4401 Magnolia Avenue
St. Louis, MO 63110
314.776.7574
ngcdev.org

Professional Grounds Management Society
720 Light Street
Baltimore, MD 21230-3816
410.223.2861
www.pgms.org

Professional Landcare Network
950 Herndon Parkway
Suite 450
Herndon, VA 20170
703.736.9666
www.landcarenetwork.org

Tree Care Industry Association
135 Harvey Road
Suite 101
Londonderry, NH 03053
603.314.5386
www.tcia.org

Sally Driscoll/Editor

Health & Fitness Center Manager

Snapshot

Career Cluster: Business Administration; Hospitality & Tourism; Sales & Service

Interests: Physical activity, managing others, customer service

Earnings (Yearly Average): $53,582

Employment & Outlook: Slower Than Average Growth Expected

OVERVIEW

Sphere of Work

Health and fitness center managers supervise retail, private, and organizational exercise facilities. In addition to ensuring the maintenance of all club equipment and facilities, they also supervise staff and resolve customer complaints and may play a role in small-scale marketing and promotion initiatives. Health and fitness center managers are also responsible for the recruitment, assessment, and billing related to external vendors such as janitorial staff, pool cleaners, vending machine companies, and laundry facilities that help health clubs function every day.

Work Environment

Health and fitness center managers traditionally split their time between interacting with clients in and around health and fitness center facilities and conducting traditional executive duties in administrative settings. Visibility is an important characteristic of successful health and fitness center managers, who must be available to assist staff members as well as customers throughout the day. Many managers of large health and fitness centers also supervise a small staff of assistant managers who share in the center's management responsibilities.

Profile

Working Conditions: Work Indoors

Physical Strength: Light Work

Education Needs: Junior/Technical/ Community College, Bachelor's Degree

Licensure/Certification: Recommended

Physical Abilities Not Required: N/A

Opportunities For Experience: Internship, Volunteer Work, Part-Time Work

Holland Interest Score*: ESR

* See Appendix A

Occupation Interest

Health center management attracts a wide variety of professionals. Some health and fitness center managers undertake the position as a means of transitional employment while pursuing postsecondary education in the field—such as chiropractic or physical therapy studies— or coursework in business and executive management. Others come to the position through having worked as a fitness trainer or instructor and recognize the job as a significant step up in their career. Health center management almost exclusively attracts health-conscious and physically active individuals who are by nature team players eager to use their knowledge to assist others in a friendly and productive manner.

A Day in the Life—Duties and Responsibilities

The daily responsibilities of health and fitness center managers are diverse. In addition to ensuring that all center equipment is in proper functioning order, they must supervise all staff and also interview, hire, and oversee training for new employees. Health and fitness center managers are also responsible for addressing the concerns and complaints of both staff members and clientele and must act quickly to ensure that such concerns are addressed.

Health and fitness center managers may also have considerable input into their center's financial health, reviewing budgets and maximizing investments in equipment and tools. They may also be responsible for reviewing the center's membership roster to ensure that member dues are organized and up to date. Health and fitness center managers may play an important role in promotional activities and marketing initiatives designed to attract new members.

Health and fitness center managers who oversee exercise facilities that are part of larger organizational hierarchies—such as country clubs, resort hotels, or golf clubs—are typically required to attend occasional manager meetings in which they discuss how they are approaching and meeting the overall goals of the organization with other facility supervisors.

Duties and Responsibilities

- Hiring and firing personnel
- Coordinating staff
- Attending to day-to-day activities of the club
- Making sure staff is well trained, properly qualified, and certified or licensed
- Holding classes or seminars for new club staffers
- Performing administrative duties, such as payroll and bookkeeping
- Marketing the fitness center to attract new customers
- Overseeing all equipment upkeep and general maintenance

WORK ENVIRONMENT

Physical Environment

Health and fitness center managers may work as independent business owners or as executive staff members in larger organizations such as hotels, resorts, and golf clubs. They typically split their time between the health center and an office environment.

Relevant Skills and Abilities

Communication Skills
- Speaking effectively

Interpersonal/Social Skills
- Asserting oneself
- Providing support to others

Organization & Management Skills
- Coordinating tasks
- Managing people/groups
- Paying attention to and handling details

Other Skills
- Understanding and having knowledge of fitness and exercise

Human Environment

Extensive collaboration and communication skills are required of the position. Health and fitness center managers interact with customers, colleagues, and outside vendors on a daily basis and must be skilled in handling customer questions and complaints.

Technological Environment

Health and fitness center managers use a variety of administrative technologies, ranging from telephone, e-mail, and web conferencing to financial-management software.

Familiarity with the intricacies of modern exercise equipment is also important.

EDUCATION, TRAINING, AND ADVANCEMENT

High School/Secondary

High school students can best prepare for a career in health and fitness center management with courses in geometry, biology, chemistry, physical education, nutrition, health, and computers. Summer programs, volunteer work, and internships at health centers or similar facilities can familiarize students with the day-to-day procedures of operation.

Suggested High School Subjects
- Applied Communication
- Biology

- Business
- Business English
- Business Math
- First Aid Training
- Geometry
- Health Science Technology
- Physical Education
- Physiology
- Social Studies
- Sociology

Famous First

The first gymnasium to offer systematic instruction was that of the Round Hill School for Boys in Northampton, Mass. It was opened in 1823 by John Cogswell and George Bancroft. The instructor in Latin, Charles Beck, served as the gym instructor. A few years later the first men's collegiate gymnastics program (which included all manner of physical movement and exercise) opened at Harvard University; and in 1862 the first women's gym program was launched at Mount Holyoke College in South Hadley, Mass., just a few miles from Northampton.

Postsecondary

There are several associate- and bachelor-level postsecondary programs in the United States dedicated to health center facilities management. Coursework in health center management instructs students on the basics of small business management as well as fitness program development, equipment maintenance, and basic nutrition. Health and fitness management students should also take courses in anatomy, kinesiology, and exercise physiology.

Related College Majors
- Business Administration & Management
- Health & Physical Education
- Hospitality Management

- Parks, Recreation & Leisure Studies
- Physical Education Teaching & Coaching
- Public Health
- Sport & Fitness Administration/Management

Adult Job Seekers

Health and fitness center managers traditionally work regular business hours, though their responsibilities may require long workdays and occasional weekend work. The increased cultural awareness of health and fitness in the United States has made health and fitness center management a rapidly growing field. Individuals with management experience in other industries can easily parlay their skills into a new position in health center management through supplemental education or certification.

Professional Certification and Licensure

While states do not explicitly require certification or licensure for non-instructional health and fitness center positions, completion of a certificate program can be beneficial for aspiring health center professionals. Such certification can give prospective managers higher visibility in the job market and serve as proof of their experience with customer service, marketing, and gym safety. Prospective health and fitness center managers should consult credible professional associations within the field and follow professional debate as to the relevance and value of any certification program.

Additional Requirements

Health and fitness center management is a people-centric position that requires patience, understanding, and camaraderie with both fellow staff members and center members. Ideal candidates for health and fitness center management positions have proven leadership abilities and are enthusiastic about helping others meet their health and fitness goals.

EARNINGS AND ADVANCEMENT

Advancement for health and fitness center managers occurs by climbing the career ladder in prestigious centers. Many health and fitness center managers also work toward opening their own centers. Earnings of health and fitness center managers depend on the type, size, geographic location and prestige of the center and whether the center is public or private. Earnings also depend on the education, experience, and responsibilities of the individual. Median annual earnings of health and fitness center managers were $53,582 in 2012. Many health and fitness center managers also receive bonuses for bringing in and signing up new members.

Health and fitness center managers may receive paid vacations, holidays, and sick days; life and health insurance; and retirement benefits. These are usually paid by the employer. Health and fitness center managers are also allowed to use the center facilities at no cost.

EMPLOYMENT AND OUTLOOK

General and operations managers, of which health and fitness center managers are a part, held about 1.9 million jobs nationally in 2012. Employment is expected to grow slower than the average for all occupations through the year 2022, which means employment is projected to increase 3 percent to 6 percent. However, as more people begin to recognize the importance of personal fitness, the need for health and fitness center managers may increase and employment prospects improve. Opportunities for employment can be found in traditional health centers and also in places like resort and hotel spas and cruise ships.

Related Occupations
- Fitness Trainer & Instructor
- Recreation Program Director

> ## *Conversation With . . .*
> ## *RYAN GROLL*
> ### Health and Fitness Center Manager, 2 years

1. What was your individual career path in terms of education/training, entry-level job, or other significant opportunity?

In high school, I got my first job in a health and fitness center working for minimum wage. When I turned 18, I got my first ACE personal training certification. I got my bachelor's degree from the University of Maryland in kinesiology. To get into the school is extremely difficult, so I had to take classes at Anne Arundel Community College and boost my credentials. When I finished, I pursued personal training at the University of Maryland, at 24 Hour Fitness in Annapolis, and moved up to master trainer. At night, I went to school for my master's in exercise physiology from McDaniel College. The owner of the club where I now work lives on the Eastern Shore of Maryland and used to commute an hour to the gym in Annapolis. I met him, we hit it off, and he would ask me for ideas. He wanted to open his own gym. He liked some of the ideas I had to offer, one thing led to another, and he brought me on as independent contractor to consult on equipment and how the fitness side of the gym would be run. Finally, he asked me if I wanted to be fitness director. At that time we also had a general manager, so the owner, GM and I worked hand-in-hand to build this from scratch, from the HR handbook to how we keep our clients. Six months after the business opened, we were doing phenomenally, the GM moved on and I stepped into that role, too.

Our area has a lot of weekenders and vacationers. It's a completely different crowd on weekends. The second home-owners come in at 10 or 11 o'clock to train, vs. the 9-to-5ers, who want to get in and out.

2. What are the most important skills and/or qualities for someone in your profession?

Being very knowledgeable is very important so your clients will get results and they won't get hurt. Equal or more is your charisma and confidence. You can be the smartest trainer out there, but if your clients don't trust you, you're not going to make a dramatic impact in their life. If you don't practice what you preach your clients can't take you seriously.

3. What do you wish you had known going into this profession?

When I first started, I thought clients would always come to me and that it would be easy as long as I was smart and knew what I was doing. I figured out that with more planning and relationships, years down the road those relationships blossom. Word of mouth is always best. You've got to talk to everybody, give out as much information as you can – and when something clicks and somebody wants to see a trainer, they will come to you.

4. Are there many job opportunities in your profession? In what specific areas?

The opportunity is there if you make it. If you want to be an independent contractor, go to the more dense cities; there's more of a need and want for that kind of service. East Coast and West Coast are big in fitness, and you do have to realize it's a service.

5. How do you see your profession changing in the next five years? What role will technology play in those changes, and what skills will be required?

As technology gets better, it helps and hinders. People think they can do more things on their own, with more apps and forums online, and they utilize that vs. going to a trainer. One thing technology can never erase is the accountability and motivation you get from a personal trainer.

6. What do you enjoy most about your job? What do you enjoy least?

I still love to impact people's lives. That's the whole reason I got into this industry. I'm glad I'm in an industry I'm passionate about. One of the harder things is that you can't really disconnect from your job. You'll have clients emailing you with their questions and concerns on a Saturday, or you'll text them: "Hey, hope you had a good workout." As a manager, the challenging part is to teach what I know to other trainers. Working with clients came naturally for me. I had to step back and realize it takes more than a month or two. You have to let them work out things and be there to help if they have questions.

7. Can you suggest a valuable "try this" for students considering a career in your profession?

Spend more time in the gym. I can't stress it enough. I brought on three new trainers and told them: you don't have clients yet, but be here to build confidence, build experience, and increase your awareness. Clients see you and they talk to you; they talk to you and they want to train with you. Also, you constantly have to stay on top of new trends and technology.

SELECTED SCHOOLS

Although it may not be necessary in every case to have a college degree to obtain work as a health and fitness center manager, many employers do prefer candidates with either an associates' or bachelor's degree in business, sports management, or a similar subject. Below are listed some of the more prominent institutions in this field.

Endicott College
376 Hale Street
Beverly, MA 01915
978.927.0585
www.endicott.edu

Indiana University, Bloomington
107 S. Indiana Avenue
Bloomington, IN 47405
812.855.4848
www.iub.edu

SUNY Cortland
38 Graham Avenue
Cortland, NY 13045
607.753.2011
www.cortland.edu

Tulane University
6823 St. Charles Avenue
New Orleans, LA 70118
504.865.5000
tulane.edu

University of Michigan
500 S. State Street
Ann Arbor, MI 48109
734.764.1817
www.umich.edu

University of Oregon
1585 E. 13th Avenue
Eugene, OR 97403
541.346.1000
uoregon.edu

University of Tampa
401 W. Kennedy Boulevard
Tampa, FL 33606
813.253.3333
www.ut.edu

University of Texas, Austin
1823 Red River Street
PO Box 8058
Austin, TX 78713
512.475.7440
www.utexas.edu

University of Tulsa
800 S. Tucker Drive
Tulsa, OK 74104
918.631.2000
www.utulsa.edu

West Chester University
700 S. High Street
West Chester, PA 19382
610.436.1000
www.wcupa.edu

MORE INFORMATION

American Fitness Professionals and Associates
1601 Long Beach Boulevard
P.O. Box 214
Ship Bottom, NJ 08008
800.494.7782
www.afpafitness.com

Club Managers Association of America
1733 King Street
Alexandria, VA 22314
703.739.9500
www.cmaa.org

Mid-Atlantic Club Management Association
5734 Wheelwright Way
Haymarket, VA 20169
888.596.2262
www.macmaclubs.org

National Gym Association
P.O. Box 970579
Coconut Creek, FL 33097
954.344.8410
www.nationalgym.com

National Independent Health Club Association
165 8th Avenue
Suite 1
Granite Falls, MN 56241
320.722.0084
www.nihca.org

John Pritchard/Editor

Hotel/Motel Manager

Snapshot

Career Cluster: Business Administration; Hospitality & Tourism; Sales & Service

Interests: Handling many projects at once, problem solving, customer service

Earnings (Yearly Average): $54,800

Employment & Outlook: Slower Than Average Growth Expected

OVERVIEW

Sphere of Work

Hotel and motel managers ensure that all operations of a lodging establishment or property are carried out in an efficient and profitable manner. Hotels will generally have a general manager, while motels, which are designed and built to accommodate motorists (and which often provide direct access to rooms from a central parking lot) may be managed by an owner if operated independently. In general, hotel and motel managers hire and terminate employees, develop and implement budgets, oversee

marketing for their location, make and enforce hotel policies, approve repairs and renovations, and are active in the community. Hotel general managers that oversee larger and luxury properties will coordinate with departmental managers to ensure that each aspect of the property operates effectively and that guests' every need is met. Hotel managers usually achieve their positions after many years of working their way upward through various departments and properties. In an independent setting, such as a bed and breakfast, the owner is responsible for all aspects of the business, from housekeeping to bookkeeping.

Profile

Working Conditions: Work Indoors
Physical Strength: Light Work
Education Needs: On-The-Job Training, Technical/Community College, Bachelor's Degree
Licensure/Certification: Recommended
Physical Abilities Not Required: No Heavy Labor
Opportunities For Experience: Military Service, Part-Time Work
Holland Interest Score*: ESR

* See Appendix A

Work Environment

Hotel and motel managers spend the majority of their time in the hotel or motel in which they work. Depending on the size of the lodging facility, they may frequently attend meetings with department managers, external consultants, and other individuals to discuss marketing, customer service, employee relations, and internal operations. In general, a hotel is a busy, complex environment, with many separate parts working in concert with one another. It is the hotel manager's responsibility to keep this system operating smoothly. A motel, while less complex, is equally comprised of many separate parts working in concert, from the front desk to facility maintenance and housekeeping, all of which might fall upon the shoulders of a manager-owner in an independent setting. As a result, both hotel and motel managers often work long hours and maintain a very active schedule.

Occupation Interest

Hotel and motel managers are at the heart of a thriving lodging establishment. It is a high-profile position that gives the manager a role to play in every part of a hotel or motel facility. Hotel and motel managers have the opportunity to direct the activities of the entire staff, serve as the public face of the property or business, and find ways to increase revenues, productivity, and efficiency. Their jobs are rarely routine or confined to one area of operation, which means that the manager is frequently mobile and constantly interacting with others in every part of the property. Those who enjoy projects, problem solving, and decision making may find hotel management a fulfilling occupation.

A Day in the Life—Duties and Responsibilities

The job responsibility of a hotel or motel manager typically varies with the size of the property and the number of employees. Most managers develop the property's annual budgets, assess sales revenues and expenses, plan marketing strategies, and hire and terminate employees (larger properties will have a human resources department responsible for employee relations). When the property is in need of repairs, the manager will be involved with the decision-making process, such as approving design plans and expenses, and hiring contractors. Furthermore, hotel and motel managers enact security policies designed to keep guests and their belongings safe while on the property. Finally, the manager must comply with all local ordinances and regional and national laws governing lodging establishments.

Hotel and motel managers must also work closely with mid-level managers and their departments to ensure that their respective areas are operating smoothly on a day-to-day basis. For a larger facility, this might include working with high-level managers responsible for areas such as catering, facility management, and human resources. In a smaller facility, this might include working with the supervisors of the various departments, from the front desk to housekeeping. Hotel and motel managers typically create or approve new company-wide policies, including employee benefits, sales reporting protocols, reservations systems, and housekeeping standards, or are responsible for reporting or communicating these policies as they are passed down to the property level from a corporate body.

In smaller properties, a hotel and motel manager may have additional responsibilities, such as managing the front desk and reservations, selling meeting space, and even making repairs. Regardless of whether the property is large or small, one of the most important jobs a manager has is ensuring that the guest is satisfied. A manager must do his or her best to field and address guest complaints and concerns in such a way that customers are satisfied and likely to return.

Duties and Responsibilities

- Making decisions concerning personnel, services, and room rates
- Resolving problems with guests
- Planning budgets and authorizing purchases
- Coordinating the activities of the front office, kitchen and dining room, and other areas
- Hiring personnel
- Overseeing upkeep and maintenance
- Delegating authority and assigning tasks to department heads

OCCUPATION SPECIALTIES

Resident Managers

Resident Managers live in hotels or motels and are on call 24 hours a day to resolve any problems or emergencies.

Front Office Managers

Front Office Managers supervise the front office activities and take care of reservations, room assignments, unusual requests, inquiries, and guests' complaints.

Lodging Facilities Managers

Lodging Facilities Managers supervise and maintain temporary or permanent lodging facilities such as small apartment houses, hotels, motels, trailer parks, tourist camps, and resorts.

Convention Services Managers

Convention Services Managers coordinate the activities of the large hotels' various departments for meetings, conventions, and other special events.

WORK ENVIRONMENT

Physical Environment

Hotel and motel managers spend the majority of their time in either the main lobby or in an office within the hotel. Such "high traffic" locations are sometimes the scene of tense encounters, should there be trouble with a guest. It is important that the manager be accessible to defuse problematic situations and take these encounters to a less visible location. Hotel managers may also go off-site to meet with other managers and business and community leaders, as well as external vendors and contractors.

Relevant Skills and Abilities

Organization & Management Skills
- Following instructions
- Paying attention to and handling details
- Performing routine work

Technical Skills
- Working with machines, tools, or other objects

Other Skills
- Using set methods and standards in your work

Work Environment Skills
- Working outdoors
- Working with plants

Human Environment

The hotel and motel manager must interact and coordinate with a wide range of people. He or she must work with his or her employees, ensuring that they are performing professionally and that their respective departments are meeting guests' needs. They must also meet frequently with external parties, such as contractors, business leaders, community officials, and consultants. Most importantly, they interact constantly with the guests—greeting them in the lobby, answering any questions they may have, and attempting to address their concerns and complaints.

Technological Environment

The hotel and motel manager generally uses basic office technology, including telecommunication (voice, video, and Internet) equipment. The manager will also need to understand certain software used for reservations, accounting, housekeeping, and other hotel operations.

EDUCATION, TRAINING, AND ADVANCEMENT

High School/Secondary

High school students who want to become hotel managers are encouraged to take a number of courses in business, math, and communications. They may also wish to take hospitality courses, such as food service and shop classes to give them a better understanding of these aspects of a hotel. Some high schools offer the American Hotel and Lodging Education Institute's Lodging Management Program, which give participants credit toward university-level hotel management studies. Students are further encouraged to find a part-time or summer job working at a hotel or motel, working at the front desk, in housekeeping, or in a restaurant.

Suggested High School Subjects
- Accounting
- Building & Grounds Maintenance
- Business Law
- Business Math
- College Preparatory
- English
- Food Service & Management
- Geography
- Psychology
- Speech

Famous First

The first modern first-class hotel was the Tremont House in Boston, opened in 1829. It had 170 rooms, each renting at a rate of $2 per day—meals included. Guests were allowed to rent a single private room instead of sharing one with strangers, as was common at the time. Amenities included a personal room key (instead of asking a manager or assistant to unlock the door), gaslights for illumination, and a fresh cake of soap to accompany the washbowl and pitcher. In addition, the Tremont was the first hotel with indoor toilets and bathtubs featuring plumbing, instead of outhouses and tubs requiring the use of buckets. Guests did, however, have to go down to the basement to use them, as they were not on every floor much less in every room.

College/Postsecondary

Many hotel managers today receive further training in hotel services at junior and community colleges or receive their bachelor's degree from a hospitality program at a four-year university. Training programs are also often available at vocational and technical schools. Interested students should consider pursuing internships at hotels.

Related College Majors
- Enterprise Management & Operation
- Hospitality Administration/Management
- Hotel/Motel & Restaurant Management
- Travel-Tourism Management

Adult Job Seekers

Adults who seek a job as a manager of a hotel or motel may benefit from joining a professional trade association. Such organizations provide a wide range of networking opportunities for those people who seek a managerial post.

Professional Certification and Licensure

A large number of hotel managers also complete a Certified Hotel Administrator or Certified Lodging Manager certification, which is available through a number of hotel-oriented educational foundations and institutions. Consult credible professional associations within the field, and follow professional debate as to the relevancy and value of any certification program. completion of a written exam.

Additional Requirements

Hotel and motel managers must be highly experienced in the industry and be proven leaders. They must have strong communications skills and exceptional business acumen. Furthermore, they must be gracious and diplomatic, essential characteristics for someone who works in the hospitality industry.

EARNINGS AND ADVANCEMENT

Earnings of hotel and motel managers depend on the type, size and location of the establishment, the segment of the hotel industry in which they are employed and the manager's duties and responsibilities. Mean annual earnings of hotel and motel managers were $54,800 in 2012. The lowest ten percent earned less than $29,290, and the highest ten percent earned more than $89,530.

Hotel and motel managers may receive paid vacations, holidays, and sick days; life and health insurance; and retirement benefits. These are usually paid by the employer. In addition, they may receive benefits such as living quarters, meals, parking facilities and laundry services.

Metropolitan Areas with the Highest
Employment Level in this Occupation

Metropolitan area	Employment	Employment per thousand jobs	Hourly mean wage
Los Angeles-Long Beach-Glendale, CA	810	0.21	$27.72
Washington-Arlington-Alexandria, DC-VA-MD-WV	710	0.30	$34.03
San Diego-Carlsbad-San Marcos, CA	520	0.41	$25.82
Orlando-Kissimmee-Sanford, FL	430	0.42	$30.46
San Francisco-San Mateo-Redwood City, CA	400	0.40	$33.46
Santa Ana-Anaheim-Irvine, CA	400	0.28	$27.11
Houston-Sugar Land-Baytown, TX	390	0.15	$23.65
Phoenix-Mesa-Glendale, AZ	380	0.22	$32.48

Source: Bureau of Labor Statistics

Fun Fact

The International Hotel and Restaurants Association began as the All Hotelman Alliance founded in 1869 at Hotel Trier, Koblenz, Germany, by a group of 45 "hotelmen."

Source: IH&RA

EMPLOYMENT AND OUTLOOK

There were approximately 51,000 hotel and motel managers employed nationally in 2012. Employment is expected to grow slower than the average for all occupations through the year 2022, which means employment is projected to increase 0 percent to 5 percent. Business travel will continue to grow, and increased domestic and foreign tourism will also create demand for additional hotels and motels. However, many of these new hotels will be smaller, limited-service hotels that will not need as many managers as full-service hotels. Most openings are expected to occur as experienced hotel and motel managers transfer to other occupations, in part because of long hours and stressful working conditions. Job opportunities are expected to be best for persons with college degrees in hotel or hospitality management.

Employment Trend, Projected 2012–22

Total, All Occupations: 11%

Management Occupations: 7%

Hotel/Motel Managers: 1%

Note: "All Occupations" includes all occupations in the U.S. Economy. Source: U.S. Bureau of Labor Statistics, Employment Projections Program

Related Occupations
- Food Service Manager
- Property & Real Estate Manager

Related Military Occupations
- Food Service Specialist

Conversation With . . .
STEVE GORDON
Hotel Manager
25 years in the industry

1. What was your individual career path in terms of education/training, entry-level job, or other significant opportunity?

I went to college and earned my degree in business, then moved to California from the east coast. I took a job as a bellhop at a full-service hotel in Santa Monica. I worked there while I looked for a job in business, but after awhile I realized I was making pretty good money and I liked the position. I loved where I worked. There was something new every day. So I stayed and was promoted fairly quickly. I became bell captain and worked my way up to the front desk, then to night auditor, then front desk supervisor all the way up to general manager.

2. What are the most important skills and/or qualities for someone in your profession?

The most important quality is being able to communicate with anybody. You also need patience and a quest to serve and help people. If you're on the operations side as I am, it's good to have some skill in accounting and being able to understand the business side of running a hotel.

3. What do you wish you had known going into this profession?

I wish I had known how flexible you have to be to be successful. If you want to advance, you have to be able to be willing to move anywhere they ask you, or to where the opportunities are. That's really tough for some people. Once you have a family, you don't want to move them around all over the place because you don't know how long you'll be somewhere.

4. Are there many job opportunities in your profession? In what specific areas?

It depends on how the economy is doing. The hotel industry is the first to get hit in a poor economy and one of the last to recover. If you've got a thriving economy, people are going to be buying hotels and building hotels. There will be a lot of opportunities to move around. In a tough economy, one of the first things to get cut is business travel and that hurts hotels.

You'll find more job opportunities if you're flexible and willing to relocate. There are more job opportunities in limited-service hotels. Those are the ones that don't offer all of the amenities. There are fewer full-service hotels around and they like to hire people with more experience.

5. How do you see your profession changing in the next five years? What role will technology play in those changes, and what skills will be required?

The profession is going to change because of technology. The way you check someone in, the way you get into your guest room, the way you pay for services are all changing because of technology. Your [computer] tablet and your cell phone will control everything that you do in a hotel. You'll check in online, pick your room, unlock your door, order room service, make reservations at the hotel restaurant, all with your cell phone. People who understand the technology will be ahead.

6. What do you enjoy most about your job? What do you enjoy least?

What I enjoy most is speaking to the guests and speaking to the people who work with me all day long. Most of the time, you're talking with happy people. There are, of course, people who have travel issues and are not having a great experience and it's your job to change that. But most of the time they're from somewhere else and they're interesting and they want to ask you questions about the area and that's fun. A lot of the people who work here have a passion for hospitality and everyone tends to be in an upbeat mood.

What I enjoy least is sitting behind my desk at my computer.

7. Can you suggest a valuable "try this" for students considering a career in your profession?

I think it's key to do internships, but even if you don't do that, working in a hotel is a great summer job. Even if you just work at the front desk, you'll see what people do in other departments. You'll be able to tell whether this is something that you're passionate about or not.

SELECTED SCHOOLS

In many cases today it is preferred that hotel and motel managers have a college degree prior to being hired, in addition to having experience in the industry. Candidates can acquire relevant training at a community college or vocational school. For those interested in pursuing a bachelor's degree in hospitality management, below are listed some of the more prominent institutions in this field.

Cornell University
School of Hotel Administration
Statler Hall
Ithaca, NY 14853
607.225.9393
www.hotelschool.cornell.edu

Kansas State University
Department of Hospitality
Management and Dietetics
119 Justin Hall
Manhattan, KS 66506
785.532.5500
www.he.k-state.edu/hmd/

Michigan State University
School of Hospitality Business
Epley Center
645 N. Shaw Lane
East Lansing, MI 48824
517.353.9211
hospitalitybusiness.broad.msu.ed

Northern Arizona University
W.A. Franke College of Business
Hotel and Restaurant Management
20 W. McConnell Drive
Flagstaff, AZ 86011
928.523.5232
franke.nau.edu/hrm

Penn State University
School of Hospitality Management
201 Mateer Building
University Park, PA 16802
814.865.1853
www.hhdev.psu.edu/shm

Purdue University
Department of Hospitality and
Tourism Management
Stone Hall, Rm. 106
700 W. State Street
West Lafayette, IN 47907
765.494.4643
www.purdue.edu/hhs/htm

University of Central Florida
Rosen College of Hospitality
Management
9907 Universal Boulevard
Orlando, FL 32819
407.903.8000
hospitality.ucf.edu

University of Nevada, Las Vegas
Harrah College of Hotel
Administration
4505 Maryland Parkway
Box 456013
Las Vegas, NV 89154
702.9.895.3161
www.unlv.edu/hotel

Virginia Tech
Department of Hospitality and
Tourism Management
362 Wallace Hall
Blacksburg, VA 24061
540.231.5515
www.htm.pamplin.vt.edu

Washington State University
School of Hospitality Business
Management
Todd Hall 342
PO Box 644724
Pullman, WA 99164
509.335.5766
www.business.wsu.edu/academics/
hospitality

MORE INFORMATION

**American Hotel & Lodging
Association**
1201 New York Avenue, NW
Suite 600
Washington, DC 20005-3931
202.289.3100
www.ahla.com

**American Hotel and Lodging
Educational Institute**
800 N. Magnolia Avenue
Suite 300
Orlando, FL 32803
800.349.0299
www.ahlei.org

Michael Auerbach/Editor

Housekeeper

Snapshot

Career Cluster(S): Hospitality & Tourism; Human Services
Interests: Maintenance, working with your hands, helping others
Earnings (Yearly Average): $21,820
Employment & Outlook: Average Growth Expected

OVERVIEW

Sphere of Work

Housekeepers are responsible for room cleanliness and upkeep both in commercial lodging facilities and in private residences. They perform basic cleaning and room maintenance tasks such as collecting trash and soiled linens, changing bedsheets, and cleaning toilets, showers, and sinks. In the commercial hospitality industry, housekeepers are regulated by strict guidelines so that the quality and appearance of guest rooms are maintained in a uniform manner throughout an establishment. Private housekeepers are often responsible for dealing with the particular requests of their individual clients. Many housekeeping professionals are independent contractors who have

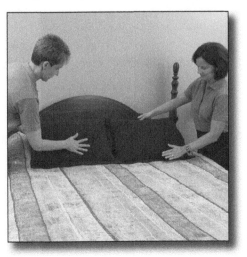

a variety of clients. Some private housekeepers are live-in residents in their places of employment.

Work Environment

Housekeepers work primarily in guest quarters that are inhabited by hotel guests on a short-term basis and in the bedrooms, kitchens, bathrooms, and other rooms of private residences. While large hospitality establishments separate housekeeping duties into particular tasks, employing teams comprising bed makers, linen cleaners, and bathroom cleaners, smaller establishments require housekeepers to perform all of the duties necessary to complete a guest room's required daily maintenance.

Profile

Working Conditions: Work Indoors
Physical Strength: Medium Work
Education Needs: No High School Diploma, On-The-Job Training
Licensure/Certification: Usually Not Required
Physical Abilities Not Required: No Strenuous Labor
Opportunities For Experience: Part-Time Work
Holland Interest Score*: ESR

* See Appendix A

Occupation Interest

Housekeeping attracts individuals from several professional and educational backgrounds. Since little to no formal education is required and much of the training for the position is done on the job, job seekers of all ages and skill sets are frequently employed as housekeepers.

A Day in the Life—Duties and Responsibilities

Housekeepers spend their days cleaning private rooms and common areas in hotels and private residences. In addition to daily maintenance such as the removal of trash and soiled linens, housekeepers are also in charge of sweeping, vacuuming, organizing kitchen spaces, and mopping floors. Housekeepers who are employed by hotels and other commercial establishments are also responsible for replenishing toiletries and furnishing fresh linens, in addition to cleaning and maintaining public spaces such as elevators, lobbies, and business centers. Those employed by individuals or private residences may be charged with a variety of specific duties, from preparing meals to tending to laundry and other household chores.

Duties and Responsibilities

- Sweeping, mopping, and waxing floors
- Vacuuming carpets
- Removing trash
- Cleaning ovens, refrigerators, and microwaves in private kitchens
- Cleaning bathrooms
- Washing dishes
- Changing and making beds
- Doing laundry
- Dusting and polishing furniture

WORK ENVIRONMENT

Relevant Skills and Abilities

Communication Skills
- Speaking effectively

Interpersonal/Social Skills
- Cooperating with others
- Working as a member of a team

Organization & Management Skills
- Coordinating tasks
- Following instructions
- Meeting goals and deadlines
- Performing routine work
- Working quickly when necessary

Physical Environment

Housekeepers work in hotels, private residences, and private clubs. They may also clean any number of different businesses after their hours of operation, including banks, schools, museums, and other public and commercial establishments.

Human Environment

While most housekeepers work alone, they may also work in concert with small teams of other housekeeping staff members.

Technological Environment

Housekeeping does not require extensive technical expertise, although some of the cleaning tools and supplies used by housekeepers require precautionary safety measures.

EDUCATION, TRAINING, AND ADVANCEMENT

High School/Secondary

No formal educational training is required to become a housekeeper. Workers who are new to the field are trained on the job by experienced or senior staff. Professionals enter the field of housekeeping from a variety of different professional backgrounds, including building maintenance, food service, and other custodial positions. High-school-level course work related to home economics can be beneficial.

Suggested High School Subjects
- Building & Grounds Maintenance
- Custodial Service
- English
- Health Science Technology

Famous First

The first law enacted to protect domestic workers was Britain's Master and Servant Act of 1823. In fact, this act was one of the first pieces of legislation to regulate relations between employers and employees period. Although the law heavily favored employers, requiring workers to show them obedience and loyalty and not to organize against them (as in a trade union), it did ostensibly ensure that workers would be paid for performing their assigned duties; if they were not, they had legal recourse. In practice, however, the reverse was true. It was masters, not servants, who took advantage of the law and filed suits in court—for non-performance of duties—against their servants. In 1864, for example, over 10,000 workers were sent to prison under the law, whereas not a single employer was jailed.

Postsecondary

Individuals interested in a career in housekeeping management can benefit from associate- or certificate-level coursework in food-service management, hospitality management, or small-business management. Many housekeeping managers for large commercial establishments gain experience as small-business owners prior to seeking management opportunities at the large-scale, commercial level.

Adult Job Seekers

Many young workers, students, and new professionals work in housekeeping as a temporary means of employment or as a bridge to another vocation. Most housekeepers in the hospitality industry work set, standard hours that revolve around guest check-in and departure times.

Professional Certification and Licensure

No certification or licensure is required.

Additional Requirements

Individuals interested in pursuing employment as a housekeeper should possess the ability to accurately follow detailed instructions and be able to work well with fellow team members. Housekeepers must be physically capable of handling the stooping, kneeling, and crouching involved in standard maintenance tasks. They must also be able to complete tasks quickly in the face of closely approaching deadlines.

EARNINGS AND ADVANCEMENT

Earnings of housekeepers depend on geographic location and the housekeeper's responsibilities, experience, abilities and number of hours worked. Mean annual earnings of housekeepers were $21,820 in 2012. The lowest ten percent earned less than $16,430, and the highest ten percent earned more than $30,980.

Most private housekeepers have very limited or no health insurance, retirement plans or unemployment benefits. Those who live with their employers may be given room and board, health insurance, a car, vacation days, and education benefits.

Metropolitan Areas with the Highest
Employment Level in this Occupation

Metropolitan area	Employment[1]	Employment per thousand jobs	Hourly mean wage
New York-White Plains-Wayne, NY-NJ	34,240	6.64	$17.13
Chicago-Joliet-Naperville, IL	21,040	5.78	$11.39
Los Angeles-Long Beach-Glendale, CA	20,700	5.35	$11.00
Las Vegas-Paradise, NV	19,530	23.86	$14.35
Washington-Arlington-Alexandria, DC-VA-MD-WV	17,010	7.26	$12.07
Atlanta-Sandy Springs-Marietta, GA	16,510	7.30	$9.21
Orlando-Kissimmee-Sanford, FL	13,140	12.99	$9.88
Phoenix-Mesa-Glendale, AZ	11,840	6.84	$9.68

[1]Does not include self-employed. Source: Bureau of Labor Statistics

EMPLOYMENT AND OUTLOOK

Nationally, there were approximately 1.4 million housekeepers employed in 2012. Private households, hotels and motels, hospitals, nursing homes and other residential care facilities employed the largest percentages of these workers. Although cleaning jobs can be found in all cities and towns, most are located in highly populated areas where there are many office buildings, schools, apartment houses, nursing homes, and hospitals.

Employment is expected to grow slightly better than the average for all occupations through the year 2022, which means employment is projected to increase 9 percent to 15 percent. As families become more pressed for time, they are hiring cleaning services to perform a variety of tasks in their homes. In addition, housekeepers will be needed to clean the growing number of residential care facilities for the elderly. Many jobs will be available because of the need to replace the large number of workers who leave this occupation. Those who are interested in entering this field should find jobs easily.

Employment Trend, Projected 2012–22

Building and Grounds Maintenance Occupations: 13%

Housekeepers: 13%

Total, All Occupations: 11%

Note: "All Occupations" includes all occupations in the U.S. Economy. Source: U.S. Bureau of Labor Statistics, Employment Projections Program

Related Occupations
• Gardener & Groundskeeper

Conversation With . . .
ANITA ALFONSO
Housekeeper, 3 years

1. What was your individual career path in terms of education/training, entry-level job, or other significant opportunity?

I came here from Bosnia three years ago. A woman from my country brought me to apply for this job. She is my supervisor now. I started working part time, doing turndown service, which is putting chocolate on the bed, making sure the room is clean after the housekeeper is through. It was very good. It was from 3 p.m. to 9 p.m.

After I had my baby, I needed a job where I could work in the morning. That's when I became a housekeeper, cleaning rooms.

2. What are the most important skills and/or qualities for someone in your profession?

For me, the most important thing is to know English very well. Most guests speak English and sometimes when they ask something, it's very difficult to understand. For me, it's very important to know English so I can give them what they need and to make sure everything is good with that. I also like to talk with guests so they feel comfortable and welcome in the hotel. You should always be nice, always be smiling.

3. What do you wish you had known going into this profession?

I wish I had more time to prepare my English before I looked for a job. I just came to this country when I started the job and it was very hard at first. I always had to run and check with somebody, ask, "What does that mean?" But everybody was nice.

The only bad thing was my English. Everything else I adapted to very well. There are no special things to know as a hotel housekeeper. If you are organized, and know exactly what you're going to do, everything is easy.

4. **Are there many job opportunities in your profession? In what specific areas?**

    Yes. There are open positions in housekeeping from time to time.

5. **How do you see your profession changing in the next five years? What role will technology play in those changes, and what skills will be required?**

    In our hotel, nothing has changed. The only thing is, before, we had to use punch cards [to sign in at the beginning of the shift]. Now we put our hand in a [biometric hand scanner]. Otherwise everything is the same.

6. **What do you enjoy most about your job? What do you enjoy least?**

    I hate making the bed. I don't like to vacuum under the bed, either. That's because I get back pain. I like to clean the bathroom. When I'm done and everything is shiny in the bathroom. Nice and shiny and clean smelling. I love it.

7. **Can you suggest a valuable "try this" for students considering a career in your profession?**

    If you keep your home clean and everything is nice, your job as a housekeeper in a hotel is going to be very easy because you already know what rooms need. It's not necessary to have training. It's just up to you how you're going to do it. I recommend practicing cleaning the bathroom. That's where you spend the most time when you're cleaning. Use lots of hot water with a sponge and with cream cleanser. No sprays.

SELECTED SCHOOLS

It is not expected that housekeepers receive training beyond high school; indeed, a high school diploma itself is not required in many cases. For individuals seeking to operate their own commercial maid service, however, a degree from a technical or community college is likely to prove beneficial.

MORE INFORMATION

Association of Residential Cleaning Services International
7870 Olentangy River Road
Suite 302
Columbus, OH 43235
614.547.0887
www.arcsi.org

Cleaning Management Institute
19 British American Boulevard West
Latham, NY 12110-2197
518.640.9155
www.cminstitute.net

International Executive Housekeepers Association, Inc.
1001 Eastwind Drive, Suite 301
Westerville, OH 43081-3361
800.200.6342
www.ieha.org

International Janitorial Cleaning Services Association
2011 Oak Street
Wyandotte, MI 48192
734.252.6189
www.ijcsanetwork.com

International Sanitary Supply Association
7373 N. Lincoln Avenue
Lincolnwood, IL 60712
800.225.4772
www.issa.com

John Pritchard/Editor

Interior Designer

OVERVIEW

Sphere of Work

Interior designers are responsible for the aesthetic aspects of the interior of a building or specific space, whether it is commercial or residential. They deal with how colors, textures, light, furniture, and space work together to develop safe, functional, and attractive design solutions that meet client needs.

Commercial designers work on large projects such as hotels and restaurants, while residential designers focus on private homes. Some designers are involved in the design and planning of architectural components, such as crown molding, built-in bookshelves, and building layouts. As such, interior designers often consult blueprints and have an understanding of building and fire codes. All interior designers must work within a client's budget, charging customers for time, drawings, materials, and workroom labor.

Work Environment

Because interior designers spend much of their time with clients and vendors pricing individual aspects of each job, they are not constantly working in an office environment. Job functions outside of the office can include time spent shopping for necessary items and materials. When they are in their offices (or working from their homes), interior designers spend many hours placing orders, following up, and making creative decisions. Some designers work in a shop where the "storefront" displays gift-type items, with design services within for those interested clients; others work in furniture showrooms, which are open to the public.

Profile

Working Conditions: Work Indoors
Physical Strength: Light Work
Education Needs: Technical/
  Community College, Bachelor's Degree
Licensure/Certification:
  Recommended
Physical Abilities Not Required: No
  Heavy Work
Opportunities For Experience:
  Internship, Part-Time Work
Holland Interest Score*: AES

* See Appendix A

Occupation Interest

Individuals attracted to the interior design profession need to be strategic in visualizing what a customer needs or envisions— creativity gives interior designers the ability to explain an idea or concept to a client and then sell it. They should take notice of their surroundings and have an interest in physical spaces and their functionality. Interior designers need patience, business sense, and the ability to use interpersonal communication to work with a team and manage client expectations. They should be willing to negotiate and mediate to solve problems, and be savvy shoppers with attention to detail. Because they are continually dealing with client budgets, interior designers need to be financially astute.

A Day in the Life—Duties and Responsibilities

Typical daily tasks of an interior designer include determining client needs, agreeing to a budget and deadlines, and understanding how a space will be used. Designers estimate costs and put together a plan, often using computer-aided design (CAD) software, which makes it easier to revise the plans as changes occur. Once the design concept is completed, interior designers coordinate with contractors' work schedules. They follow up on the whereabouts of furnishings or decorative items they are tracking, and communicate with workroom members about installation schedules. Interior designers must also communicate with clients about re-selection of items that may have become discontinued or unavailable for their deadline. They collaborate with everyone from electricians to builders for designs that are safe and meet construction requirements.

Interior designers might select everything required in a design plan, from fabric to paint to furniture, and/or work with other professionals such as drapery experts and carpet installers. They will also review catalogues and order samples, examine space and equipment requirements, and develop new business contacts. Interior designers must manage their time effectively, and when necessary, make customers aware of unavoidable problems that could delay a specific job, such as inaccurate orders or delays in product shipping.

Duties and Responsibilities

- Developing design plans based on function of a space and client's preferences
- Collecting and presenting fabric, material, and color samples
- Estimating costs and evaluating them in relation to client's budget
- Presenting detailed design plans for client approval
- Working with vendors to obtain required materials and labor
- Overseeing installation and/or application of design elements

WORK ENVIRONMENT

Physical Environment

In large design firms, interior design offices are typically in well-lit, comfortable settings that reflect the designer's style. Their hours of operation align with typical business hours. Smaller design firms or self-employed contractors adjust their workday to meet client needs, which means they may be on-site at a showroom or client location after the traditional workday. Although the bulk of interior design work is done indoors, interior designers may also be asked to design outdoor spaces such as covered entrances or patios and decks.

Transferable Skills and Abilities

Communication Skills
- Expressing thoughts and ideas clearly
- Speaking and writing effectively

Creative/Artistic Skills
- Being skilled in art or design

Interpersonal/Social Skills
- Cooperating with others
- Working as a member of a team

Organization & Management Skills
- Coordinating tasks
- Managing people/groups

Research & Planning Skills
- Researching ideas
- Solving problems
- Laying out a plan

Human Environment

An interior designer's work space is usually functional, aesthetically pleasing and busy, with creative and inspirational people who not only enjoy the job, but have a good working relationship with peers and colleagues, clients, and third-party contacts. Because personal tastes and preferences are involved, however, interior designers must be prepared to sometimes work with finicky or difficult clients.

Technological Environment

Interior designers use computer-aided software (such as computer-aided design and drafting, or CADD) to help with the actual design process. Designers are increasingly using computers and smartphones to view, price, and order products such as stocks of fabric from any location.

OCCUPATION SPECIALTIES

Kitchen and Bath Designers

Kitchen and Bath Designers specialize in kitchens and bathrooms and have expert knowledge of the variety of cabinets, fixtures, appliances, plumbing, and electrical solutions for these rooms.

Lighting Designers

Lighting Designers focus on the effect of lighting for home, office, and public spaces. For example, lighting designers may work on stage productions, in gallery and museum spaces, and in healthcare facilities, to find appropriate light fixtures and lighting effects for each space.

Sustainable Designers

Sustainable Designers use strategies to improve energy and water efficiencies and indoor air quality, and they specify environmentally preferable products, such as bamboo and cork for floors.

EDUCATION, TRAINING, AND ADVANCEMENT

High School/Secondary

Some high schools offer courses related to interior design. Otherwise, high school students interested in pursuing an interior design career should take basic art classes, learn about the color wheel and the use of different textiles, and work to develop basic business and math skills.

Students should maintain good study habits and participate in a related extracurricular activity, such as projects or clubs involving art, graphic design, or business. High school students should consider applying for interior design firm internships that may later qualify them for apprenticeships or lead to paid positions.

Suggested High School Subjects

- Applied Math
- Arts
- Blueprint Reading
- Clothing & Textiles
- English
- Family & Consumer Sciences
- Graphic Communications
- Interior Design
- Mechanical Drawing
- Merchandising

Famous First

The first notable interior decorating firm was Herter Brothers, founded in New York City after the Civil War. The brothers, Gustave and Christian, began operating an upholstery business and branched out from there into furniture making and cabinetry. Later they incorporated paneling and ceiling design into their business, and eventually offered everything from flooring, carpeting, and draperies to general furnishings. Among their most prominent clients were the Vanderbilts and Jay Gould.

Postsecondary

College students interested in an interior design career should take courses in art, design, business, and the sciences, which can help them in their understanding of the basics of textiles. (The subfield of textile design requires numerous chemistry classes.) Psychology classes can help students work more effectively with other people in the creative field. Many cities offer career-specific training programs at design schools or colleges. Upon completion of a bachelor's degree, interior designers are ready for a formal design apprenticeship program.

Postsecondary students will benefit from internships and volunteer opportunities at showrooms, interior design offices, or as assistants to designers who are constantly on the road. These activities can lead to entry-level employment with various companies.

Related College Majors
- Art, Architecture, and Decoration
- Fashion Design
- Interior Design
- Textile Design

Adult Job Seekers

Joining interior design professional industry organizations encourages networking, which can help adult job seekers without a college degree gain access to the interior design profession as assistants to working professionals. These organizations and associations generally list available job openings and offer mentoring services to help those new in the field plan their career and educational choices. Professional Certification and Licensure: Through the National Council for Interior Design Qualification (NCIDQ), interior designers can be accredited with licenses after testing that includes passing knowledge of computer-aided design, drawing, perspectives, spatial planning, color and fabrics, architecture, codes, measurements, lighting and building specifications, and ergonomics. Once they demonstrate sufficient knowledge to pass test requirements, interior designers advertise their new credentials.

Most often, however, professional certification and licensure is not required in the interior design field.

Additional Requirements

Interior designers need to be familiar with CADD software and be quick to react to changing trends. They should be able to adapt quickly when clients change their minds about a design element, and should understand basic customer service skills and concepts. In some cases, interior designers may have to absorb the cost of materials or items purchased that cannot be returned. They need to understand different aspects of the industry: clients, distributors, wholesale showrooms, builders, sales people, and architects. It is helpful for interior designers to have excellent collaborative skills, and to be comfortable working as members of a team.

EARNINGS AND ADVANCEMENT

Earnings of interior designers vary widely with the specialty, type of employer, number of years of experience, and reputation of the individual. Among salaried interior designers, those in large specialized design and architectural firms tend to earn higher and more stable salaries. Interior designers working in retail stores usually earn a commission, which can be irregular.

For residential design projects, self-employed interior designers and those working in smaller firms usually earn a per-hour consulting fee, plus a percentage of the total cost of furniture, lighting, artwork, and other design elements. For commercial projects, they might charge a per-hour consulting fee, charge by the square footage, or charge a flat fee for the whole project.

Mean annual earnings of interior designers were $52,970 in 2012. The lowest ten percent earned less than $25,670 and the highest ten percent earned more than $86,900.

Interior designers may receive paid vacations, holidays, and sick days; life and health insurance; and retirement benefits. These are usually paid by the employer. Self-employed interior designers have to provide their own benefits.

Metropolitan Areas with the Highest Employment Level in this Occupation

Metropolitan area	Employment[1]	Employment per thousand jobs	Hourly mean wage
New York-White Plains-Wayne, NY-NJ	2,540	0.49	$31.70
Los Angeles-Long Beach-Glendale, CA	1,820	0.47	$29.95
Atlanta-Sandy Springs-Marietta, GA	1,330	0.59	$23.27
Washington-Arlington-Alexandria, DC-VA-MD-WV	1,200	0.51	$31.14
Chicago-Joliet-Naperville, IL	1,150	0.32	$28.57
San Francisco-San Mateo-Redwood City, CA	1,140	1.13	$34.42
Dallas-Plano-Irving, TX	1,050	0.50	$25.38
Seattle-Bellevue-Everett, WA	950	0.68	$24.33

[1]Does not include self-employed. Source: Bureau of Labor Statistics

EMPLOYMENT AND OUTLOOK

Interior designers held about 55,000 jobs nationally in 2012. Employment of interior designers is expected to grow about as fast as the average for all occupations through the year 2022, which means employment is projected to increase 8 percent to 15 percent. Rising demand for the professional design of homes, offices, restaurants and other retail establishments, in addition to institutions like hospitals and nursing homes, should create job growth for interior designers. Although competition is strong, this field is expected to grow.

Employment Trend, Projected 2012–22

Interior Designers: 13%

Total, All Occupations: 11%

Arts, Design, and Entertainment Occupations: 7%

Note: "All Occupations" includes all occupations in the U.S. Economy. Source: U.S. Bureau of Labor Statistics, Employment Projections Program

Related Occupations
- Fashion Designer
- Florist
- Hotel & Motel Manager

Conversation With . . .
ROBYN ELIZABETH ENANY
Interior Designer, 14 years

1. What was your individual career path in terms of education/training, entry-level job, or other significant opportunity?

I studied child development in school but I've also always done design on the side. I was always very good with color. During my first marriage, we ran three insurance offices. I was then divorced and needed something that would give me a little bit more growth and financial security. I was approached by a doctor friend and got a job in the medical field. Still, I was doing interior design on the side. Along the way, I worked for a family furniture company doing their showcases, floor plans, and window displays. After I remarried, we moved to a manor house in Maryland. I did the whole house, top to bottom, as well as a 2600-square-foot rental. When we moved back to California three years later, I knew that design was my love and took classes at Long Beach Day College. I started my first gig through a contractor with a good-sized piece of property, met other contractors, and it just developed from there.

My tourism clients have included a few restaurants, mostly along Long Beach. Here, you're dealing with a whole different spectrum from typical clients; owners and investors dealing with millions of dollars, and contractors and architects. You have to keep designs user-friendly, think of all different sizes of people and accommodate not just seating but seating arrangements, both inside and out. Also consider the storefront: how inviting is it? And restaurants should include rooms for conferences or parties that need to be insulated from the rest of the space. Where's the bar? Where's the private space?

2. What are the most important skills and/or qualities for someone in your profession?

You have to be knowledgeable about design and have a good listening ear. If you're not comprehending the client's needs, your job won't go anywhere.

3. What do you wish you had known going into this profession?

Every job is a learning curve for me. I love it. I can do 20 kitchens and each will have a different hiccup. But there are some similarities, so you grab the best for the next job.

4. Are there many job opportunities in your profession?

Many. There are many people out there who don't know how to pull a paint palette together. So it's very beneficial for them to spend a day with me. They may just want the assurance of what furnishings to buy. Since many people are uncomfortable with or unsure of how to decorate their homes, there will always be a need for interior designers.

5. How do you see your profession changing in the next five years? What role will technology play in those changes, and what skills will be required?

Everything is CAD (computer-aided design) now. These programs are not cheap. I do 20-20 Design programs, and we get all the measurements–skylights, windows, everything–and at the end of the day the client is sent, say, an aerial view of their new kitchen, how it looks when the cabinets are opened up, what the cabinets contain, the entrances, the exits …everything. The more visual, the more people want it.

The thing is, you can be very computer literate but you don't want to limit your time to be onsite with clients. Technology notwithstanding, you still need to go out and meet clients, show them what you've done for other clients and give them a good visual.

You have to be a good listener and be on the side of your client. It's a process. They have to trust us.

6. What do you enjoy most about your job? What do you enjoy least?

I love working with people. I enjoy challenges, such as when I turn a dysfunctional kitchen turn into a downright gorgeous one.

What I enjoy least is when my material is on backorder, or when they assure me backorder is 6 to 8 weeks, then tell me the vendor doesn't make it anymore.

7. Can you suggest a valuable "try this" for students considering a career in your profession?

I bring students interested in interior design along to first consultations. They can see how you conduct yourself around clients. Seventy percent of this is public relations and etiquette; the client needs to trust you fully. I remember bringing a 19-year-old along. At the end of an hour and a half, two-hour consult with a client, we got in the car and she said, "You gave them so many options. Why don't you tell them what you want?" And I said: "Because this is not my home." I always give clients two or three layouts. Give clients a say in a particular project, they feel part of it. That is very important.

SELECTED SCHOOLS

Students interested in a career in interior design are generally advised to obtain an associates' degree or a bachelor's degree in the subject. There are over 200 bachelor's degree programs available, according to the Council for Interior Design Accreditation (CIDA). The CIDA website (see address below) provides a comprehensive listing by state, and is the best place to begin researching schools.

MORE INFORMATION

American Society of Interior Designers
608 Massachusetts Avenue, NE
Washington, D.C. 20002-6006
202.546.3480
www.asid.org

Association of Interior Design Professionals
113 N. Main Street
Kernersville, NC 27284
336.310.4819
www.aidponline.com

Council for Interior Design Accreditation
206 Grandville Avenue
Suite 350
Grand Rapids, MI 49503-4014
616.458.0400
accredit-id.org

National Council for Interior Design Qualification
1602 L Street NW
Suite 200
Washington, DC 20036-5681
202.721.0220
www.ncidq.org

Interior Design Educators Council
9100 Purdue Road
Suite 200
Indianapolis, IN 46268
317.328.4437
www.idec.org

Interior Design Society
164 S. Main Street
Suite 404
High Point, NC 27260
336.884.4437
www.interiordesignsociety.org

International Interior Design Association
222 Merchandise Mart, Suite 567
Chicago, IL 60654
888.799.4432
www.iida.org

Susan Williams/Editor

Pilot

Snapshot

Career Cluster: Transportation; Hospitality & Tourism
Interests: Aviation, navigation, geography, engineering technology, physics, math and geometry
Earnings (Yearly Average): $129,760 (airline); $80,140 (commercial)
Employment & Outlook: Decline Expected

OVERVIEW

Sphere of Work

Pilots are professionals who use aircraft to transport people and freight, take photographs, launch weapons, dust crops, perform rescue missions, and other tasks. Most pilots are airline pilots and co-pilots, transporting passengers and cargo to and from their destinations. A small number of pilots are commercial pilots, and their duties can include spreading seeds for reforestation, conducting test flights, tracking military and criminal targets, monitoring traffic, and even fighting fires. The main vehicles used by pilots are large commercial airplanes, smaller fixed-wing aircraft and jets, military aircraft, and helicopters.

Work Environment

Pilots work in a variety of environments. Most pilots work in the airline industry, flying regional, national, and international routes for major commercial airlines. Many pilots are in the military, using their aircraft for attacks and rescues, as well as surveillance and mapping purposes. Many pilots in the commercial industry got their start in the military, although this has declined in recent years.

In addition to commercial and military pilots, some pilots work in agriculture and forestry, flying over crops to dust with pesticides and to drop seeds in areas being reforested. Still other professional pilots work in the media industry, flying over traffic and incident scenes. In each of these environments, the work of a pilot is complex and potentially dangerous. Flying is also a demanding career choice, requiring that the pilot spend a great deal of time away from home.

Profile

Working Conditions: Work Indoors

Physical Strength: Light Work

Education Needs: Technical/ Community College, Bachelor's Degree

Licensure/Certification: Required

Physical Abilities Not Required: No Heavy Labor

Opportunities For Experience: Military Service

Holland Interest Score*: IRE

* See Appendix A

Occupation Interest

Most people pursue their training as a pilot because of the excitement of such positions. Indeed, pilots sometimes travel all over the world using state of the art aviation equipment and technology. It is an exciting field, but comes with significant responsibility. As a rule, the pilot who has been designated pilot in command (PIC)—of any aircraft, small or large—has a legal obligation for and the final authority regarding that aircraft under Federal Aviation Administration (FAA) regulations. This means that the PIC is responsible for the safety of the aircraft, ultimately determines the aircraft's route, commands the flight crew, and holds the responsibility for the safe passage of any passengers. In the case of an emergency, the pilot is in command and has the authority to deviate from standard practice or make a decision that differs from the direction given by the control tower.

Pilots serve in the military, in commercial airline industry, can work for public or private entities fighting fires, transporting patients in crisis, or serving the agricultural sector. Pilots are essential to any industry or sector that needs safe and swift transport, or has needs best provided by air.

A Day in the Life—Duties and Responsibilities

The specific responsibilities of a pilot vary a great deal based on the industry in which he or she works. Overall, however, a pilot's primary responsibilities are to ensure the safety of the plane and its passengers and satisfy the requirements of his or her employers. To this end, pilots will conduct thorough safety and systems checks on a plane before departing, a process known as a "pre-flight," or a pre-flight inspection. During such reviews, the pilot will use a checklist to make sure all safety equipment, navigation technology, and other systems are operating normally. The pilot will check the plane's logs to review any issues the plane may have had in its previous flights and review weather reports and flight plans. A pilot oversees the plane's "pushback" and taxi from a gate or terminal before takeoff. During flight, the pilot will communicate with passengers, the flight crew, and air traffic control with any updates. When it is time to land, a pilot runs another series of checks, communicating with the tower of the receiving airport and re-checking landing gear and systems.

In addition to sharing many of the responsibilities described above, pilots who do not work for airlines have a number of other tasks. Helicopter pilots, for example, often photograph accident sites and conduct tours while flying their vehicles. Crop dusters and seeders must often load their payloads in addition to operating their airplanes. Many pilots who do not work for a major airline must also perform their own administrative tasks and business development activities in addition to flying.

Duties and Responsibilities

- Reviewing and confirming flight plans and passenger/cargo data
- Performing pre-flight inspection of the aircraft and its systems
- Contacting control tower by radio to receive take-off/landing instructions
- Controlling the airplane in flight, either manually or using autopilot
- Logging flight information
- Communicating with the crew and passengers
- Holding final responsibility for the aircraft, the crew and passengers, and the cargo
- Meeting scheduling requirements as specified by airline or commercial or private client

OCCUPATION SPECIALTIES

Airline Pilots

Airline pilots fly for airlines that transport people and cargo on a fixed schedule.

Commercial Pilots

Commercial Pilots fly aircraft on a contract basis; they are involved in charter flights, rescue operations, firefighting, aerial photography, and crop dusting.

Co-Pilots

Co-Pilots are generally junior officers and pilots-in-training.

Flight Engineers

Flight Engineers are responsible for monitoring, operating, and maintaining aircraft systems.

Navigators

Navigators establish the position of the plane and direct the course of airplanes on flights, using navigational instruments, atmospheric observations, or basic reasoning.

Executive Pilots

Executive Pilots fly company-owned aircraft to transport company officials or customers.

Helicopter Pilots

Helicopter Pilots fly helicopters for purposes such as transporting passengers and cargo, search and rescue operations, fighting fires, and reporting on traffic and weather conditions.

WORK ENVIRONMENT

Relevant Skills and Abilities

Communication Skills
- Speaking effectively

Interpersonal/Social Skills
- Asserting oneself
- Demonstrating leadership

Organization & Management Skills
- Making decisions
- Meeting goals and deadlines
- Performing duties that change frequently

Research & Planning Skills
- Researching information
- Laying out a plan
- Using logical reasoning

Technical Skills
- Performing scientific, mathematical, and technical work

Physical Environment

A pilot primarily works at airports or similar aviation centers and landing sites. Military pilots may also be found on aircraft carriers and other naval ships. Each of these environments tend to be complex and extremely busy, with many working parts, including safety, luggage and cargo, air traffic control, fuel services, repair crews, and other elements all coming into contact with one another. Pilots for commercial airlines will often have layovers in distant cities where they must seek accommodation. The airline covers the cost of these overnight stays.

Human Environment

Pilots must work with a wide range of people on the ground and on board their planes. Such parties include maintenance crews, security personnel, flight attendants, air traffic controllers, luggage handlers and, of course, the passengers. Pilots must interact directly with many of these individuals, while communicating and coordinating with others on the ground while in flight. Pilots are sometimes responsible for unruly passengers. As part of the Homeland Security Act of 2002, some pilots have been deputized and are federal law enforcement officers, called Federal Flight Deck Officers.

Technological Environment

Pilots must work with what are often extremely complex pieces of engineering. As part of the pre-flight check, they must carefully examine each of these systems to ensure that they are running properly. During flight, they must be skilled with automatic pilot systems, weather gauges, communications equipment, and safety measures. Military pilots must also work with weapons systems. Helicopter and other pilots who work outside of the airline industry may also be expected to work with photographic equipment, payload release systems (such as crop dusters and firefighting helicopters and planes), and other systems.

EDUCATION, TRAINING, AND ADVANCEMENT

High School/Secondary

High school students interested in becoming pilots are encouraged to study such sciences as physics, math and geometry, and geography. Additionally, because communication with passengers, ground personnel, and passengers is critical to many pilots, aspiring pilots are encouraged to take courses that build verbal skills, such as English.

Suggested High School Subjects
- Algebra
- Applied Math
- Applied Physics

- Blueprint Reading
- College Preparatory
- Computers
- English
- Geography
- Geometry
- Physics
- Trigonometry

Famous First

The first transcontinental jet airplane passenger service began in January 1959, when an American Airlines Boeing 707 flew from Los Angeles to Idlewild, N.Y. The plane held four crew members and 112 passengers, and completed the flight in just over four hours. The pilot was Captain Charles Macatee of Huntington, N.Y. Passengers were charged about $160 for one-way and $300 for round-trip. Macatee, a senior pilot, retired several years later. The plane itself, however, continued in service for the next 28 years.

Postsecondary

Many pilots receive postsecondary certification, such as an associate's degree, from a junior and/or community college. However, as the field of aviation is extremely competitive, pilots are encouraged to obtain at least a bachelor's degree in a related field and/or obtain direct pilot training through the military or civilian flight schools. In the past, many commercial pilots were ex-military. While no longer the trend, the military is a viable option for those seeking pilot training.

Related College Majors
- Aeronautical Engineering
- Aircraft Piloting & Navigation
- Aviation
- Engineering (General)

Adult Job Seekers

Pilot jobs are very difficult to obtain due to the competitive nature of the industry. It is essential for pilots, particularly those aspiring to gain employment with a major airline, to log the most flight hours possible in order to have a chance at obtaining a better job. Many pilots begin their careers at small, regional carriers or gain their training through the military. For those pilots leaving the military, training in civilian regulations is necessary.

Professional Certification and Licensure

The central authority regulating pilots in the civilian arena is the Federal Aviation Administration (FAA). Pilots must receive their licenses from the FAA through a series of tests (including a written exam as well as a physical examination) and logged time in both flight simulators and in the air with qualified FAA officials. During the course of their careers, pilots should also receive separate licensure for flying through bad weather using instruments only. Airline pilots must also log 1,500 hours of FAA-approved flight time and certification in instrument and night flying. Physical exams and additional training are required on a yearly basis.

Additional Requirements

Pilots should demonstrate a strong attention to detail and be able to work long hours in stressful situations. They are expected to remain physically fit, with good hearing and eyesight. Furthermore, most airline pilots must undergo company orientation to assimilate the corporation's best practices and policies. When a pilot reaches sixty years of age, he or she usually must consider retirement.

EARNINGS AND ADVANCEMENT

Earnings depend on the employing airline; number of hours and miles flown; size, speed and type of plane; the pilot's length of service and the type of flight (international or domestic). Extra pay may be provided for night and international flights. Pilots who fly jet aircraft usually earned higher salaries than nonjet pilots. Pilots working outside the airlines earned lower salaries.

Mean annual earnings of airline pilots were $129,760 in 2012. The lowest ten percent earned less than $66,970, and the highest ten percent earned more than $176,384.

Mean annual earnings of commercial pilots were $80,140 in 2012. The lowest ten percent earned less than $38,520, and the highest ten percent earned more than $134,990.

Pilots may receive paid vacations, holidays, and sick days; life and health insurance; and retirement benefits. These are usually paid by the employer. Employers provide pilots with hotel accommodations during layovers, transportation between hotels and airports, and an expense account when they are away from home. Pilots employed by airlines may also receive free or reduced fare flights for themselves and family members.

Metropolitan Areas with the Highest Employment
Level in this Occupation (Airline Pilot)

Metropolitan area	Employment	Employment per thousand jobs	Annual mean wage[1]
Atlanta-Sandy Springs-Marietta, GA	7,150	3.16	n/a
Chicago-Joliet-Naperville, IL	5,530	1.52	$130,920
New York-White Plains-Wayne, NY-NJ	4,440	0.86	$166,080
Los Angeles-Long Beach-Glendale, CA	2,440	0.63	$125,570
Washington-Arlington-Alexandria, DC-VA-MD-WV	2,360	1.01	$109,800
Denver-Aurora-Broomfield, CO	2,340	1.90	$91,740

[1]Hourly figures not available. Source: Bureau of Labor Statistics

Metropolitan Areas with the Highest Employment
Level in this Occupation (Commercial Pilot)

Metropolitan area	Employment	Employment per thousand jobs	Annual mean wage[1]
Houston-Sugar Land-Baytown, TX	1,910	0.72	$97,970
Dallas-Plano-Irving, TX	1,180	0.56	$93,990
Phoenix-Mesa-Glendale, AZ	1,060	0.61	$65,810
Los Angeles-Long Beach-Glendale, CA	910	0.24	$84,210
Fort Lauderdale-Pompano Beach-Deerfield Beach, FL	610	0.85	$90,810
Atlanta-Sandy Springs-Marietta, GA	600	0.26	$99,820

[1]Hourly figures not available. Source: Bureau of Labor Statistics

EMPLOYMENT AND OUTLOOK

There were approximately 104,000 pilots employed nationally in 2012. About two-thirds worked for airlines. Many others worked as flight instructors at local airports or for large businesses that fly company cargo and executives in their own airplanes or helicopters. Some also worked for federal, state and local governments.

Employment of airline pilots is expected to decline through the year 2022, which means employment is projected to decrease 1 percent to 8 percent. Demand for air travel is expected to increase somewhat as the population and economy continue to grow. However, airlines will likely attempt to increase profitability over the next decade by increasing the average number of passengers per flight and eliminating routes with low demand. The result will be fewer flights and fewer pilot jobs. Job opportunities will be better with the regional airlines and low-fare carriers, which are growing faster than the more well-known major airlines. Job opportunities with air cargo carriers also are expected to be better than with passenger airlines.

Employment of commercial pilots is projected to grow 9 percent from 2012 to 2022, about as fast as the average for all occupations. Commercial pilots are projected to add jobs in various industries, including ambulance services and support activities for air transportation.

In general, pilots who have logged the greatest number of flying hours in the more sophisticated equipment typically have the best prospects. For this reason, military pilots often have an advantage over other applicants.

Employment Trend, Projected 2012–22

Total, All Occupations: 13%

Commercial Pilots: 9%

Airline and Commercial Pilots: 13%

Total, All Occupations: 11%

Note: "All Occupations" includes all occupations in the U.S. Economy. Source: U.S. Bureau of Labor Statistics, Employment Projections Program

Related Occupations
- Airplane Navigator
- Airplane Pilot
- Flight Engineer
- Helicopter Pilot
- Space Operations Officer
- Special Operations Officer

Conversation With . . .
JAMES P. ANDRIES
Commercial Airline Pilot, 30 years

1. What was your individual career path in terms of education/training, entry-level job, or other significant opportunity?

I always thought planes were cool and wanted to learn to fly. Whenever I had a few extra bucks, I took flying lessons. I earned a Bachelor of Career Arts at Dallas Baptist University. College degree in hand, I joined the Air Force and flew jets for seven years. After leaving the Air Force, I was hired by a major airline, where I've worked for over 25 years. I hate to make people think they need all this education for a job in aviation, because that's not true. But opportunities for pilots without a college degree generally involve smaller airplanes and much lower pay. A college degree is important if you want to fly corporate, military, or airline. (Embry-Riddle and Florida Institute of Technology have well regarded flight programs.)Two myths: that you have to be superhuman fit, and two, you have to be a strong in science and math. Average health and a degree in any field will open most doors in aviation.

The best way to become a professional pilot is through a university program or the military. I chose the Air Force because with more types of planes, the chances of getting to fly the planes I wanted were better. If you choose the military path, realize when you sign on the dotted line, your future could include combat operations.

As airlines go, so goes the rest of the industry. If the airlines are hiring, everyone moves up the ladder, from regional on up.

A pilot has a lot of opportunity to enjoy destinations. Upcoming, I have two trips to Moscow and one trip to Amsterdam. I can explore and sightsee while on layover (required rest) between work days.

2. What are the most important skills and/or qualities for someone in your profession?

At the most basic level, flying is a blend of eye-hand coordination and academic skill. You need to pass a course that includes simulator and academic training for each new aircraft. Training is ongoing for professional pilots. We typically go once a year for simulator and re-testing on our aircraft. We are required to pass an Aviation Medical exam once or twice a year, depending on age and flight position.

3. **What do you wish you had known going into this profession?**

Training can be very expensive.

4. **Are there many job opportunities in your profession? In what specific areas?**

There are lots of options. You can stay local as a flight instructor or fly cargo and charter operations. Most pilots eventually want to move on to bigger and faster airplanes with more pay. Jobs include regional airlines, corporate flying, military flying and major airlines. At major airlines, you can work as an instructor in the training department, or you can fly the line from one city to another. I mostly fly international routes from New York to Europe.

I think we're fixing to get into the best period, in terms of career opportunities, that we've seen in 30 years. My generation was part of a big hiring boom. Projected retirement is approximately 7,000 pilots over 10 years at just one airline.

5. **How do you see your profession changing in the next five years? What role will technology play in those changes, and what skills will be required?**

Over the next five years we're going to crank into this big hiring of pilots. All the airlines are taking new aircraft orders. New aircraft bring new technology: new efficiencies, safety, Wi-Fi. Pilots will become less Wright Brothers (fly by feel) and more systems manager. Technology is the future and our friend. But at any time, autopilot or various systems could fail. The pilot is always in command and ready to take over manually if required.

6. **What do you enjoy most about your job? What do you enjoy least?**

I have always loved flying planes. My desk is at 35,000 feet traveling at 8 miles per minute, and the view is spectacular.

Unfortunately, most pilots spend a lot of time away from home. Pilots and flight attendants are gone three to five days at a time and work most holidays. If you get on with a major airline, after many years your quality of life will improve.

7. **Can you suggest a valuable "try this" for students considering a career in aviation?**

The biggest issue is your gut feeling when you're flying an airplane. Get a flight instructor to take you up on a nice sunny day with very little wind. That's flying at its best. He or she will let you take the stick and explore the world of flying. Something inside is going to click and say, "This is way cool," or "I am terrified." Future pilots will say, "This is really cool. Let's do it again."

I'd like young people to know this is within their reach. It's a competitive field, but if you want a job in aviation, pursue it. Just remember, it isn't all about flying around on a sunny day. We're paid for those days when the hydraulic system goes and you're landing in 600 feet of visibility in a snowstorm. Professional pilots can make good money; I believe they earn it.

SELECTED SCHOOLS

A variety of colleges and universities offer programs in aviation or related fields. There are also numerous private aviation academies. The website of Flying Magazine (see below) provides a list of accredited institutions. Below are shown some of the more prominent of these.

Arizona State University
College of Technology and Innovation
7231 E. Sonoran Arroyo Mall
330 Stanton Hall
Mesa, AZ 85212
480.7275232
innovation.asu.edu

Embry-Riddle Aeronautical University, Daytona Beach
600 S. Clyde Morris Boulevard
Daytona Beach, FL 32114
386.226.6000
daytonabeach.erau.edu

Embry-Riddle Aeronautical University, Prescott
3700 Willow Creek Road
Prescott, AZ 86301
928.777.6600
prescott.erau.edu

Ohio State University
Center for Aviation Studies
Bolz Hall, Suite 228
2036 Neil Avenue
Columbus, OH 43210
614.292.2405
aviation.osu.edu

Purdue University
College of Technology
West Lafayette, IN 47907
765.494.4935
tech.purdue.edu/departments/
aviation-technology

Southern Illinois University
College of Applied Sciences and Arts
665 N. Airport Road
Murphrysboro, IL 62901
618.453.8898
aviation.siu.edu

University of Nebraska, Omaha
Aviation Institute
120 CB
6001 Dodge Street
Omaha, NE 68182
402.554.3424
www.unomaha.edu/ai

University of North Dakota
Department of Aviation
Twamley Hall Room 429
264 Centennial Drive Stop 7144
Grand Forks, ND 58202
800.225.5863
aviation.und.edu

University of Oklahoma
Department of Aviation
1700 Lexington
Norman, OK 73069
405.325.7231
www.aviation.ou.edu

Western Michigan University
College of Aviation
Kalamazoo, MI 49008
269.964.6375
www.wmich.edu/aviation

MORE INFORMATION

Aircraft Owners and Pilots Association
421 Aviation Way
Frederick, MD 21701
301.695.2000
www.aopa.org

Air Line Pilots Association, International
1625 Massachusetts Avenue, NW
Washington, DC 20036
703.689.2270
www.alpa.org

Federal Aviation Administration
800 Independence Avenue, SW
Washington, DC 20591
866.835.5322
www.faa.gov

Flying Magazine
460 N. Orlando Avenue
Suite 200
Winter Park, FL 32789
407.628.4802
www.flyingmag.com

International Society of Women Airline Pilots
723 S. Casino Center Boulevard
2nd Floor
Las Vegas, NV 89101-6716
www.iswap.org

Michael Auerbach/Editor

Property & Real Estate Manager

Snapshot

Career Cluster: Business Administration; Hospitality & Tourism; Sales & Service

Interests: Real estate, business administration, budgeting, finance, marketing

Earnings (Yearly Average): $63,570

Employment & Outlook: Average Growth Expected

OVERVIEW

Sphere of Work

To some real estate professionals, the positions of property manager and real estate manager are interchangeable. To others, a property manager is a type of real estate manager who is in charge of a large property or several properties, whether commercial or residential. In either case, property and real estate managers strive to maintain and maximize the financial value of income-producing properties by marketing the properties to prospective tenants, deciding the amount of rent to charge, minimizing property expenditures, and physically maintaining the properties.

Work Environment

Residential property and real estate managers are responsible for properties in which people live, such as time-share units, apartment complexes, condominiums, and single-family rental houses. They also oversee commercial properties such as shopping centers and marinas. In the case of residential properties they may interact with tenants at any time, day or night, because unlike most commercial properties, residential properties are in use twenty-four hours a day. Some residential property and real estate managers even live in their properties so that they are available in case of emergencies.

Commercial properties house businesses and can run the gamut from office buildings to warehouses to strip malls to tiny kiosks. Each type of commercial property has its unique demands, which property and real estate managers must be able to meet. For instance, a medical office building may need special insurance or maintenance because of the medical equipment it houses, while a bank may require extra security around its facility. Commercial property and real estate managers should have the expertise to handle these situations. Tenant satisfaction is important to all property and real estate managers because satisfied tenants, residential and commercial alike, are more likely to renew their leases.

Profile

Working Conditions: Work Indoors

Physical Strength: Light Work

Education Needs: Technical/ Community College, Bachelor's Degree

Licensure/Certification: Required

Physical Abilities Not Required: No Heavy Labor

Opportunities For Experience: Military Service

Holland Interest Score*: IRE

* See Appendix A

Occupation Interest

Property and real estate management may appeal to people who are already real estate professionals, such as agents or brokers, but desire a slight career change. A background in real estate sales is helpful for property and real estate managers, as knowledge acquired about the real estate market through such work carries over well into the property and real estate management field. Training in other forms of business and/or hospitality management is also useful.

Prospective property and real estate managers must be detail-oriented workers able to multitask, delegate responsibility, and resolve disputes. Because they are the link between property owners and tenants, good communication skills are imperative.

A Day in the Life—Duties and Responsibilities

There are many kinds of property and real estate managers. A manager's property portfolio may consist of only a single property, or it may consist of multiple properties within one geographic region or even throughout several regions. Some managers have on-site offices, while others visit their properties on a regular basis. Because of this variation, responsibilities differ from manager to manager, despite the shared goal of making their properties as profitable as possible.

The workday for on-site property and real estate managers takes place partly in the office. There, they schedule building and security system maintenance, showings of vacant units, and meetings with tenants; make calls; meet with coworkers and clientele; market vacant units; and settle tenant disputes. They also create financial reports tracking property income and expenses for property owners. Other financial responsibilities of property and real estate managers may include collecting rent checks, recording transactions, creating budgets, and determining strategies to increase revenue and decrease expenses.

Property and real estate managers are also responsible for inspecting the landscaping, interior common areas, vacant units, elevators, stairwells, and parking lots of their properties. During these property inspections, managers check for damage, determine what improvements need to be made to increase tenant appeal, and ensure that the properties continue to meet government building codes and relevant lease laws.

Duties and Responsibilities

- Marketing vacant space to prospective tenants
- Establishing rental rates
- Negotiating and preparing lease and rental contracts
- Collecting rents and fees
- Disbursing funds for taxes, mortgages, payroll and insurance
- Ensuring safe use of the property
- Negotiating for maintenance services

WORK ENVIRONMENT

Physical Environment

Property and real estate managers typically work in offices and frequently visit the properties they manage to make sure everything is well kept and in working order. On-site property and real estate managers usually spend most, if not all, of their workdays at their properties and may even live there, as in the case of on-site residential property managers.

Relevant Skills and Abilities

Communication Skills
- Persuading others

Interpersonal/Social Skills
- Being sensitive to others
- Cooperating with others

Organization & Management Skills
- Performing duties that change frequently
- Selling ideas or products

Research & Planning Skills
- Developing evaluation strategies
- Solving problems

Other Skills
- Working with data or numbers as well as with people

Human Environment

Pilots must work with a wide range of people on the ground and on board their planes. Such parties include maintenance crews, security personnel, flight attendants, air traffic controllers, luggage handlers and, of course, the passengers. Pilots must interact directly with many of these individuals, while communicating and coordinating with others on the ground while in flight. Pilots are sometimes responsible for unruly passengers. As part of the Homeland Security Act of 2002, some pilots have been deputized and are federal law enforcement officers, called Federal Flight Deck Officers.

Technological Environment

Property and real estate managers use various software applications to keep tenant records, generate maintenance work orders, create budgets for their properties, and perform other administrative tasks. They also rely on standard office equipment such as fax machines, telephones, copiers, and scanners.

EDUCATION, TRAINING, AND ADVANCEMENT

High School/Secondary

High school students can prepare for careers in property or real estate management with courses in business, English, and social sciences. Part-time work for a property management or real estate company can provide an excellent introduction to the field.

Suggested High School Subjects
- Applied Communication
- Applied Math
- Building & Grounds Maintenance
- Business
- College Preparatory
- English

Postsecondary

A college degree is not always necessary to become a property or real estate manager. However, having completed courses, a degree, or a postsecondary certificate in real estate, finance, or business administration can add to a property or real estate manager's professional capability and provide a competitive edge. Many universities offer undergraduate and graduate degree programs in real estate.

Related College Majors
- Business Administration
- Hospitality Management
- Real Estate

Adult Job Seekers

Employers that hire property and real estate managers include property management companies, full-service and development real estate companies, insurance companies, banks, and government agencies. Adult job seekers can benefit from networking with real estate professionals and joining professional associations such as the

Institute of Real Estate Management (IREM). Networking can alert job seekers to job openings that have not yet been made public, while professional property management associations often post openings on their job boards.

Before pursuing education in real estate or business administration and obtaining the necessary licensure, those interested in property and real estate management may first choose to seek employment in property management support. By working as an assistant to a property or real estate manager or as part of an on-site maintenance team, for example, an aspiring manager can gain valuable on-the-job property management training.

Professional Certification and Licensure

Licensure requirements for property and real estate managers vary from state to state. A real estate license is necessary in most states, and in a few, a separate property management license is as well.

Managers of federally subsidized public housing properties are required to obtain certification, but other real estate and property managers are not. Optional certification offered by professional real estate associations may be beneficial for career advancement. Candidates are typically required to complete a degree program and coursework, pass an exam, and adhere to a code of professional ethics.

Additional Requirements

As property and real estate managers often spend a significant amount of time driving between properties, a driver's license is essential. An interest in both business administration and people or customer service will prove useful as well.

EARNINGS AND ADVANCEMENT

Mean annual earnings of property and real estate managers were $63,570 in 2012. The lowest ten percent earned less than $26,600, and the highest ten percent earned more than $113,400.

Property and real estate managers may receive paid vacations, holidays, and sick days; life and health insurance; and retirement benefits. These are usually paid by the employer. They may also use company cars, and some managers in land development may receive a small share of ownership in projects they develop.

Metropolitan Areas with the Highest Employment Level in this Occupation (Airline Pilot)

Metropolitan area	Employment [1]	Employment per thousand jobs	Hourly mean wage
Los Angeles-Long Beach-Glendale, CA	6,830	1.76	$35.55
Chicago-Joliet-Naperville, IL	4,760	1.31	$28.17
Houston-Sugar Land-Baytown, TX	4,590	1.74	$38.23
Phoenix-Mesa-Glendale, AZ	4,100	2.37	$23.26
Dallas-Plano-Irving, TX	3,920	1.87	$30.05
Santa Ana-Anaheim-Irvine, CA	3,910	2.77	$37.19
New York-White Plains-Wayne, NY-NJ	3,470	0.67	$47.89
San Francisco-San Mateo-Redwood City, CA	3,350	3.35	$43.70

[1]Does not include self-employed. Source: Bureau of Labor Statistics

EMPLOYMENT AND OUTLOOK

Property and real estate managers held about 300,000 jobs nationally in 2012. About one-half were self-employed. Around another one-fourth worked in offices of real estate agents and brokers. Others worked for government agencies that manage public buildings.

Employment is expected to grow about the same as the average for all occupations through the year 2022, which means employment is projected to increase 9 percent to 15 percent. Opportunities are best for those with a college degree in business administration, real estate, or a related field. Growth in the number of apartments and offices should require more property managers. In addition, the number of older people will grow during the next decade, increasing the need for various types of suitable housing, such as assisted-living facilities and retirement communities. There will be demand for property and real estate managers to operate these facilities, especially for those who have a background in the operation and administrative aspects of running a health unit.

Related Occupations
- Building Manager
- Hotel/Motel Manager
- Real Estate Sales Agent

Conversation With . . .
LEIGH LAWSON
Real Estate Manager
26 years in the industry

1. What was your individual career path in terms of education/training, entry-level job, or other significant opportunity?

I always knew I wanted to go into a real estate career and groomed myself toward it early on. My father built spec houses. I gobbled up glamorous real estate books, and studied castles and grounds and interiors. I also studied ballet from age 3 and was in competitions so I traveled a lot, which is the best education when dealing with the hospitality and international real estate industry. The more knowledge and acceptance of another culture you possess, the more successful you can be.

I graduated from the College of William and Mary with a bachelor's degree in business management, then immediately got my real estate license. I then deemed it important to learn the art of financing. If you don't know financing and how it is all entangled and what a buyer is about to embark on for the 30-year length of most mortgages, then you won't be a very good realtor. I got into a loan officer/management training program with First Washington Mortgage in McLean, Va., and did everything. In 1988, I went into real estate full-time in Newport Beach, California. I was "Rookie of the Year" because I did what no other realtor did: figured out how to make a down market work for me and my clients. Nobody wanted to do rentals but I did because nothing was selling. My office was next to the University of California, Irvine and to a number of beach communities. So, I did 122 rentals and made a lot of splash and cash.

At one time I thought I wanted to be a builder/developer, but later found that I'm not that technical. I'm more of a marketing person. That's what I do best.

My company's property management division manages a lot of properties for the government, including U.S. Naval Academy people who get shipped out, or people in the area who own houses and rent them by the week for the academy graduation. We also do a lot for the Baltimore Orioles and the Baltimore Ravens. The baseball players are more transient because they get traded a lot. They spend a lot of money, and they want to be as close to Oriole Park at Camden Yards as possible. Very high end. The Ravens are more stable. They want bigger houses, their wives and girlfriends are more in control, and they're more out in Baltimore County where their training facility is located. We also network with hotels and do vacation rentals. People may stay in the same place every year but as they get elderly they may need a house that is handicapped accessible. Or they want to bring their pets.

2. What are the most important skills and/or qualities for someone in your profession?

Don't have an ego. I see so many realtors who make it all about them. Real estate is and should be about helping buyers and sellers buy and sell their homes, or helping renters find their homes. Homes are peoples' go-to places when they are happy and sad and seek solitude and peace. We are the catalyst and confidant to make dreams a reality, and to keep that dream a reality.

3. What do you wish you had known going into this profession?

To start a 401K retirement account.

4. Are there many job opportunities in your profession? In what specific areas?

Real estate has endless job opportunities. On the property management side, one could manage apartments for resorts, the government (including housing for military, the elderly, and Section 8), hotels and hotel chains, co-ops, cruise lines, or even commercial property management.

You could also pursue real estate with title companies; builders and their representatives; loan companies; architectural firms; retail firms such as Home Depot or Lowes; electrical, plumbing, HVAC/AC; or other related industry associations such as the home builders' associations or the National Association of Realtors or the local realtors' associations.

5. How do you see your profession changing in the next five years? What role will technology play in those changes, and what skills will be required?

The first thing buyers, sellers or renters do is go online. They do their searching before they call a realtor. I have sold homes where I have never met the people. We can do electronic signatures on contracts so we do that, especially with the military and government. But, people will always need someone to value their homes. Realtors bring together a meeting of the minds between buyer and seller. You need to bring a professional into the situation to get the best value for your home. People use property managers when time is of the essence and they don't have time to go place to place and do all the research. If you want to do real estate, know your technology and keep up with any application available.

6. What do you enjoy most about your job? What do you enjoy least?

I love my job of real estating! It's the greatest because of its flexibility. Those who don't like knowing what they will be doing every day won't enjoy this type of job. I also love meeting and talking with new people, and going to functions and events.

7. Can you suggest a valuable "try this" for students considering a career in your profession?

Try working for a real estate office or for a realtor, builder, or loan company before you actually go into the field full-time. Not all are the same and your personality will not always gel with whomever you are working with. It may take a few tries before you say, "This is cool."

SELECTED SCHOOLS

Most colleges and universities have programs in business administration; many also have concentrations in real estate. Training in hospitality management is equally valuable for aspiring property and real estate managers. For some jobs completion of a two-year program at a community college or vocational school may be sufficient. Interested students are advised to consult with a school guidance counselor. Below are listed some of the more prominent institutions in this field.

New York University
School of Continuing and
Professional Studies
7 E. 12th Street, Suite 921
New York, NY 10003
212.918.7100
www.scps.nyu.edu

**University of California,
Berkeley**
Haas School of Business
Baker Faculty Building, F602
Berkeley, CA 94720
510.643.6105
groups.haas.berkeley.edu

University of Connecticut
School of Business
2100 Hillside Road, Unit 1041
Storrs, CT 06269
860.486.3040
www.business.uconn.edu

University of Florida
Heavener School of Business
233 Bryan Hall
PO Box 117160
Gainesville, FL 32611
352.273.0165
catalog.ufl.edu/ugrad/current

University of Georgia
Terry College of Business
Brooks Hall
301 Herty Drive
Athens, GA 30602
706.542.8100
www.terry.uga.edu

**University of Illinois, Urbana
Champaign**
College of Business
1055 Business Instructional Facility
515 E. Gregory Drive
Champaign, IL 61820
217.333.2747
www1.business.illinois.edu

University of Pennsylvania
Wharton School
3620 Locust Walk
Philadelphia, PA 19104
215.898.3030
www.wharton.upenn.edu

**University of Southern
California**
Marshall School of Business
3670 Trousdale Parkway
Los Angeles, CA 90089
213.740.8674
www.marshall.usc.edu

University of Texas, Austin
McCombs School of Business
2110 Speedway, Stop B6000
Austin, TX 78712
512.471.5921
www.mccombs.utexas.edu

University of Wisconsin, Madison
Wisconsin School of Business
975 University Avenue
Madison, WI 53706
608.262.1550
bus.wisc.edu

MORE INFORMATION

Building Owners & Managers Association International
1101 15th Street, NW, Suite 800
Washington, DC 20005
202.408.2662
www.boma.org

Building Owners & Managers Institute International
1 Park Place, Suite 475
Annapolis, MD 21401
800.235.2664
www.bomi.org

Community Associations Institute
6402 Arlington Boulevard
Suite 500
Falls Church, VA 22024
703.970.9220
www.caionline.org

Institute of Real Estate Management
430 N. Michigan Avenue
Chicago, IL 60611-4090
800.837.0706
www.irem.org

National Apartment Association
201 North Union Street, Suite 200
Alexandria, VA 22314
703.518.6141
www.naahq.org

National Association of Residential Property Managers
638 Independence Parkway
Suite 100
Chesapeake, VA 23320
800.782.3452
www.narpm.org

National Property Management Association
4025 Tampa Road, Suite 1203
Oldsmar, FL 34677
813.475.6998
www.npma.org

Property Management Association
7508 Wisconsin Avenue, 4th Floor
Bethesda, MD 20814
301.657.9200
www.narpm.org

Jamie Aronson Tyus/Editor

Recreation Program Director

Snapshot

Career Cluster: Hospitality & Tourism; Human Services; Sports & Entertainment

Interests: Physical education, recreational activities, planning events and programs

Earnings (Yearly Average): $48,215

Employment & Outlook: Faster Than Average Growth Expected

OVERVIEW

Sphere of Work

Recreation program directors work for private institutions as well as municipalities, developing and coordinating recreation needs for residents and visitors, including children, seniors, and adults. Recreation program directors develop these recreation programs by assessing community or service audience recreation needs; hiring and evaluating recreation workers and additional staff; overseeing the safety and maintenance of grounds, equipment, and facilities; promoting the recreation program to the community; planning events; scheduling programs; keeping records on program

happenings and staff; and fundraising through direct solicitation
and grant-writing. Recreation program directors manage both public
and private recreation programs through a variety of host agencies
or institutions such as schools, camps, resorts, public agencies,
retirement facilities, and hospitals.

Work Environment

Recreation program directors spend their workdays overseeing
recreation programs in a wide variety of indoor and outdoor settings,
including schools, public recreation centers, private resorts, indoor
childcare centers, playgrounds, sports fields, swimming pools,
residential facilities, or day camps. A recreation program director's
work environment may involve extremes of heat, cold, or noise.
Given the diverse demands of the recreation profession, recreation
program directors may need to work a combination of days, evenings,
weekends, vacation, and summer hours to ensure program success.

Profile

Working Conditions: Work Both
Indoors and Outdoors
Physical Strength: Light Work
Education Needs: Technical/
Community College, Bachelor's Degree
Licensure/Certification:
Recommended
Physical Abilities Not Required: No
Heavy Labor
Opportunities For Experience:
Internship, Military Service Part-Time
Work
Holland Interest Score*: ESA
* See Appendix A

Occupation Interest

Individuals drawn to the
recreation field tend to be
charismatic, intelligent, and
organized people who have the
ability to quickly assess situations,
utilize resources, and solve
problems. Successful recreation
program directors are responsible
leaders who display effective time
management skills, a strong sense
of initiative, and a concern for
individuals and society. Recreation
program directors should enjoy
physical activity and spending
time with a wide range of people, including those with special needs
and those from diverse cultural, social, and educational backgrounds.

A Day in the Life—Duties and Responsibilities

The daily occupational duties and responsibilities of recreation
program directors will be determined by the individual's area of
job specialization and work environment. Recreation program
directors must be able to assess the recreational needs and abilities

of individuals, groups, or the local community. Before their busy season, they typically spend time interviewing, hiring, and evaluating recreation workers and staff, including food service workers and maintenance crews. They spend a portion of each day supervising seasonal and full-time recreation workers, such as lifeguards, coaches, and activity leaders, and overseeing the safety, upkeep, and maintenance of grounds, equipment, and facilities. Recreation program directors promote the recreation program to the local community through flyers, websites, e-mails, and press releases. They also plan and schedule program events such as tournaments, nature studies, leagues, dances, team sports, and classes, and periodically brainstorm new ways to recruit volunteers for all aspects of the recreation program. Conducting program assessment and evaluation through surveys and feedback requests is one way in which recreation program directors can gain an understanding of the success of their programming.

Recreation program directors have many legal, financial, and administrative responsibilities, such as ensuring that their recreation program meets national requirements for safety and the Americans with Disabilities Act, planning the short-term and long-term recreation program budget, and conducting background checks on staff, volunteers, and contractors. Recreation directors are sometimes responsible for raising money for programming through grant-writing, fundraising, and donation requests. Part of the job involves keeping the recreation program in the public eye so that it will continue to attract patrons and contributions. The recreation program

Duties and Responsibilities

- Developing and overseeing recreational programs
- Setting up schedules and activities
- Soliciting financial resources
- Coordinating human resources
- Directing specialized activities and events
- Publicizing and promoting programs to the community
- Maintaining facilities in good working order
- Ensuring safety of all patrons and staff
- Dealing with emergencies as necessary

director may represent the recreation program at conferences and meetings, including local and national recreation society meetings, or meet periodically with institutional supervisors, such as parks and recreation department commissioners, facility owners, or other stakeholders.

All recreation program directors are responsible for accurate record keeping on program safety, accidents, and staff performance.

WORK ENVIRONMENT

Physical Environment

The immediate physical environment of recreation program directors varies based on the program's focus and location. Recreation program directors spend their workdays coordinating activities in a wide variety of settings including schools, public recreation centers, indoor childcare centers, ice skating rinks, hospitals, playgrounds, sports fields, pools and aquatic centers, residential facilities, or day camps. Most recreation directors spend part of their work day outdoors, but the majority of their time is spent inside an office.

Relevant Skills and Abilities

Communication Skills
- Promoting an idea
- Speaking effectively

Interpersonal/Social Skills
- Asserting oneself
- Being sensitive to others
- Motivating others

Organization & Management Skills
- Coordinating tasks
- Demonstrating leadership
- Managing people/groups

Other Skills
- Being physically active

Human Environment

Recreation program directors work with a wide variety of people and should be comfortable meeting with colleagues, supervisors, program benefactors, staff, children, the elderly, people with physical disabilities, and families. Because they represent the program to the public and function in a supervisory or administrative role, they should enjoy meeting new people and spending much of their job managing others. Excellent communication skills are an advantage.

Technological Environment

Recreation program directors must be comfortable using computers to access information and records, Internet communication tools for e-mail, social media, and program websites, and cell phones to ensure availability during on-call hours or in case of an emergency. Those recreation program directors coordinating a specialized recreation program, such as metalworking or a ropes course, may also need to be comfortable training others in the use of techniques they have just learned themselves. They should be certified in CPR and other lifesaving techniques, and be at ease using related equipment.

EDUCATION, TRAINING, AND ADVANCEMENT

High School/Secondary

High school students interested in pursuing a career as a recreation program director should prepare themselves by developing good study habits. High school study of physical education, foreign language, public safety, sociology, psychology, and education will provide a strong foundation for work as a recreation program director or college-level work in the field. High school students interested in this career path will benefit from seeking part-time or seasonal work that exposes the students to diverse groups of people and recreational activities. They can also obtain certification in lifesaving techniques through their school or town.

Suggested High School Subjects
- Accounting
- Algebra
- Applied Communication
- Arts
- Business
- Business Law
- Business Math
- Crafts
- English
- Physical Education
- Social Studies

Famous First

The first summer camp for boys was Camp Comfort in Milford, Conn, established in 1861. It was founded by Frederick William Gunn, founder of The Gunnery prep school. The camp took 50 boys on a two-week camping trip. Today there are about 7,000 overnight camps and 5,000 day camps in the United States; together they serve over 10 million children.

College/Postsecondary

Postsecondary students interested in becoming recreation program directors should earn an associate's or bachelor's degree in recreation or physical education. A small number of colleges (accredited by the National Recreation and Park Association) offer the bachelor's of parks and recreation degree. Courses in physical education, education, public safety, business management, accounting, and foreign languages may also prove useful in future recreation work. Postsecondary students can gain work experience and potential advantage in their future job searches by securing internships or part-time employment in parks and recreation departments or private recreation programs.

Related College Majors
- Adapted Physical Education/Therapeutic Recreation
- Parks, Recreation & Leisure Facilities Management
- Parks, Recreation & Leisure Studies
- Physical Education Teaching & Coaching
- Sport & Fitness Administration/Management

Adult Job Seekers

Adults seeking employment as recreation program directors should have, at a minimum, an associate's or bachelor's degree in recreation or a related field and extensive program directing experience. Some recreation programs require their directors to hold a master's degree and second language proficiency. Adult job seekers should educate themselves about the educational and professional license requirements of their home states and the organizations where they seek employment, and may benefit from joining professional associations that offer help with networking and job searches. Professional recreation associations, such as the American Camping Association and the Society of State Directors of Health, Physical Education & Recreation, generally offer job-finding workshops and maintain lists and forums of available jobs.

Professional Certification and Licensure

Professional certification and licensure is not required of general recreation program directors. Directors of specialized recreation programs, such as swimming or parks and recreation, may be required to earn specialized certification as a condition of employment. Lifeguard certification, pool operations certification, and CPR/First Aid certification is offered by the American Lifeguard Association and requires coursework and passing an examination. The National Recreation and Park Association (NRPA) certificate is offered in therapeutic recreation, park management, outdoor recreation, industrial or commercial recreation, and camp management. It also requires a bachelor's degree or its equivalent in education and work experience, as well as passing a national examination. Ongoing professional education is required for continued certification in both lifesaving techniques and NRPA disciplines.

Additional Requirements

Successful recreation program directors will be knowledgeable about the profession's requirements, responsibilities, and opportunities. High levels of integrity and personal and professional ethics are required of recreation program directors, as professionals in this role interact with staff in subordinate roles and have access to personal information. Membership in professional recreation associations is encouraged among all recreation program directors as a means of building status within a professional community and networking.

In most states, the names of those people working in the field of recreation are almost always required to be submitted for a criminal record check. This includes employees, volunteers, and those delivering special programs.

EARNINGS AND ADVANCEMENT

Recreation program directors advance based on their experience. Certification by the National Recreation and Park Association helps advancement. Recreation program directors had mean annual earnings of $48,215 in 2012.

Recreation program directors may receive paid vacations, holidays, and sick days; life and health insurance; and retirement benefits. These are usually paid by the employer.

Metropolitan Areas with the Highest Employment Level in this Occupation (Recreation Workers)

Metropolitan area	Employment	Employment per thousand jobs	Hourly mean wage[1]
New York-White Plains-Wayne, NY-NJ	15,200	2.95	$14.66
Chicago-Joliet-Naperville, IL	10,870	2.99	$12.02
Los Angeles-Long Beach-Glendale, CA	9,640	2.49	$12.21
Washington-Arlington-Alexandria, DC-VA-MD-WV	4,680	1.99	$14.80
Oakland-Fremont-Hayward, CA	4,080	4.20	$13.39
Phoenix-Mesa-Glendale, AZ	4,030	2.33	$12.63
Boston-Cambridge-Quincy, MA	3,980	2.32	$12.20
Philadelphia, PA	3,900	2.14	$13.15

[1]Figures are for all recreation workers, not specifically for directors. Source: Bureau of Labor Statistics

EMPLOYMENT AND OUTLOOK

Recreation workers, of which recreation program directors are a part, held about 310,000 jobs nationally in 2012. About one-third worked in the park and recreation departments of local governments. About another one-fourth worked in nursing and residential care facilities and civic and social organizations, such as the Boy Scouts or Girl Scouts or the YMCA/YWCA. Employment is expected to grow about as fast as the average for all occupations through the year 2022, which means employment is projected to increase 10 percent to 19 percent. This is primarily due to people spending more time and money on recreation. However, employment growth may be limited by budget constraints facing State and local governments over the next decade.

Employment Trend, Projected 2012–22

Personal Care and Service Occupations: 21%

Recreation Workers: 14%

Total, All Occupations: 11%

Note: "All Occupations" includes all occupations in the U.S. Economy. Source: U.S. Bureau of Labor Statistics, Employment Projections Program

Related Occupations
- Fitness Trainer and Aerobics Instructor
- Health Club Manager
- Park Ranger
- Recreation Worker

Related Occupations
- Caseworker & Counselor

Conversation With . . .
STACEY COMISHOCK
Activities and Aquatics Director
17 years in the industry

1. What was your individual career path in terms of education/training, entry-level job, or other significant opportunity?

I have a degree in environmental studies from the University of Vermont. My intended career path was to teach agriculture education or environmental education in school districts. I tried it for awhile. It was a long commute. So, I decided to work at Smugglers Notch for a winter. I lived only 20 minutes away. I started out in the group vacations department as an administrator. I booked groups, did customer service, scheduled ski lessons and rentals, put together rooming lists, and planned meals and other activities. After two years, I was approached by the activities department with a full-time year-round supervisor position as a vendor administrator. I worked with vendors who offered snowmobile tours, dog sled treks, canoe and kayak rentals, etc. to our guests. I learned about resort operations. Seven years ago I was asked to take over as activities director.

2. What are the most important skills and/or qualities for someone in your profession?

Organization is a wonderful skill to have in any type of profession. You also need to be very personable. Not only are you dealing with staff constantly, but you're also dealing with the guests. You have to make a connection to people, be gregarious. It's not for the shrinking violet. Since we're on stage a lot, you need to be comfortable with being out there, being on a microphone. That's not something I was necessarily okay with when I started, but it's just something that comes along with practice. And you need to be willing to work hard. No day is the same in this industry .It's not for someone who likes the mundane.

3. What do you wish you had known going into this profession?

I didn't know it was going to be a profession. I think that's how it starts with a lot of people. It's just a job that they take temporarily. For a lot of people it becomes their permanent career. It sucks you in because it's so exciting and interesting. It's rewarding, creative and fun. A lot of people come to hang out and end up staying. I wish I had known it was okay to have a job in the customer service industry because a lot of people say "When are you going to get a real job?" This is a real job. You're creating memories for people.

4. Are there many job opportunities in your profession? In what specific areas?

There are. You have to be willing to work hard. You have to be willing to work your way up. Put your time in as the ski instructor, for example, or the desk person. Show that you're committed to the job and someone will notice that and guide you in your career path. The tourism industry is growing. The problem is a lot of the jobs are seasonal, but if you're willing to work hard, you can work in different places and string those seasons together.

5. How do you see your profession changing in the next five years? What role will technology play in those changes, and what skills will be required?

Technology is changing everything that we do. It's making us more efficient in our industry. It's also really calling us to task. In the past, word of mouth was how we gained our clients. These days it's instantaneous. If a guest has a bad experience, they're going to post it online right away. We're on display constantly. That has affected how we train our staff and do customer service in general. On the other side, technology is making it easier to communicate with our guests and among ourselves. We can get information to each other faster and to our guests in real-time, through text messaging.

Any basic computer skills will be helpful if you plan to go into this industry. Anyone in this industry should be able to use [Microsoft] Excel.

6. What do you enjoy most about your job? What do you enjoy least?

What I enjoy most is the creativity. I love creating the programming for the resort. Finding programs and activities that work and that guests really enjoy is my favorite part. That's the skill that I carried through from doing agriculture education and creating lesson plans.

My least favorite part is staffing. Staffing sometimes is a nightmare. But it usually always works out.

7. Can you suggest a valuable "try this" for students considering a career in your profession?

Definitely try to get a summer job in a field that you're excited about. Working for a park department, being a lifeguard, working at a family entertainment center or a resort- anywhere where you're seeing lots of people. Customer service isn't for everybody, so it's great to go and try that out.

SELECTED SCHOOLS

Many community colleges and four-year colleges and universities offer programs in physical education; a number of them also offer programs in parks and recreation management, arts and crafts management, and related fields. Interested student are advised to consult with a school guidance counselor.

MORE INFORMATION

American Academy for Park and Recreation Administration
P.O. Box 1040
Mahomet, IL 61853
217.586.3360
www.aapra.org

American Alliance for Health, Physical Education, Recreation & Dance
1900 Association Drive
Reston, VA 20192-1598
800.213.7193
www.aahperd.org

American Camping Association
5000 State Road 67 North
Martinsville, IN 46151
765.342.8456
www.acacamps.org

American Lifeguard Association
8300 Boone Boulevard, 5th Floor
Vienna, VA 22182
703.761.6750
www.americanlifeguard.com

Employee Services Management Association
P.O. Box 10517
Rockville, MD 20849
www.esmassn.org

National Council for Therapeutic Recreation Certification
7 Elmwood Drive
New City, NY 10956
845.639.1439
nctrc@NCTRC.org
www.nctrc.org

National Recreation and Park Association
22377 Belmont Ridge Road
Ashburn, VA 20148-4501
800.626.6772
www.nrpa.org

Society of State Directors of Health, Physical Educ. & Recreation
1900 Association Drive, Suite 100
Reston, VA 20191-1599
703.390.4599
www.thesociety.org

YMCA of the USA
101 N. Wacker Drive
Chicago, IL 60606
800.872.9622
www.ymca.net

Simone Isadora Flynn/Editor

Reservation & Ticket Agent

Snapshot

Career Cluster: Hospitality & Tourism; Sports & Entertainment

Interests: Customer service, sales, data entry, hospitality

Earnings (Yearly Average): $33,580

Employment & Outlook: Slower Than Average Growth Expected

OVERVIEW

Sphere of Work

Reservation and ticket agents record and finalize reservations for transportation, lodging, event attendance, and facility and equipment rental. They work in a variety of industries, from tourism, transportation, and travel to entertainment and sports. Many of the duties and responsibilities of reservation agents combine those of data-entry specialists, customer-service representatives, and sales representatives.

Work Environment

Reservation and ticket agents work in a variety of settings. Many work in call centers and administrative settings, while others work at ticket kiosks and retail counters in airports, train stations, stadiums, and theaters. Reservation agents for large airline or travel companies work in administrative settings throughout the year, while ticket agents may work in ticket kiosks or box offices on a seasonal or per-event basis.

Profile

Working Conditions: Work Indoors
Physical Strength: Light Work
Education Needs: On-The-Job Training
High School Diploma Or G.E.D.
Licensure/Certification: Usually Not
  Required
Physical Abilities Not Required: No
  Heavy Labor
Opportunities For Experience:
  Internship, Volunteer Work
Holland Interest Score*: CES

* See Appendix A

Occupation Interest

Reservation and ticket agents come from a variety of professional and academic backgrounds. Many ticket agents are seasonal, part-time, or temporary employees. Reservation and ticket agents are often entry-level employees eager to acquire professional experience out of high school or college. Others utilize the role as a foundation for a long-term career in hospitality, entertainment administration, or event management. Anyone interested in becoming reservation or ticket agents should be able to handle a fast-paced and often highly stressful work environment. It is important to also enjoy interacting with the general public.

A Day in the Life—Duties and Responsibilities

The responsibilities and duties of reservation and ticket agents vary in complexity given their particular industry. Reservation agents are responsible for taking customer requests for tickets, services, or facility and equipment rental and entering them into a database. They may also take financial information and reiterate the rights and regulations granted to customers upon purchase of their rental agreement, in addition to details regarding cancellations, transfers, and exchanges.

Reservation agents also act as sales representatives, providing clients with available options and attempting to determine the particulars of their reservation and how best to accommodate their needs. This is a particularly common responsibility of reservation specialists in the tourism, hospitality, and transportation industries. Agents are often required to enumerate available accommodations, on-site activities, and other amenities. Reservation agents in the tourism and rental transportation industry must also inform customers of insurance options and any relevant medical or visa requirements.

Ticket agents employed at entertainment venues and sporting events may simply sell tickets to customers, a temporary or event-only role they may conduct in addition to other administrative functions during non-event hours.

Duties and Responsibilities

- Answering questions about schedules and fares
- Planning routes and computing ticket costs
- Making reservations
- Selling tickets
- Maintaining records of tickets and passenger names
- Lifting, checking, and weighing baggage
- Contacting passengers to confirm reservations
- Offering ancillary services such as trip insurance

OCCUPATION SPECIALTIES

Reservation and Ticket Agents

Reservation and Ticket Agents take and confirm passengers' reservations for hotels, airlines, bus companies, railroads, and steamship lines. They also sell and issue tickets and answer questions about itineraries, rates, and package tours. Ticket agents who work at airports also check bags and issue boarding passes to passengers.

Hotel and Motel Desk Clerks

Hotel and Motel Desk Clerks greet and register customers, issue keys, transmit and receive messages, keep records, compute bills, and collect payments. They may also make and confirm reservations.

Automobile Rental Clerks

Automobile Rental Clerks rent automobiles to customers at airports, hotels, marinas, and other locations by preparing a rental contract and informing customers about policies and procedures.

Box Office Clerks

Box Office Clerks receive ticket orders from customers and process payments. They work primarily in sports and entertainment venues, as part of the "box office," handling seat reservations and issuing and receiving tickets.

WORK ENVIRONMENT

Relevant Skills and Abilities

Communication Skills
- Expressing thoughts and ideas clearly

Interpersonal/Social Skills
- Cooperating with others
- Working as a member of a team

Organization & Management Skills
- Managing conflict
- Performing routine work

Technical Skills
- Working with technology

Physical Environment

Administrative and office settings are most common and are usually located in major metropolitan areas. In this environment, agents wear headsets and sit at computer terminals while they take incoming calls from customers. Reservation and ticket agents also work at kiosks and customer-service desks in numerous locations, including airports, train stations, resort hotels, theaters, stadiums, and specialty retail settings.

Human Environment

Strong customer-service skills are paramount, as interaction with clients and potential clients is the most significant element of the job.

Technological Environment

Reservation specialists utilize a variety of traditional administrative technologies, including telephones, e-mail, electronic databases, spreadsheets, and financial-tracking software. Travel agents use special reservation computer software in order to input travel- and airline-related codes.

EDUCATION, TRAINING, AND ADVANCEMENT

High School/Secondary

Reservation and ticket agent positions usually require a high school diploma or the equivalent. High school students can best prepare for a career as a reservation and ticket agent with courses in algebra, communications, and computers. English, writing, and public-speaking courses can also build an important foundation for future customer-service processionals.

Volunteerism and charitable work allow students to interact with a diverse array of people prior to graduation, fostering experiences that can also benefit future work in customer service. Many theaters and stadiums offer summer programs and internships that can introduce students to the field.

Suggested High School Subjects
- Applied Communication
- Business Data Processing
- English
- Foreign Languages
- Geography
- Keyboarding
- Mathematics
- Merchandising
- Speech

Famous First

The first ticket machines came out in the 1920s. They were mechanical devices used by train conductors and bus drivers to issue passenger tickets on the spot. Since the 1980s electronic computer terminals and printers have been used in a variety of ticketing applications. More recently printed tickets have started to be replaced by smartphone applications that allow users to purchase and use tickets and passes instantly via the screen.

Postsecondary

Postsecondary education is not a requirement for a career as a reservation and ticket agent, though it is often preferred. Students interested in management and executive roles within the hierarchy of tourism, sports management, or event management should pursue postsecondary course work in hospitality management, business administration, or finance.

Much of the relevant telephone and computer skills necessary to successfully function as a reservation or ticket agent are learned through on-the-job instruction from managers, supervisors, or seasoned employees. Many travel companies provide formal training programs to newly hired agents in order to ensure they have learned company and industry procedures and policies.

Related College Majors
- Business Administration
- Hospitality Management
- Retail Operations Tourism & Travel Services Marketing Operations
- Travel-Tourism Management

Adult Job Seekers

Reservation and ticket agents come to the industry from a variety of occupational and educational backgrounds. Many are entry-level employees or recent graduates who are interested in a career in hospitality, entertainment, or sports management and are eager to gain experience on the industry's ground floor. While advancement is limited, seasoned professionals with extensive backgrounds in management finance or business may be promoted to shift-lead and management positions in the field.

Professional Certification and Licensure

No specific certification or licensure is required, but U.S. federal law requires that individuals pass a background check and drug test to work in the airline industry. Both are administered by the Federal Aviation Administration (FAA).

Additional Requirements

Reservation and ticket agents must be highly organized individuals who can successfully complete a variety of different tasks within a short time frame. Sympathetic professionals with well-developed interpersonal communication skills are often the most successful in the field, as they can offer clients the highest level of service and overall satisfaction. Fluency in English and a pleasant, professional appearance are also essential. Fluency in a foreign language is not required but can increase an applicant's chances of getting hired.

EARNINGS AND ADVANCEMENT

Earnings depend on the employer, union affiliation and the employee's experience and performance. Mean annual earnings of reservation and ticket agents were $33,580 in 2012. The lowest ten percent earned less than $20,130, and the highest ten percent earned more than $47,660.

Reservation and ticket agents may receive paid vacations, holidays, and sick days; life and health insurance; and retirement benefits. These are usually paid by the employer. Reservation and ticket agents may also receive free or reduced travel and hotel rates for themselves and members of their families.

Metropolitan Areas with the Highest
Employment Level in this Occupation

Metropolitan area	Employment	Employment per thousand jobs	Hourly mean wage
New York-White Plains-Wayne, NY-NJ	9,000	1.75	$16.52
Los Angeles-Long Beach-Glendale, CA	5,770	1.49	$17.15
Miami-Miami Beach-Kendall, FL	4,780	4.78	$15.68
Orlando-Kissimmee-Sanford, FL	4,700	4.64	$13.47
Chicago-Joliet-Naperville, IL	4,330	1.19	$18.55
Salt Lake City, UT	3,900	6.28	$15.59
Washington-Arlington-Alexandria, DC-VA-MD-WV	3,610	1.54	$15.82
Las Vegas-Paradise, NV	3,200	3.91	$15.86

Source: Bureau of Labor Statistics

EMPLOYMENT AND OUTLOOK

There were approximately 135,000 reservation and ticket agents employed nationally in 2012. Over one-half were employed by airlines. Employment is expected to grow slower than the average for all occupations through the year 2022, which means employment is projected to increase 0 percent to 5 percent. The ability of passengers to make airline, train, hotel, and car reservations online is reducing the need for workers in this field. Most job openings will arise as experienced workers transfer to other jobs or retire.

Employment Trend, Projected 2012–22

Total, All Occupations: 11%

Administrative Support Occupations: 7%

Reservation and Ticket Agents: 2%

Note: "All Occupations" includes all occupations in the U.S. Economy. Source: U.S. Bureau of Labor Statistics, Employment Projections Program

Related Occupations
- Counter and Rental Clerk
- Travel Agent

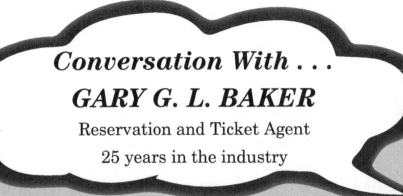

Conversation With . . .
GARY G. L. BAKER
Reservation and Ticket Agent

25 years in the industry

1. What was your individual career path in terms of education/training, entry-level job, or other significant opportunity?

I grew up in Europe, so I was around the world from a young age. Being in the Army for three years also gave me the opportunity to travel. It blossomed into an interest in other languages, cultures and foods. I speak two languages fluently – English and German – and know the Scandinavian languages. In college I worked part-time in my agency, which intertwined my interests in travel and business. I received my bachelor's degree in business management.

While traveling, I became interested in seeing sports arenas and racing venues around the world, with the ambition of driving world-famous racetracks. This led me to high-performance driving. Now, I'm a nationally recognized high-performance driving instructor. That's another way that I parlayed my love of travel into something more.

To become a Reservation Agent, college is not mandatory, but you will need a technical education and computer training.   You will use a Global Distribution System (GDS) a centralized computer system used to purchase car rentals, hotel rooms, and airline tickets. More advanced certification can also be obtained which include Certified Travel Counselor (CTC); Certified Travel Industry Executive (CTIE); or Certified Travel Associate (CTA).

2. What are the most important skills and/or qualities for someone in your profession?

Active listening and understanding clients and their needs is key. For example, a date of birth is necessary for an airline reservation, but some older ladies don't like to give their age. You need to be able to navigate that type of situation. You need to be able to convey information effectively, such as stating the month and numerical day, not just "Wednesday," when confirming a travel date.

I have had many travelers request something that isn't necessarily what the person really wants or needs. I recently had some college kids who bought airline tickets online and came into my office to get a rail pass for Europe. Their entry and exit point of Amsterdam was ineffective for what they wanted. We ended up changing their itinerary so they flew in and out of Rome, which enabled them to travel to Eastern European countries they wanted to see.

3. What do you wish you had known going into this profession?

I wish I had known that this is the best job you can have because it is one that I truly enjoy. Meeting new people and traveling the world can be so much fun.

4. Are there many job opportunities in your profession? In what specific areas?

I see myself as an advanced concierge. Your growth depends on your ability to consider each client's request successfully and develop a nurturing relationship.

5. How do you see your profession changing in the next five years? What role will technology play in those changes, and what skills will be required?

I heavily rely on advanced technology; it gives me an advantage. There are programs that can dig into things. For example, Amadeus, one of the three large GDSs, is changing from mostly services such as airline and rental car reservations to things like visa processing. We're also seeing GDS help with ancillary airline fees—probably the biggest pet peeve of any traveler. Now we'll bundle those so you have an end price.

6. What do you enjoy most about your job? What do you enjoy least?

I really enjoy the level of trust between the agent and client. What I like least is poor supplier service, as well as fees for things like baggage and seat assignments. These can diminish the trust established by the reservation agent. I'm not a fan of how the industry is becoming more a la carte. What's next, a fee to buy a seatbelt buckle or to exit the aircraft first?

7. Can you suggest a valuable "try this" for students considering a career in your profession?

Try this and see how long it takes you to "hold" this type of booking without paying for it. If, rather than enjoy the challenge of fitting these pieces together, you find this exercise frustrating, this job may not be for you:

Grandma and Grandpa live in Munich, Germany, and their daughter, son-in-law, and two grandchildren are traveling from Charlottesville, VA, to meet them. The children will then stay with their grandparents and take a trip to Italy with them while Mom and Dad enjoy a respite of their own.

Mom is flying into Munich on July 30 with her daughter, age 8. Dad and their son, 5, will leave Charlottesville on August 14 to meet them there. Mom and Dad plan to then head to France and fly back to Charlottesville from Paris on September 1st. Grandpa will bring the children back from Rome on September 20. Grandpa will need to go back to Munich on October 1st. What is the best price for all? Keep in mind that the kids will need to be with an adult at all times.

SELECTED SCHOOLS

It is not necessarily expected that reservation and ticket agents hold college degrees, but it is preferred in many cases. Many community colleges and four-year colleges and universities offer programs in business administration; a number of them also offer programs in hospitality management or related fields. Interested student are advised to consult with a school guidance counselor.

MORE INFORMATION

Airlines for America
1301 Pennsylvania Avenue NW
Suite 1100
Washington, DC 20004
202.626.4000
www.airlines.org

American Hotel and Lodging Association
1201 New York Avenue, NW
Suite 600
Washington, DC 20005-3931
202.289.3100
www.ahla.com

John Pritchard/Editor

Taxi Driver & Chauffeur

Snapshot

Career Cluster: Hospitality & Tourism, Transportation, Distribution & Logistics

Interests: Road Transportation, Urban Transportation, Hospitality

Earnings (Yearly Average): $25,140

Employment & Outlook: Faster Than Average Growth Expected

OVERVIEW

Sphere of Work

Taxi drivers and chauffeurs are members of the transportation industry. They provide an alternative form of transportation to buses and subways that tends to be more private, comfortable, and convenient, and offer another way of getting around without the need for a privately owned car. They may also take people sightseeing or on longer journeys. In addition, they sometimes pick up and deliver luggage or goods alone.

Work Environment

Taxi drivers and chauffeurs work in towns and cities throughout the world, where they typically navigate their way between airports, business districts, hotels, convention centers, restaurants, and private residences. A driver may rent his or her vehicle from a fleet company that serves a variety of customers.

A chauffeur may work for a single individual or company to whom he or she carries out many different requests. Most chauffeur assignments are pre-arranged and door-to-door, whereas the taxi driver tends to live for the moment, with each job that comes his or her way a new adventure. Chauffeurs and taxi drivers both work independently and without supervision, answering mostly to their customers rather than to bosses.

Profile

Working Conditions: Work Both Indoors And Outdoors
Physical Strength: Light To Medium Work
Education Needs: No High School Diploma, On-The-Job Training
Licensure/Certification: Required
Physical Abilities Not Required: No Heavy Labor
Opportunities For Experience: Part-Time Work
Holland Interest Score*: IRE, REC

* See Appendix A

Occupation Interest

Taxi drivers and chauffeurs must be excellent drivers, able to navigate streets during rush hour or poor weather conditions, and be intimately familiar with their cities. Punctuality, flexibility, and an overall sense of responsibility are other key qualifications. While these jobs tend to be portrayed as glamorous, some urban taxi drivers run a high risk of being robbed or assaulted. Drivers sometimes deal with unsavory situations, emergencies, and challenging personalities, although the opportunity to meet celebrities and other interesting people can be enticing.

A Day in the Life—Duties and Responsibilities

The chauffeur or taxi driver who rents his or her vehicle begins the day by picking up the cab or limo at the fleet's garage. The first stop is usually the fuel pump, where the driver makes sure the vehicle is in good working condition. The chauffeur then proceeds to the first assignment. During the course of the shift, a chauffeur's clients might include business travelers, performers, or a wedding party. The chauffeur continues from one assignment to another until the shift ends. A taxi driver may start the day with a pre-assigned fare, cruise through the business district looking for potential customers, or take a place in the designated taxi waiting area at the airport, train station, or other popular hub. A dispatcher can contact the driver at any time for a special pick-up. Customer destinations vary widely, from shopping and restaurants to medical centers to businesses and tourist attractions. Once the taxi driver determines where each fare is going, the driver sets the meter and informs the dispatcher of the intended journey.

Chauffeurs are commonly pre-paid, while the taxi driver collects money from each fare based in part on set fees. Both chauffeurs and taxi drivers depend on tips to round out their earnings. Drivers earn tips in part by the courtesy extended to the customers, which may include lifting luggage, assisting a physically handicapped customer, or stopping at a coffee shop upon request.

At the end of the shift, the driver fills out a log and prepares the car for the next day. Although there is no work to take home, many drivers spend time reading about the history of the city or keeping abreast of new restaurants and hotels.

Duties and Responsibilities

- Driving people from one place to another
- Transporting handicapped persons
- Assisting passengers in and out of the taxi
- Providing sightseeing tours
- Collecting fees
- Keeping a log book
- Reporting by radio or telephone to the taxi company dispatcher
- Handling luggage
- Picking up and delivering packages

OCCUPATION SPECIALTIES

Taxi Drivers

Taxi Drivers, or cabbies, generally use a meter to determine the fare when a passenger requests a destination. The most common ways for cabbies to provide their services are when a customer calls a central dispatcher to request a cab or the driver picks up a customer from a cabstand or in response to a curbside hail.

Chauffeurs

Chauffeurs take passengers on prearranged trips. They operate limousines, vans, or private cars.

Paratransit Drivers

Paratransit Drivers transport people with special needs, such as the elderly or those with disabilities. They operate specially equipped vehicles designed to help people with a variety of physical or other needs.

WORK ENVIRONMENT

Physical Environment

The taxi driver or chauffeur is confined to the car, except when taking breaks. Air-conditioning or heat, seats with good support, and a vehicle that is comfortable to maneuver can make the experience mostly pleasant. Sitting for long periods can cause muscular discomfort related to lack of exercise. City traffic and heavy exhaust fumes can also be detrimental to one's health, while breathing in the unpleasant odors present with some customers, such as heavy perfume or the stench of alcohol, can be another negative aspect of the work.

Relevant Skills and Abilities

Interpersonal/Social Skills
- Cooperating with others
- Working as a member of a team

Organization & Management Skills
- Following instructions
- Organizing information or materials
- Performing routine work

Work Environment Skills
- Driving a vehicle

Human Environment

For many drivers, contact with customers is the highlight of the job. Conversations may be initiated by either party and may evolve into in-depth discussions about current events or politics. Taxi drivers must be patient, sympathetic, and willing to repeat information about local events or weather several times a day. Drivers must also be comfortable taking directions from the dispatcher, interacting and often competing with other taxi drivers, and exercising tact and patience with other drivers, customers, and pedestrians.

Technological Environment

Drivers must be familiar with the basic mechanics of their vehicles, the taximeter, and communications equipment, such as two-way radios or cell phones. GPS devices, computers, calculators, credit card machines, and other small gadgets may be used as well.

EDUCATION, TRAINING, AND ADVANCEMENT

High School/Secondary

A high school diploma is not always required, although it is desirable. Most employers in the United States expect good English language skills, while knowledge of a second language can also be very useful. Basic math skills are needed to keep records and make change. Speech communications can give one confidence in relating with the public, and courses in geography will help with map-reading skills. Driver training and auto mechanics courses are vital.

Suggested High School Subjects
- Auto Shop
- Business Math
- Driver Training
- English
- First Aid Training

Famous First

The first electric taxicabs were introduced in New York City in 1897 by Samuel's Electric Carriage and Wagon Company. The firm operated twelve two-person buggies powered by battery. Within a year it was operating 62 vehicles under the name Electric Vehicle Company, and by 1899 it had 100 cars. Also in that year the first speeding ticket in the United States was issued—to a taxi driver. And later in the same year the first automobile fatality occurred, when one Henry Bliss was struck and killed by an electric taxicab.

Postsecondary

College courses in business, social sciences, communications, or foreign languages can be advantageous for drivers, especially those interested in starting their own companies. Regardless of one's educational level, most companies provide on-the-job training that lasts a week or two. A driver should then be ready to tackle the work independently.

Advancement is limited in most places. An experienced driver may be rewarded with the best routes, command a higher salary as a private chauffeur, choose to become a dispatcher, or start his or her own company.

Adult Job Seekers

There are few barriers for adults interested in beginning a new career as a taxi or limousine driver. Drivers can usually find positions that are full- or part-time, work customized hours, or work a shift that fits best with family responsibilities.

Professional Certification and Licensure

A driver's license is required. Some cities and states also require a special license for taxi drivers and chauffeurs, often referred to as a "hack" license. A commercial vehicle license may be needed for larger vans or shuttles. In addition to the license, many cities and states set minimum requirements for training and driving experience that may be measured by an examination. Drivers interested in owning their own companies or working independently may need an additional permit.

Additional Requirements

Some cities and states require a driver to be a United States citizen or legal resident. They might test the applicant's proficiency in English. A prospective driver must also be physically fit, as drivers often lift heavy luggage and need to see well. Some cities and states require a medical examination and drug testing prior to licensing.

EARNINGS AND ADVANCEMENT

Earnings depend on the geographic location of the employer, the number of hours worked, customers' tips and the driver's efforts to seek out customers. Taxi drivers and chauffeurs had mean annual earnings, including tips, of $25,140 in 2012. The lowest ten percent earned less than $17,050, and the highest ten percent earned more than $37,200.

Taxi drivers and chauffeurs usually do not receive fringe benefits given to workers of other occupations.

Metropolitan Areas with the Highest Employment Level in this Occupation

Metropolitan area	Employment[1]	Employment per thousand jobs	Hourly mean wage
New York-White Plains-Wayne, NY-NJ	10,810	2.10	$16.38
Las Vegas-Paradise, NV	10,420	12.73	$15.09
Chicago-Joliet-Naperville, IL	4,890	1.34	$13.14
Los Angeles-Long Beach-Glendale, CA	4,610	1.19	$11.55
Boston-Cambridge-Quincy, MA	3,910	2.29	$13.25
Houston-Sugar Land-Baytown, TX	3,550	1.35	$12.27
Philadelphia, PA	3,160	1.73	$11.93
Washington-Arlington-Alexandria, DC-VA-MD-WV	2,980	1.27	$14.93

[1]Does not include self-employed. Source: Bureau of Labor Statistics

Fun Fact

The literal meaning of the French word chauffeur is "stoker." How, then, did it come to have its current meaning of a professional paid driver? The earliest cars were steam-powered and operators of steam engines in France were known as stokers; soon that became a nickname for the country's first motorists. And the wealthy few who were able to afford the first cars typically hired someone to drive them.

EMPLOYMENT AND OUTLOOK

There were approximately 235,000 taxi drivers and chauffeurs employed nationally in 2012. Employment is expected to grow faster than the average for all occupations through the year 2022, which means employment is projected to increase 10 percent to 20 percent. This is due to local and suburban travel increasing as the population grows. Job opportunities may fluctuate from season to season and from month to month.

Employment Trend, Projected 2012–22

Taxi Drivers and Chauffeurs: 16%

Total, All Occupations: 11%

Motor Vehicle Operators: 9%

Note: "All Occupations" includes all occupations in the U.S. Economy. Source: U.S. Bureau of Labor Statistics, Employment Projections Program

Related Occupations
- Bus Driver

Conversation With . . .
CLAYTON DENNARD
Chauffeur, 7 years

1. What was your individual career path in terms of education/training, entry-level job, or other significant opportunity?

I was a Criminal Justice major in college and planning to go into law enforcement. During college, I worked in hospitality. I worked at resorts, hotels, restaurants. I waited tables. I got my degree and was about to go to work for the Charleston Police Department. I was doing an internship and ready to go to the police academy. I was working at a resort and saw a lack of reliable transportation. So I bought an SUV and a van and hired four guys to sit outside the resort, on Thursday, Friday and Saturday nights only. As people came out, they took them downtown, to the movies, to a restaurant. At first, we wore polo shirts and shorts and were glorified taxis. I went to a trade show in Vegas and saw there was an opportunity. We transitioned immediately to black suits and ties. We went from a few guys to having a reservation staff and reservations software.

2. What are the most important skills and/or qualities for someone in your profession?

You have to really enjoy being around people. You have to like to please other people. That's a very hospitality mindset. I hire chauffeurs that are well spoken. But you also have to known when not to respond. We're supposed to be in the background. We train in discretion. We take husbands and wives out on Friday nights and husbands and girlfriends out on Saturday nights. But the drivers are paid to drive, not to be a minister, not to be a counselor.

3. What do you wish you had known going into this profession?

I spend a lot of money on my accountants and lawyers. If I had taken some Business 101 classes, that would have been very helpful.

4. Are there many job opportunities in your profession? In what specific areas?

I think there's an opportunity for young people who are well-educated. I have to be honest with you, I go to these trade shows and there are some dummies out there. I'm 33; most of the owners are twice my age. There are a lot of opportunities with large limousine companies: LimoLink, Boston Coach–those are nationwide. They have people in reservations, drivers, trade show people. There are jobs in the big markets, the New Yorks, the LAs, the Bostons. This is a second job for a lot of people. I have retirees, policemen, firefighters working for me. There are a lot of one- and two-car operators in my town trying to get by.

5. How do you see your profession changing in the next five years? What role will technology play in those changes, and what skills will be required?

If I were a young kid in college, I would be working on smart phone apps, making reservations easier. Uber (an app that connects passengers with drivers for hire or shared rides) is backed by Google, which basically gave them a blank check to do development. The tech savvy kid can say, "Hey, I've got a platform to revolutionize your reservations system and allow you compete with Uber."

6. What do you enjoy most about your job? What do you enjoy least?

I enjoy being a part of a family's life events. Weddings are cool. I also enjoy being part of big things like Presidential debates. I enjoy being part of big things like Super Bowls.

What I enjoy least is cleaning up the cars. It can be vomit, or it can be pink boa feathers after a bachelorette party, or sand off their feet from a beach wedding. It can be food that they snuck in and got peanut butter all over the seat. It could be red wine. I feel bad for my shop vac. The other thing is holding people to their contract. People overspend on their wedding, the dress, the cake, and then want to cut back on transportation. Or someone's out for the night and they extend past their contracted time. Everything's fine Friday night, but then they see their bill Monday morning.

7. Can you suggest a valuable "try this" for students considering a career in your profession?

Go work for a major chauffeur operation for the summer. I have two interns that work for me now that get college credits. They answer phones, work as greeters at the airport, do trade shows. You have to be 25 to drive for insurance purposes, so they can't drive.

Those summer jobs are so valuable. I took my experience waiting tables and my law enforcement knowledge from college and combined them. I have law enforcement contracts, driving celebrities, politicians to the Democratic National conventions, debates.

SELECTED SCHOOLS

It is not expected that taxi drivers and chauffeurs receive training beyond high school; indeed, a high school diploma itself is not required in many cases. For individuals seeking to operate their own companies, however, a degree in business from a community college or a four-year university is likely to prove beneficial.

MORE INFORMATION

National Limousine Association
49 S. Maple Avenue
Marlton, NJ 08053
800.652.7007
www.limo.org

Taxicab, Limousine and Paratransit Association
3200 Tower Oaks Boulevard
Suite 220
Rockville, MD 20852
301.984.5700
www.tlpa.org

Sally Driscoll/Editor

Travel Agent

Snapshot

Career Cluster: Hospitality & Tourism
Interests: Travel, event planning, tourism
Earnings (Yearly Average): $36,970
Employment & Outlook: Decline Expected

OVERVIEW

Sphere of Work

Travel agents strive to provide customers with pleasant, hassle-free vacations and business trips that meet those customers' expectations. They specialize in the scheduling and preparation of travel arrangements, lodging, activities, and other travel-related services for individual clients and larger travel and tour groups. Travel agents evaluate and organize a large amount of print and web-based information and then select the most suitable travel options for their clients, often obtaining an additional discount for them. Travel agents recommend destinations, hotels, and tourist events to customers based on their interests, budget constraints, and locations. In some cases, resorts

and travel groups compensate travel agents for endorsing their companies by promoting specific vacation packages to customers.

Work Environment

Travel agents typically work in clean, comfortable, and well-lit offices. Self-employed travel agents often work out of home offices. Most work alone or among a small staff of employees consisting of administrative personnel or other travel agents. It is customary for travel agents to work at least forty hours per week; however, many work overtime, especially during peak travel seasons like holidays and school vacations. They spend most of their time behind a desk, coordinating and negotiating with airlines, cruise lines, hotels, and tourism companies via phone and Internet. They frequently meet and interact with customers to fulfill their requests and offer travel advice.

Profile

Working Conditions: Work Indoors
Physical Strength: Light Work
Education Needs: Technical/
  Community College, Bachelor's Degree
Licensure/Certification: Required
Physical Abilities Not Required: No
  Heavy Labor
Opportunities For Experience:
  Military Service, Part-Time Work
Holland Interest Score*: ECS

* See Appendix A

Occupation Interest

The travel industry is often demanding and challenging. Successful transactions frequently rely on speed, effective communication, and in-depth knowledge of national and international destinations. Prospective travel agents must be willing to operate in a fast-paced, stressful environment and should thrive under pressure. They should enjoy working with people, even when this becomes a challenge. Since people tend to hold idealized views of vacation trips, customer expectations are often difficult to fulfill. When unforeseen events occur, travel agents are sometimes blamed for a customer's poor travel experiences. Travel agents must be detail-oriented and take pride in the successful coordination and planning of events.

A Day in the Life—Duties and Responsibilities

Travel agents spend most of the workday at a desk, on the phone, and on the computer. Travel agents act as the liaison between customers and travel companies. They are responsible for calculating travel costs and making air, cruise, hotel, and rental car reservations. They also process special financial transactions for customers. Travel agents are in constant communication with vendors and clients to arrange travel and vacation packages to suit the needs of the particular customer. They consult with travelers about desired destinations, availability, budget restrictions, and any special requirements they might have. Travel agents also provide customers with information regarding national and international regulations, including travel advisories, money exchange rates, and required documentation like passports and visas. For long-term or high-profile clients, some travel agents make themselves available on an "on-call" basis to deal with any travel-related issues that arise during a client's trip. Travel agents must handle any problems related to itineraries they have booked.

Travel agents research and obtain flight information and locate high quality destination attractions, tourist exhibitions, and special deals, like group rates and discounts. Sometimes they travel to specific destinations to research the quality of a travel experience themselves, which further bolsters their credibility with clients. Many travel agents specialize in a specific geographic area or region, demographic group, or cultural preference. Specialization is increasingly advantageous due to the competitive nature of the profession and relatively slow job growth.

Duties and Responsibilities

- Arranging travel and lodging for clients
- Making airline, steamship, or rail reservations
- Booking hotel rooms, car rentals, and tours
- Collecting payment for tickets and tour packages
- Promoting, advertising and selling travel services
- Advising on travel destinations and weather conditions
- Informing clients on customs, regulations, passports, medical certificates, and currency exchange rates
- Using websites and software for optimum fares and schedules
- Visiting hotels and travel attractions for evaluations

OCCUPATION SPECIALTIES

Concierges

Concierges assist hotel guests with local restaurant reservations, transportation services (taxis, shuttles, limousines), and recommendations for local attractions and nightlife hot spots.

Automotive Club Travel Counselors

Automotive Club Travel Counselors plan trips for members, providing maps and brochures.

Reservation Clerks

Reservation Clerks make travel and hotel accommodations for guests and employees of businesses.

WORK ENVIRONMENT

Physical Environment

Most travel agents work under minimal supervision, from a small, comfortable office or out of their own homes. They sit for long periods and must communicate regularly with clients and vendors.

Human Environment

Travel agents constantly communicate with clients and customer service personnel over the phone, in person, and through e-mail. They often deal with difficult and impatient people and must maintain an outwardly pleasant attitude and an accommodating demeanor at all times. In larger offices, travel agents interact with other office personnel.

Relevant Skills and Abilities

Communication Skills
- Persuading others
- Speaking effectively

Interpersonal/Social Skills
- Being able to work independently and as a member of a team
- Cooperating with others

Organization & Management Skills
- Paying attention to and handling details
- Selling ideas or products

Technical Skills
- Using technology to process information
- Working with data or numbers

Work Environment Skills
- Traveling

Technological Environment

Travel agents use basic office equipment to help them complete their daily tasks. They routinely use phones, fax machines, calculators, computers and software, and the Internet and e-mail. They should also be highly proficient at reading and understanding maps, travel schedules, itineraries, and other related documents.

EDUCATION, TRAINING, AND ADVANCEMENT

High School/Secondary

High school students who wish to become travel agents should enroll in academic courses that emphasize business, communications, geography, foreign languages, world history, and social studies. Students should also participate in extracurricular clubs and student groups that focus on travel and tourism. It is also helpful for students to travel as much as possible, even to local or regional attractions, in order to develop a sense of how to evaluate and critique locations and exhibitions. Students can gain valuable research experience by investigating online travel sources, deals, itineraries, and popular tourist attractions across the globe.

Suggested High School Subjects
- Applied Communication
- Bookkeeping
- Business & Computer Technology
- Business Math
- College Preparatory
- Computer Science
- English
- Foreign Languages
- Geography
- History
- Social Studies
- Speech

Famous First

The first travelers checks were issued in 1891 by the American Express Company. The checks made it possible for American travelers in Europe to obtain cash—and, later, goods and services—in places where a written letter of credit from a banker was not accepted. The checks were available in $10, $20, $50, and $100 denominations. Over the past few decades travelers checks have declined in use as credit cards and automated teller machines have become more readily available.

Postsecondary

After graduating from high school, most prospective travel agents find it helpful to enroll in full- or part-time travel agent programs. Many vocational schools, public adult education programs, local community colleges, and distance learning programs offer courses in travel and tourism that provide students with a solid understanding of sales and marketing, ticketing and reservations, tour planning and development, and world geography. A small number of colleges and universities offer bachelor's and master's degrees in the travel industry.

Related College Majors
- Hospitality Management

- Tourism & Travel Services
- Travel-Tourism Management

Adult Job Seekers

Though a postsecondary degree is not considered a requirement for prospective travel agents, many employers give hiring preference to those jobseekers with demonstrated experience in the field of travel and tourism. In addition, those who have personal travel experience and proven knowledge of a specific geographic region or foreign country are likely to have an easier time finding employment. Prospective travel agents can participate in mentorships with local travel agencies. Some travel agents begin their careers as reservation clerks or agent assistants with local travel agencies.

Professional Certification and Licensure

Experienced travel agents who have worked in larger offices and wish to start their own businesses must be formally approved by companies in the travel industry. This type of accreditation ensures that a travel agent is reliable and will be prompt with payments and other transactions. Approving entities can include airlines (like the Airlines Reporting Corporation and the International Airlines Travel Agency Network), cruise lines, and railways. In order to receive approval, a travel agent's business must be financially viable and successful and must employ at least one experienced manager or travel agent.

Additional Requirements

Travel agents are responsible for providing pleasant, uncomplicated travel experiences for their customers. As more and more travel information becomes available via online sources, agents must continually add to their existing knowledge of cultures, destinations, lodging, procedures, government regulations, and attractions. They must possess impeccable research and computer skills, and they must also be able to effectively relay updated and new information to clients as it becomes available.

EARNINGS AND ADVANCEMENT

Earnings of travel agents depend on the size and geographic location of the travel agency and the individual's experience and sales ability. Travel agents starting their own agencies need the approval of organizations of air, ship and rail lines before they can receive commissions on sales. Earnings of travel agents who own their own agencies depend mainly on commissions from service fees that they charge clients.

Travel agents had mean annual earnings of $36,970 in 2012. The lowest ten percent earned less than $19,930, and the highest ten percent earned more than $57,400.

Travel agents usually receive paid vacations, holidays, and sick days; life and health insurance; and retirement benefits. These are usually paid by the employer. Self-employed agents must provide these benefits for themselves. Discounts on travel fares are also available for travel agents.

Metropolitan Areas with the Highest
Employment Level in this Occupation

Metropolitan area	Employment[1]	Employment per thousand jobs	Hourly mean wage
New York-White Plains-Wayne, NY-NJ	4,300	0.83	$18.51
Chicago-Joliet-Naperville, IL	4,180	1.15	$18.67
Los Angeles-Long Beach-Glendale, CA	3,220	0.83	$17.66
Dallas-Plano-Irving, TX	1,620	0.77	$20.40
Miami-Miami Beach-Kendall, FL	1,620	1.62	$19.71
Washington-Arlington-Alexandria, DC-VA-MD-WV	1,350	0.58	$21.64
Houston-Sugar Land-Baytown, TX	1,310	0.50	$20.03
Boston-Cambridge-Quincy, MA	1,250	0.73	$22.95

[1]Does not include self-employed. Source: Bureau of Labor Statistics

Fun Fact

According to a 2014 study by the American Society of Travel Agents, 59 percent of millennial, 53 percent of Generation X, and 58 percent of Baby Boomer leisure travelers who used travel agents believed that vacations planned with travel agents were better than those organized without their assistance. The *Value of Travel Agents study* was sponsored by Carnival Cruise Lines.

EMPLOYMENT AND OUTLOOK

There were about 73,000 travel agents employed nationally in 2012. Employment of travel agents is expected to decline through the year 2022, which means employment is projected to drop between 10 percent and 15 percent. The ability of passengers to make airline, train, hotel, and car reservations online is reducing the need for workers in this field. Most openings will occur as experienced travel agents transfer to other occupations or retire.

Employment Trend, Projected 2012–22

Total, All Occupations: 11%

Sales and Related Occupations: 7%

Travel Agents: 12%

Note: "All Occupations" includes all occupations in the U.S. Economy. Source: U.S. Bureau of Labor Statistics, Employment Projections Program

Related Occupations
- Reservation and Ticket Agent

Related Military Occupations
- Transportation Specialist

Conversation With . . .
BECKY TREAKLE
Travel Consultant
17 years in the industry

1. What was your individual career path in terms of education/training, entry-level job, or other significant opportunity?

The old adage says, 'who you know is as important as what you know." I loved to travel and was well-traveled, but my 'in' into the industry was knowing someone who owned a travel agency. I had been in retail sales in management positions and had taken time off to stay home with my kids. When I was ready to go back to work, I broached the subject with my acquaintance, who had been booking my travel. I said: "You know how much I travel; what would it take to work for you?"

My experience in sales was key to getting the job. Our industry is about sales and customer service first and foremost and most travel and hospitality jobs are exactly that: servicing the customer. My training has been first-hand. However, I strongly suggest basic travel agency training at your local community college. Airport codes, tourist areas, visa and passport information are the kinds of basic skills you need. Most people I know do a certificate-type program, or you can align yourself with a travel agency that does classes -- and there are good ones out there.

2. What are the most important skills and/or qualities for someone in your profession?

As I mentioned, having a knack for selling is a big plus. You need to listen to exactly what the client wants or needs. Internet reviews mean consumers come to you more educated than they used to. Putting your experience with different locations or resorts with what the client wants is key. Organization is another plus. And of course it is a must to go, do, and see the destinations. If you do not like to travel this is not for you.

3. What do you wish you had known going into this profession?

Networking is a huge part of what we do. Referrals are how we gather most of our business. You must learn to talk to people and go to networking events to meet new prospects. In addition, basic computer skills from Word to Excel to Powerpoint are a must.

4. **Are there many job opportunities in your profession? In what specific areas?**

Our profession has changed immensely over the last decade and if you are will to go with the changes then yes, there are many opportunities. Niche travel such as destination weddings and honeymoons are growing rapidly. People get married; it's recession-proof. We have already done the footwork: we have vetted the wedding coordinators on property so you know they will return phone calls, we know if they speak English, we know the legalities for you to go to this location and get married in a foreign country so there are no surprises on your big day. Find a niche that you are passionate about: wine, food, sports. I love football, and every ten years I lead a trip to Dublin, Ireland for the Navy-Notre Dame football game there.

5. **How do you see your profession changing in the next five years? What role will technology play in those changes, and what skills will be required?**

Technology will continue to change how we do business and how knowledgeable the consumer is about a destination or a resort. Being tech savvy is important, but going to the locations and seeing first-hand always is better than online reviews. There are a number of ways to do this. For instance, I have contacted Cancun Tourism and said, "Hey, I am coming on my own dime. Can you hook me up with some of your resort properties so I can stay there?" Some companies, countries, and resorts will have certifications – almost always online – and you have travel to finish training on the property. They treat us well, we treat them well, they treat our clients well, and we keep sending clients. But, bottom line: they can wine and dine me until the cows come home but if I don't feel my clients are getting good service or bang for their buck, I will not send them back.

6. **What do you enjoy most about your job? What do you enjoy least?**

Helping plan the perfect trip for someone who has worked hard to earn the money and the time off to go away and, of course, traveling myself.

I don't like the lack of respect given to our industry. We are not viewed as professionals, but more as order-takers. The fault does lie partially on the travel agent community which must view itself as professionals, and to expect this from other industries and peers. Our pay is not to scale for the hours we work or the training we chose to undertake to increase our knowledge.

7. **Can you suggest a valuable "try this" for students considering a career in your profession?**

Internships are great! We offer them, encourage them and even advertise at the local community college. Travel industry shows are another suggestion. Call or stop into a local travel agency. I am sure they will be more then willing to tell you all about what they do.

SELECTED SCHOOLS

Many community colleges and four-year colleges and universities offer programs in business/retail services; a number of them also offer programs in hospitality management, tourism/travel, and related fields. A variety of online travel agent schools are also available. Interested student are advised to consult with a school guidance counselor.

MORE INFORMATION

Airlines Reporting Corporation
3000 Wilson Boulevard
Suite 300
Arlington, VA 22201-3862
703.816.8000
www.arccorp.com

American Society of Travel Agents
1101 King Street
Suite 200
Alexandria, VA 22314
703.739.2782
www.asta.org

International Airlines Travel Agency Network
703 Waterford Way
Suite 600
Miami, FL 33126
877.734.2826
www.iatan.org

National Association of Career Travel Agents
1101 King Street
Suite 200
Alexandria, VA 22314
877.226.2282
www.nacta.com

The Travel Institute
148 Linden Street
Suite 305
Wellesley, MA 02482
800.542.4282
www.thetravelinstitute.com

Briana Nadeau/Editor

Waiter/Waitress

Snapshot

Career Cluster: Hospitality & Tourism

Interests: Restaurant business, hospitality industry, food service, customer service

Earnings (Yearly Average): $20,710

Employment & Outlook: Average Growth Expected

OVERVIEW

Sphere of Work

Waiters and waitresses, also commonly known as servers, are members of the service industry who attend to customers, serve food and beverages, and process payments. Waiters and waitresses are responsible for providing patrons with a pleasant dining experience and for accommodating their needs and requests. They prepare and clean tables before, during, and after service, take customer orders, and may perform additional tasks as required by the establishments where they work.

Work Environment

Waiters and waitresses work in a variety of locations, from small diners and coffee shops to hotel and cruise ship dining rooms to large restaurants and fine dining establishments. They usually work indoors (or outdoors on a patio or deck) in clean, pleasant environments; however, some establishments can be noisy, hot, and crowded. Full-time, part-time, and seasonal employment opportunities are available. Servers may be required to work split shifts or evenings, weekends, and holidays. They usually wear a uniform and are supervised by managers, owners, or head waitstaff. They frequently bend, reach, lift, and carry food. Restaurants can be busy during rush periods and highly stressful for the waitstaff.

Profile

Working Conditions: Work Indoors
Physical Strength: Light to Medium Work
Education Needs: No High School Diploma, On-The-Job Training, High School Diploma Or GED
Licensure/Certification: Usually Not Required
Physical Abilities Not Required: No Heavy Labor
Opportunities For Experience: Apprenticeship, Part-Time Work
Holland Interest Score*: CES

* See Appendix A

Occupation Interest

Individuals looking to become waiters or waitresses must be energetic, physically fit, and possess endurance. The job can be physically demanding, and waiters and waitresses should be accustomed to standing, walking, and carrying heavy objects. In addition, they must have impeccable social skills and an outgoing personality, as excellent customer service can lead to higher earnings and repeat customers. Servers must also work well under pressure and handle difficult customers with patience and respect.

A Day in the Life—Duties and Responsibilities

Waiters and waitresses spend most of their time serving and attending to customers. They greet restaurant patrons, distribute food and beverage menus, memorize and communicate menu item details and daily or weekly specials, and offer suggestions about food and beverages. Servers must ensure compliance with laws about alcohol consumption and help prevent allergic reactions. They take customer orders, bring orders to the kitchen or bar for preparation, and deliver food items and drinks to customers. Waiters and waitresses are often responsible for preparing fountain and alcoholic drinks, as well as appetizers, salads, and simple sandwiches. After a meal, waiters and waitresses must correctly total item prices, including tax, and present the final bill to customers. After customers leave, waiters and waitresses prepare for the next patrons by cleaning and tidying surfaces and delivering fresh water and new place settings to the table. They also usually refill and organize condiments, including salt and pepper, ketchup, sugar, and cream.

In fine dining establishments, waiters and waitresses often fulfill a more informative role, suggesting appropriate wine pairings and describing the composition and preparation of menu items. They may also assemble salads, prepare meats, and flambé desserts at tableside.

In many restaurants, owners or managers provide their waitstaff with one or two meals (depending on the shift length) before or after their shift. At the end of a shift, waiters and waitresses commonly tally and divide their tips among restaurant employees who have contributed to the service, including bartenders and bus staff.

Duties and Responsibilities

- Presenting menus and taking customer orders
- Suggesting dinner courses and informing customers of specials of the day
- Explaining preparation of items on the menu
- Serving courses from kitchen and service bars
- Preparing beverages, fountain drinks, salads and sandwiches
- Filling salt, pepper, sugar, cream, condiment and napkin containers
- Clearing tables or counters of dirty dishes
- Cleaning table tops

WORK ENVIRONMENT

Physical Environment

Waiters and waitresses work in a dining room or outdoor section of a small or large dining establishment. They take food from the kitchen, which can be hot and noisy, to the dining room, which is normally cool, quiet, and clean. They risk slipping, falling, colliding with doors or other people, and receiving cuts and burns.

Human Environment

Waiters and waitresses spend the majority of their day working with other wait staff, restaurant managers and owners, bartenders, chefs and line cooks, hosts and hostesses, bus staff, and restaurant patrons.

Relevant Skills and Abilities

Communication Skills
- Expressing thoughts and ideas
- Speaking effectively

Interpersonal/Social Skills
- Being able to remain calm
- Cooperating with others
- Working as a member of a team

Organization & Management Skills
- Handling challenging situations
- Paying attention to and handling details
- Performing routine work

Technological Environment

Waiters and waitresses use a number of tools and devices to aid them in their daily activities. They constantly handle order slips, serving trays, tableware and cutlery, pens and pencils, and bills and receipts. In many restaurants, waiters and waitresses must learn how to use electronic ordering machines, food preparation machines, cash registers, and computers.

EDUCATION, TRAINING, AND ADVANCEMENT

High School/Secondary

High school students looking to become waiters and waitresses should study courses related to travel and tourism, food and nutrition, communications, economics, English, and basic mathematics. In specialty restaurants, it is often helpful for waiters and waitresses to have some familiarity with a foreign language. Students should practice memorizing scripts and text and recite them in front of friends or family members. They should also begin to recognize different methods of food preparation and start to develop an educated palate. They can visit local restaurants, diners, or coffee shops to see how those businesses operate and to observe the wait staff in action.

Suggested High School Subjects
- Business Math
- English
- Family & Consumer Sciences
- Food Service & Management
- Mathematics

Famous First

The first sociological study of the world of waitressing was James P. Spradley's *The Cocktail Waitress: Woman's Work in a Man's World*, published in 1975. Since then a few of other studies have come out, along with a number of autobiographies by professional waitresses. Crime and mystery novels involving waitresses have a somewhat longer pedigree.

College/Postsecondary

An undergraduate degree is not necessary for people looking to become waiters or waitresses; however, formal training in hospitality and food service can strengthen a candidate's credentials and increase their opportunities for employment and promotion. Many vocational education programs teach students the fundamentals of working in and managing a restaurant or other food establishment. They learn about the selection, purchasing, storage, preparation, and serving of food items. They also train in nutrition, travel and tourism, home economics, safety, sanitation, and food preparation equipment.

Adult Job Seekers

Many prospective waiters and waitresses begin as bus staff at a restaurant or dining establishment. Others begin by seeking part-time or seasonal employment with restaurants in heavy tourist or resort areas. Vocational programs or unions may help with job placement. Through entry-level positions, prospective servers can learn the service industry and become familiar with restaurant operations. They also get to know other members of the wait staff, which can eventually ease their transition from entry-level workers to full-time waiters or waitresses. Experienced waiters and waitresses may move into host or hostess roles, find employment in specialized settings, or advance to supervisory positions.

Professional Certification and Licensure

Dining establishments that serve alcohol require waiters and waitresses to be at least eighteen or twenty-one years old, depending on the state. In some states, waiters and waitresses must successfully pass a food-handling exam. Those interested in bartending in addition to their serving duties usually need to pass a separate bartending exam to earn a bartending license, in accordance with state regulations.

Additional Requirements

Waiters and waitresses must have aptitude for arithmetic and problem solving, as well as an excellent memory, as they juggle simultaneous customer requests and demands. They must be able to think on their feet and make decisions quickly and effectively. Employers consistently look to hire waiters and waitresses who are warm, engaging, and reliable. Because waiters and waitresses rely heavily on tips as a large part of their income, it is in their best interest to treat all customers with respect and consideration.

EARNINGS AND ADVANCEMENT

Earnings depend on the type, geographic location, and customers of the restaurant, and the employee's skill and personality. For most waiters and waitresses, higher earnings are usually the result of receiving more in tips rather than higher hourly wages. Tips generally average between ten and twenty percent of the guests' checks, so those working in busy restaurants tend to earn the most. Waiters and waitresses had mean annual earnings, including tips, of $20,710 in 2012. The lowest ten percent earned less than $16,210, and the highest ten percent earned more than $29,510.

Waiters and waitresses may receive paid vacations, holidays, and sick days; life and health insurance; and retirement benefits. These are usually paid by the employer. Free or reduced-charge meals may also be available.

Metropolitan Areas with the Highest Employment Level in this Occupation (Recreation Workers)

Metropolitan area	Employment	Employment per thousand jobs	Hourly mean wage
New York-White Plains-Wayne, NY-NJ	76,400	14.81	$11.76
Los Angeles-Long Beach-Glendale, CA	64,290	16.61	$10.40
Chicago-Joliet-Naperville, IL	49,830	13.69	$10.72
Houston-Sugar Land-Baytown, TX	46,660	17.67	$9.72
Atlanta-Sandy Springs-Marietta, GA	44,190	19.54	$9.41
Washington-Arlington-Alexandria, DC-VA-MD-WV	37,870	16.16	$11.67
Dallas-Plano-Irving, TX	37,290	17.78	$10.11
Phoenix-Mesa-Glendale, AZ	32,960	19.05	$9.98

Source: Bureau of Labor Statistics

Fun Fact

Menus on tablet computers was reported as the top trend in dinning for 2014, according to the National Restaurant Association's "What's Hot" culinary forecast.

EMPLOYMENT AND OUTLOOK

There were approximately 2.4 million waiters and waitresses employed nationally in 2012. Employment is expected to grow slower than the average for all occupations through the year 2022, which means employment is projected to increase 3 percent to 9 percent. This slower growth is due to the popularity of take-out food and self-service or carryout options in restaurants that do not require waiters and waitresses. However, these workers will continue to be needed as the population expands and people enjoy eating out at restaurants. Many job openings will occur as workers in this occupation change jobs frequently.

Employment Trend, Projected 2012–22

Total, All Occupations: 11%

Food Service Occupations: 9%

Waiters and Waitresses: 6%

Note: "All Occupations" includes all occupations in the U.S. Economy. Source: U.S. Bureau of Labor Statistics, Employment Projections Program

Related Occupations
- Bartender
- Flight Attendant
- Food Service Manager

Conversation With . . .
PATTI YOUNG
Waitress, 23 years

1. What was your individual career path in terms of education/training, entry-level job, or other significant opportunity?

I did not have any sort of career path in mind when I began this job. I had been working for Raytheon [Company] for many years and had just been laid off. Having never taken more than a couple classes at a college, I decided to give waitressing a shot.

2. What are the most important skills and/or qualities for someone in your profession?

Everyday life as a waitress is extremely tedious work. You must possess high people skills. It is very difficult at times to work so closely with the public. You come in contact with so many various personalities. Some guests are very easygoing where others are a bit more impatient. You try to make sure to smile at all times and treat each guest

to the best of your ability.

3. What do you wish you had known going into this profession?

I came into this profession as a server totally blind. I wasn't even sure I could do it. It isn't an easy job. Funny thing is, I wish I knew how well you could do moneywise before I began because once you start making great tips, you rely on this money every day and you don't want to change jobs and actually have to wait for a paycheck!

4. Are there many job opportunities in your profession? In what specific areas?

There are millions of job opportunities in the server fields. Everyone needs to eat. People enjoy going out to eat and to be waited on once in awhile after working all day or just to enjoy some down time with family and friends. There is also always room for advancement if you decide to further yourself and get into the management aspect of a restaurant.

5. How do you see your profession changing in the next five years? What role will technology play in those changes, and what skills will be required?

It is quite a scary thought to think about how being a waitress could change quite soon. I believe that eventually we won't exist anymore. I have actually been to restaurants where you can order at the table using a small computer. It is fun and easy but so impersonal. I love interacting with my customers, meeting their children, hearing funny stories. I have many regular customers and they enjoy chatting with me as well. I

hope that in the future, it's not the case that everyone orders off a computer with no contact from a human being.

6. What do you enjoy most about your job? What do you enjoy least?

I enjoy my customers the most. I have people who come in and ask for me to be their server because they enjoy my company and appreciate the attention and good service I offer them. I take pride in my work. It makes me happy when I make people happy. There are bad sides to every profession and I think the worst thing about my job is unhappy customers. Sometimes no matter what you do, bend over backwards, they still are not satisfied. This is very frustrating. Of course the number one worst part of the job is when we're not tipped. We work for a very small wage per hour and try to do our best to earn a tip. Tips are our lifeline.

7. Can you suggest a valuable "try this" for students considering a career in your profession?

The only thing I can offer anyone who is thinking about becoming a server is to realize that you need to have a level head. You can't show anger and you have to be able to deal with many situations. The customer is always right and that is very difficult for some people to grasp. You can't argue with the guest so you need to have a very easygoing personality. Friendliness is a must! I assume most people looking for a job in my field will probably be doing it as a stepping stone before heading into a different career. I had no intentions of always being a server but after 23 years in one place I have grown to know it so well that I probably will never leave.

SELECTED SCHOOLS

It is not necessarily expected that waiters and waitresses receive training beyond high school; indeed, a high school diploma itself is not a requirement in many cases. For individuals seeking to operate their own restaurants, however, a degree in food service or hospitality management from a community college or four-year university is likely to prove beneficial.

MORE INFORMATION

Culinary Workers Union
Local 226
1630 S. Commerce Street
Las Vegas, NV 89102
702.385.2131
www.culinaryunion226.org

National Restaurant Association
Educational Foundation
175 W. Jackson Boulevard
Suite 1500
Chicago, IL 60604-2814
800.765.2122
www.nraef.org

Simone Isadora Flynn/Editor

What Are Your Career Interests?

This is based on Dr. John Holland's theory that people and work environments can be loosely classified into six different groups. Each of the letters above corresponds to one of the six groups described in the following pages.

Different people's personalities may find different environments more to their liking. While you may have some interests in and similarities to several of the six groups, you may be attracted primarily to two or three of the areas. These two or three letters are your "Holland Code." For example, with a code of "RES" you would most resemble the Realistic type, somewhat less resemble the Enterprising type, and resemble the Social type even less. The types that are not in your code are the types you resemble least of all.

Most people, and most jobs, are best represented by some combination of two or three of the Holland interest areas. In addition, most people are most satisfied if there is some degree of fit between their personality and their work environment.

The rest of the pages in this booklet further explain each type and provide some examples of career possibilities, areas of study at MU, and co-curricular activities for each code. To take a more in-depth look at your Holland Code, take a self-assessment such as the SDS, Discover, or a card sort at the MU Career Center with a Career Specialist.

Realistic *(Doers)*

People who have athletic ability, prefer to work with objects, machines, tools, plants or animals, or to be outdoors.

Are you?		Can you?	Like to?
practical	independent	fix electrical things	tinker with machines/vehicles
straightforward/frank	ambitious	solve electrical problems	work outdoors
mechanically inclined	systematic	pitch a tent	be physically active
stable		play a sport	use your hands
concrete		read a blueprint	build things
reserved		plant a garden	tend/train animals
self-controlled		operate tools and machine	work on electronic equipment

**Career Possibilities
(Holland Code):**

Air Traffic Controller (SER)	Dental Technician (REI)	Laboratory Technician (RIE)	Property Manager (ESR)
Archaeologist (IRE)	Farm Manager (ESR)	Landscape Architect (AIR)	Recreation Manager (SER)
Athletic Trainer (SRE)	Fish and Game Warden (RES)	Mechanical Engineer (RIS)	Service Manager (ERS)
Cartographer (IRE)	Floral Designer (RAE)	Optician (REI)	Software Technician (RCI)
Commercial Airline Pilot (RIE)	Forester (RIS)	Petroleum Geologist (RIE)	Ultrasound Technologist (RSI)
Commercial Drafter (IRE)	Geodetic Surveyor (IRE)	Police Officer (SER)	Vocational Rehabilitation
Corrections Officer (SER)	Industrial Arts Teacher (IER)	Practical Nurse (SER)	Consultant (ESR)

Investigative *(Thinkers)*

People who like to observe, learn, investigate, analyze, evaluate, or solve problems.

Are you?		Can you?	Like to?
inquisitive	intellectually self-confident	think abstractly	explore a variety of ideas
analytical	Independent	solve math problems	work independently
scientific	logical	understand scientific theories	perform lab experiments
observant/precise	complex	do complex calculations	deal with abstractions
scholarly	Curious	use a microscope or computer	do research
cautious		interpret formulas	be challenged

**Career Possibilities
(Holland Code):**

Actuary (ISE)	Chemical Engineer (IRE)	Geologist (IRE)	Physician, General Practice (ISE)
Agronomist (IRS)	Chemist (IRE)	Horticulturist (IRS)	Psychologist (IES)
Anesthesiologist (IRS)	Computer Systems Analyst (IER)	Mathematician (IER)	Research Analyst (IRC)
Anthropologist (IRE)	Dentist (ISR)	Medical Technologist (ISA)	Statistician (IRE)
Archaeologist (IRE)	Ecologist (IRE)	Meteorologist (IRS)	Surgeon (IRA)
Biochemist (IRS)	Economist (IAS)	Nurse Practitioner (ISA)	Technical Writer (IRS)
Biologist (ISR)	Electrical Engineer (IRE)	Pharmacist (IES)	Veterinarian (IRS)

Artistic *(Creators)*

People who have artistic, innovating, or intuitional abilities and like to work in unstructured situations using their imagination and creativity.

Are you?		Can you?	Like to?
creative	original	sketch, draw, paint	attend concerts, theatre, art
imaginative	introspective	play a musical instrument	exhibits
innovative	impulsive	write stories, poetry, music	read fiction, plays, and poetry
unconventional	sensitive	sing, act, dance	work on crafts
emotional	courageous	design fashions or interiors	take photography
independent	complicated		express yourself creatively
Expressive	idealistic		deal with ambiguous ideas
	nonconforming		

Career Possibilities
(Holland Code):

Actor (AES)	Copy Writer (ASI)	Interior Designer (AES)	Medical Illustrator (AIE)
Advertising Art Director (AES)	Dance Instructor (AER)	Intelligence Research Specialist	Museum Curator (AES)
Advertising Manager (ASE)	Drama Coach (ASE)	(AEI)	Music Teacher (ASI)
Architect (AIR)	English Teacher (ASE)	Journalist/Reporter (ASE)	Photographer (AES)
Art Teacher (ASE)	Entertainer/Performer (AES)	Landscape Architect (AIR)	Writer (ASI)
Artist (ASI)	Fashion Illustrator (ASR)	Librarian (SAI)	Graphic Designer (AES)

Social *(Helpers)*

People who like to work with people to enlighten, inform, help, train, or cure them, or are skilled with words.

Are you?		Can you?	Like to?
friendly	cooperative	teach/train others	work in groups
helpful	generous	express yourself clearly	help people with problems
idealistic	responsible	lead a group discussion	do volunteer work
insightful	forgiving	mediate disputes	work with young people
outgoing	patient	plan and supervise an activity	serve others
understanding	kind	cooperate well with others	

Career Possibilities
(Holland Code):

City Manager (SEC)	Historian (SEI)	Park Naturalist (SEI)	Teacher (SAE)
Clinical Dietitian (SIE)	Hospital Administrator (SER)	Physical Therapist (SIE)	Social Worker (SEA)
College/University Faculty (SEI)	Psychologist (SEI)	Police Officer (SER)	Speech Pathologist (SAI)
Community Org. Director (SEA)	Insurance Claims Examiner (SIE)	Probation and Parole Officer (SEC)	Vocational-Rehab. Counselor (SEC)
Consumer Affairs Director (SER)Counselor/Therapist (SAE)	Librarian (SAI)	Real Estate Appraiser (SCE)	Volunteer Services Director (SEC)
	Medical Assistant (SCR)	Recreation Director (SER)	
	Minister/Priest/Rabbi (SAI)	Registered Nurse (SIA)	
	Paralegal (SCE)		

Enterprising *(Persuaders)*

People who like to work with people, influencing, persuading, leading or managing for organizational goals or economic gain.

Are you?
self-confident
assertive
persuasive
energetic
adventurous
popular

ambitious
agreeable
talkative
extroverted
spontaneous
optimistic

Can you?
initiate projects
convince people to do things
  your way
sell things
give talks or speeches
organize activities
lead a group
persuade others

Like to?
make decisions
be elected to office
start your own business
campaign politically
meet important people
have power or status

**Career Possibilities
(Holland Code):**

Advertising Executive (ESA)
Advertising Sales Rep (ESR)
Banker/Financial Planner (ESR)
Branch Manager (ESA)
Business Manager (ESC)
Buyer (ESA)
Chamber of Commerce Exec
  (ESA)

Credit Analyst (EAS)
Customer Service Manager
  (ESA)
Education & Training Manager
  (EIS)
Emergency Medical Technician
  (ESI)
Entrepreneur (ESA)

Foreign Service Officer (ESA)
Funeral Director (ESR)
Insurance Manager (ESC)
Interpreter (ESA)
Lawyer/Attorney (ESA)
Lobbyist (ESA)
Office Manager (ESR)
Personnel Recruiter (ESR)

Politician (ESA)
Public Relations Rep (EAS)
Retail Store Manager (ESR)
Sales Manager (ESA)
Sales Representative (ERS)
Social Service Director (ESA)
Stockbroker (ESI)
Tax Accountant (ECS)

Conventional *(Organizers)*

People who like to work with data, have clerical or numerical ability, carry out tasks in detail, or follow through on others' instructions.

Are you?
well-organized
accurate
numerically inclined
methodical
conscientious
efficient
conforming

practical
thrifty
systematic
structured
polite
ambitious
obedient
persistent

Can you?
work well within a system
do a lot of paper work in a short
  time
keep accurate records
use a computer terminal
write effective business letters

Like to?
follow clearly defined
  procedures
use data processing equipment
work with numbers
type or take shorthand
be responsible for details
collect or organize things

**Career Possibilities
(Holland Code):**

Abstractor (CSI)
Accountant (CSE)
Administrative Assistant (ESC)
Budget Analyst (CER)
Business Manager (ESC)
Business Programmer (CRI)
Business Teacher (CSE)
Catalog Librarian (CSE)

Claims Adjuster (SEC)
Computer Operator (CSR)
Congressional-District Aide (CES)
Cost Accountant (CES)
Court Reporter (CSE)
Credit Manager (ESC)
Customs Inspector (CEI)
Editorial Assistant (CSI)

Elementary School Teacher
  (SEC)
Financial Analyst (CSI)
Insurance Manager (ESC)
Insurance Underwriter (CSE)
Internal Auditor (ICR)
Kindergarten Teacher (ESC)

Medical Records Technician
  (CSE)
Museum Registrar (CSE)
Paralegal (SCE)
Safety Inspector (RCS)
Tax Accountant (ECS)
Tax Consultant (CES)
Travel Agent (ECS)

BIBLIOGRAPHY

Hospitality and Hotel Management

Burns, Jennifer Bobrow, *Career Opportunities in Travel and Hospitality*. New York: Checkmark Books, 2010.

Fenich, George G., *Meetings, Expositions, Events, and Conventions: An Introduction to the Industry*. Upper Saddle River, NJ: Prentice Hall, 2011.

Inghilleri, Leonardo, and Micah Solomon, *Exceptional Service, Exceptional Profit: The Secrets of Building a Five-Star Customer Service Organization*. New York: AMACON, 2010.

Michelli, Joseph A., *The New Gold Standard: 5 Leadership Principles for Creating a Legendary Customer Experience Courtesy of The Ritz-Carlton Hotel Company*. New York: McGraw-Hill, 2008.

Stiel, Holly, *The Art & Science of the Hotel Concierge*. Washington, DC: American Hotel & Lodging Association, 2011.

Sturman, Michael C., Jack B. Corgel, and Rohit Verma, eds., *The Cornell School of Hotel Administration on Hospitality: Cutting Edge Thinking and Practice*. Hoboken, NJ: Wiley, 2001.

Tomsky, Jacob, *Heads in Beds: A Reckless Memoir of Hotels, Hustles, and So-Called Hospitality*. New York: Anchor Books, 2012.

Restaurant and Food Services

Arduser, Lora, and Douglas R. Brown, *Waitstaff Training Handbook*. Ocala, FL: Atlantic Publishing Group, 2005.

Chalmers, Irena, *Food Jobs*. New York: Beaufort Books, 2008.

Dornenburg, Andrew, and Karen Page, *Becoming a Chef,* rev. ed. Hoboken, NJ: Wiley, 2003.

Eguaras, Louis, with Matthew Frederick, *101 Things I Learned in Culinary School*. New York: Grand Central Publishing, 2010.

Foley, Ray, *Bartending for Dummies*. Indianapolis: For Dummies, 2010.

Hayes, Ronald, *Creating Your Culinary Career*. Hoboken, NJ: Wiley, 2013.

Hill, Kathleen Thompson, *Career Opportunities in the Food and Beverage Industry*. New York: Checkmark Books, 2010.

Kirkham, Mike, Peggy Weiss, and Bill Crawford, *The Waiting Game: The Essential Guide for Wait Staff and Managers*. Berkeley, CA: Ten Speed Press, 2002.

Regan, Mardee Haiden, *The Bartender's Best Friend: A Complete Guide to Cocktails, Martinis, and Mixed Drinks*. Boston: Houghton Mifflin Harcourt, 2010.

Ruhlman, Michael, *The Making of a Chef: Mastering Heat at the Culinary Institute of America*. New York: Holt Paperbacks, 2009.

Smilow, Rick, *Culinary Careers: How to Get Your Dream Job in Food*. New York: Clarkson Potter, 2010.

Thomas, Michele, Annette Tomei, and Tracy Biscontini, *Culinary Careers for Dummies*. Indianapolis: For Dummies, 2011.

Wentz, Bill, *Food Service Management: How to Succeed in the High-Risk Restaurant Business: By Someone Who Did*. Ocala, FL: Atlantic Publishing Group, 2008.

Leisure, Gaming, Travel, and Transportation

Eichenberger, Jerry, *Your Pilot's License*, 8th ed. New York: McGraw-Hill Professional, 2012.

Field, Shelly, *Career Opportunities in Casinos and Casino Hotels*, 2nd ed. New York: Ferguson Publishing, 2009.

Gorham, Ginger, and Susan Rice, *Travel Perspectives: A Guide to Becoming a Travel Professional*, 4th ed. Stamford, CT: Cengage, 2006.

Meriwether, Douglas, *The Dao of Doug: The Art of Driving a Bus*. San Franciso: Balboa Press, 2013.

Mosher, Matt, *CDL—Commercial Driver's License Exam: Complete Prep for the Truck and Bus Driver's License Exams*, 5th ed. Piscataway, NJ: REA, 2011.

Plaut, Melissa, *Hack: How I Stopped Worrying About What to Do with My Life and Started Driving a Yellow Cab*. New York: Villard, 2008.

Poole, Heather, *Cruising Attitude: Tales of Crashpads, Crew Drama, and Crazy Passengers at 35,000 Feet*. New York: William Morrow, 2012.

Ross, Craig, Brent Beggs, and Sarah J. Young, *Mastering the Job Search Process in Recreation and Leisure Services*. Sudbury, MA: Jones & Bartlett, 2010.

Smith, Patrick, *Cockpit Confidential: Everything You Need to Know about Air Travel*. New York: Sourcebooks, 2013.

Weinick, Suzanne, *Essential Careers in Aviation*. New York: Rosen Publishing, 2012.

Health, Fitness, and Beauty

American College of Sports Medicine, *ACSM's Career and Business Guide for the Fitness Professional*. Philadelphia: Lippincott Williams & Wilkins, 2012.

American Kinesiology Association, *Careers in Sport, Fitness, and Exercise*. Champaign, IL: Human Kinetics, 2011.

Ganchy, Sally, *A Career as a Cosmotologist*. New York: Rosen Publishing, 2012.

Kauffman, Robert B., *Career Development in Recreation, Parks, and Tourism*. Champaign, IL: Human Kinetics, 2009.

Kenworthy, Kate, *The Everything Guide to Becoming a Personal Trainer*. Avon, MA: Adams Media, 2007.

St. Michael, Melyssa, *Becoming a Personal Trainer for Dummies*. Indianapolis: For Dummies, 2004.

Interior Design, Floral Design, and Landscaping

American Institute of Floral Design, *AIFD Guide to Floral Design: Terms, Techniques, and Traditions*. Baltimore: AIFD, 2012.

Asay, Nancy, and Marciann Patton, *Careers in Interior Design*. New York: Fairchild Books, 2010.

Ferguson's, *Landscaping and Horticulture (Careers in Focus)*. New York: Ferguson Publishing, 2008.

Hale, Robert, and Thomas L. Williams, *Starting Your Career as an Interior Designer*. New York: Allworth Books, 2009.

Peterson's, *Green Careers in Building and Landscaping*. Lawrenceville, NJ: Peterson's, 2010.

Piotrowski, Christine M., *Becoming an Interior Designer: A Guide to Careers*, 2nd ed. New York: Wiley, 2008.

Administrative Services, Event Management, and Property Management

France, Sue, *The Definitive Executive Assistant and Managerial Handbook*. Philadelphia: Kogan Page, 2012.

Iannucci, Lisa, and Melissa Prandi, *The Complete Idiot's Guide to Success as a Property Manager*. New York: Alpha Books, 2009.

Malouf, Lena, *Events Exposed: Managing and Designing Special Events*. New York: Wiley, 2012.

Quible, Zane K, *Administrative Office Management*, 8th ed. Upper Saddle River, NJ: Prentice Hall, 2004.

INDEX